# THE SELECTED LETTERS OF
# LAURA INGALLS WILDER

# THE SELECTED LETTERS OF
# LAURA INGALLS WILDER

---

*Laura Ingalls Wilder*

**Edited by William Anderson**

---

HARPER PERENNIAL

NEW YORK • LONDON • TORONTO • SYDNEY • NEW DELHI • AUCKLAND

A hardcover edition of this book was published in 2016 by HarperCollins Publishers.

THE SELECTED LETTERS OF LAURA INGALLS WILDER.
Copyright © 2016 by William Anderson. All rights reserved.
Printed in the United States of America. No part of this book may be used or
reproduced in any manner whatsoever without written permission except in the
case of brief quotations embodied in critical articles and reviews. For information,
address HarperCollins Publishers, 195 Broadway, New York, NY 10007.

HarperCollins books may be purchased for educational, business, or sales
promotional use. For information, please e-mail the Special Markets
Department at SPsales@harpercollins.com.

Letters © 2016 Little House Heritage Trust
Introduction, annotations, footnotes, explanatory text, photograph captions © 2016 William
Anderson

COVER: Laura Ingalls Wilder at the age of thirty-nine,
photographed in Kansas City, 1906. (*Laura Ingalls Wilder Home Association*)

Images not credited are courtesy of the author.

FIRST HARPER PERENNIAL EDITION PUBLISHED 2017.

*Designed by Jo Anne Metsch*

Library of Congress Cataloging-in-Publication Data has been applied for.

ISBN 978-0-06-241969-9 (pbk.)

HB 04.11.2024

*To all of those who first read these letters and preserved them,*
*and to all who will enjoy reading them within this book.*

# CONTENTS

# ACKNOWLEDGMENTS

Creating this book was a process of many years. Dozens of Laura Ingalls Wilder's letters were shared with me from diverse sources. Eventually, I organized the correspondence by year and filed it away. Finally, I decided that this collection is too significant to languish in a file cabinet.

I am grateful to the Little House Heritage Trust, to Abigail MacBride, its trustee, and to Noel Silverman, its counsel, for the opportunity to weave together this last major unpublished Wilder collection. Appreciation is also due to Roger MacBride, who, years ago, encouraged this book but said, "Wait awhile." His suggestion was a wise one, because scores of additional Laura Ingalls Wilder letters were unearthed in the ensuing years.

The staff at the Herbert Hoover Presidential Library and Museum has always been helpful and informative in making the Wilder and Lane papers available to me and hundreds of other researchers. Archivist Matthew Schaefer has been especially valuable during the making of this book, particularly during a last-minute research glitch. Jeff Corrigan of the State Historical Society of Missouri provided letters and historic photos, as did the Burton Historical Collection, located at the Detroit Public Library. My editors at HarperCollins, Kate Morgan Jackson and Tara Weikum, led me to letters to and from the great Ursula Nordstrom, and directed me to the George Bye Collection at Columbia University. The amazing Garth Williams was always a font of anecdotes dealing with the illustrating of the Little House books.

For over fifty years, the venerable Aubrey Sherwood of De Smet, South Dakota, did more than anyone to foster Laura Ingalls Wilder's legacy. He was always magnanimous in sharing his store of anecdotes and copies of his Wilder correspondence with me. Both Aubrey and his fellow South Dakotan Alvilda Myre Sorenson were tireless in making their state aware of the Little House books. Their treasured Wilder letters appear in this book.

My long and friendly association with the home sites of Laura Ingalls Wilder has helped lend context to my editing and annotation of these letters. These locales include museums and preserved home sites in Pepin, Wisconsin; Independence, Kansas; Burr Oak, Iowa; Spring Valley, Minnesota; Malone, New York; Walnut Grove, Minnesota; De Smet, South Dakota; Keystone, South Dakota; and Mansfield, Missouri. My great appreciation extends to all the volunteers and staff who enable these places to thrive.

It is a satisfying feeling to include letters that Laura Ingalls Wilder wrote to members of the now-gone generation who were the first to memorialize her. These people include Harold and Della Gordon, Neta Seal, Aubrey and Laura Sherwood, Everett Lantz, Charles Lantz, Vera McCaskell, Dorothy Smith, Alvilda Sorenson, Hazel Gilbert Failing, and Clara Webber. I am blessed that this original fellowship of Wilder enthusiasts welcomed me into their circle when I started research on the subject. Clara Webber commented on the bond that "Wilder people" forge: "I always instantly like any admirer of the Little House books!"

Those who shared letters, information, and advice during this book project are many. These include Barbara M. Walker, Dr. John Miller, Yumiko Taniguchi, Jean Coday, Cheryl Harness, and Connie Neumann.

I am indebted to the initial editor of this book, Maya Ziv. She is an author's dream, extending generous laissez-faire tactics as I worked through the writing and compiling process. When I worried about length, she simply said, "The book can be what it will be." Later on, Sofia Ergas Groopman added her own sparkling savvy to the editing process. David Michael, general factotum, always responded to remedy my skimpy computer skills.

My sincere appreciation to everyone who was involved in the making of this book. In an era when letter writing is a diminished art, we have an opportunity to share this historical and literary treasure trove in *The Selected Letters of Laura Ingalls Wilder*. This book is both a reminder of a bygone era of genuine communication and another visit with Laura Ingalls Wilder, pioneer and author.

—WILLIAM ANDERSON

# INTRODUCTION

## *"Certainly You May Call Me Laura"*

*The Selected Letters of Laura Ingalls Wilder* is perhaps the final collection of unpublished writings from the author of the Little House books. There no longer remains a well of her words left to print.

Since Laura Ingalls Wilder's death in 1957, readers have welcomed the publication of her remaining writings: *On the Way Home, The First Four Years, West from Home,* and *A Little House Sampler,* each published by HarperCollins. In 2015, *Pioneer Girl: The Annotated Autobiography* was released by South Dakota Historical Society Press. *Pioneer Girl* was Laura Ingalls Wilder's apprentice book-length manuscript. It is a memoir of her frontier youth, culminating with her 1885 marriage to Almanzo Wilder in De Smet, South Dakota. The book became a runaway bestseller. By happenstance, this volume of letters was assembled while *Pioneer Girl* was being prepared for publication.

Although Laura Ingalls Wilder's readers know her younger self well from her Little House books, the adult Laura is more elusive. Her later written introspections are scarce, save for columns she wrote for the *Missouri Ruralist* during her middle-age years. She kept no regular diaries, except for brief trip journals. The letters included in this book are a window into her philosophy and her experiences as a farmer's wife, a mother, a journalist, and an author of classic books. In these letters, we hear the public and private voice of the woman behind the literary legend. For this reason, these letters deserve to be read. Most of them were written from her final home, Rocky Ridge Farm in Mansfield, Missouri.

This book contains some of the four hundred–plus letters of Laura Ingalls Wilder that are held in public and private collections. The letters published here span Laura's life from 1894, when she was twenty-seven, through 1956, when she was eighty-nine. This is only a fraction of her lifetime correspondence. Sad to say, many of her letters are lost to history.

Laura penned literally thousands of responses to her readers during the last twenty-plus years of her life as an author. "I cannot bear to disappoint a child," she told her editor, Ursula Nordstrom, when discussing her steady deliveries of fan mail. Her replies were always heartfelt. Examples of them are included in the following pages, though not all that have been unearthed. Many of her fan mail responses are similar in content. The sampling herein is typical, and shows Laura's sincere regard for her reading public.

The correspondence of Laura Ingalls Wilder and her writer daughter, Rose Wilder Lane, was first collected by Roger Lea Mac-Bride. Roger was Rose's longtime attorney. "He adopted me as a spare grandmother when he was 14," she explained. When Rose died in 1968, Roger inherited a formidable task: honoring the wishes of his close friend, and tending the legacy of the Little House books.

Roger discovered boxes and files of Rose's papers in her Danbury, Connecticut, home. Her colorful correspondents ranged from the actress Sarah Bernhardt to U.S. president Herbert Hoover. Most significant among the papers was the correspondence from Laura Ingalls Wilder, some fifty years' worth. Laura's letters to Rose confirm the close collaboration between the two in the writing of the Little House books. Indeed, Rose was her mother's writing coach and mentor as

early as 1910, and their teamwork endured through the publication of
the eighth Little House book in 1943. Particularly enlightening are
Laura's and Rose's letters written between 1936 and 1939, while writing *On the Banks of Plum Creek*, *By the Shores of Silver Lake*, and *The
Long Winter*. Theirs was a symbiotic relationship. Rose's vast experience as a successful journalist, novelist, and short-story writer provided the expertise that enhanced Laura's native talent as a storyteller.
In turn, Laura's pioneer memories contributed grist for Rose's top-
paid magazine fiction and bestselling books like *Let the Hurricane
Roar* and *Free Land*.

To bring together the scattered correspondence of mother and
daughter, Roger MacBride canvassed people and places possessing
their written words. He ultimately assembled a panoramic collection. Of these, Laura's letters to her husband, Almanzo Wilder,
whom she called Manly, written during a 1915 trip to visit Rose in
San Francisco, surfaced in their Rocky Ridge farmhouse. They
were simply too good not to publish. The result was *West from
Home: Letters of Laura Ingalls Wilder, San Francisco, 1915* (Harper &
Row, 1974). Laura's letters home reveal her wit, descriptive powers,
and lively interest in the world. Her trip to see the 1915 San Francisco World's Fair, also known as the Panama-Pacific International
Exposition, had another purpose as well. "I intend to try to do some
writing that will count," Laura confided to her husband. Rose found
time from her own writing deadlines for the *San Francisco Bulletin*
to tutor Laura in journalism.

Transcribing Laura's handwritten letters was a herculean task,
performed admirably by Roger MacBride's secretary, Karen Cox. I
consulted these transcripts when I researched and wrote several
books, including *Laura Ingalls Wilder: A Biography* (HarperCollins,
1992). Ultimately, the immense cache of Wilder-Lane materials was
deposited at the Herbert Hoover Presidential Library and Museum
in West Branch, Iowa. Dwight Miller was a key figure in organizing
and archiving these thousands of papers. Over the years the archive

has been studied by innumerable scholars; many significant books and articles have resulted.

The reader of this book will observe considerable gaps in the scope of Laura's letters. As Barbara Walker, the author of *The Little House Cookbook* (Harper & Row, 1979), has noted: "The final Little House after-story is essentially a sad one; of four daughters there remain no progeny." With no interested descendants around, great segments of the family's written records vanished.

We have none of Laura's introspections on such family sorrows as Rose's unsuccessful marriage and her 1918 divorce from Gillette Lane. We know little of Laura's role in the nurture of her aging mother and her blind sister, Mary, in their final years. Nor can we share Laura's grief at the deaths of her parents and her three sisters. Never does she write about her loss of an infant son and grandson, or of Manly's debilitated vigor after suffering polio during their early marriage. There are no remaining words to shed light on these life experiences.

Laura summarized the dispersal of her family's heirlooms and keepsakes when writing to Aubrey Sherwood, the editor of the *De Smet News*, in 1952. "Things from our old home," she explained, "were scattered as were Carrie's later and I do not know what happened to them."

For the scholar, the greatest loss is the decades of letters that Laura sent to her family in De Smet after leaving there in 1894. Such correspondence would be a gold mine of information to add to the skimpy facts known of the earliest years of Laura, Manly, and Rose in Missouri. Laura's parents and sisters were savers; such letters were tucked away in their house on Third Street in De Smet.

In 1946 the Ingalls home was emptied of its remainders. Vera McCaskell, a De Smet native, remembered the leftovers as a hoard of musty quilts, clothing, trunks, dishes, and antiquated remnants of housekeeping. Post-Depression prairie people were eager to dispose of such reminders of hard times. Who cared for stacks of Mary Ingalls's raised print and Braille books and papers? Or piles of letters tied together with string?

Vera witnessed a flurry of paper descend from a second-floor window onto a truck bed bound for the town dump. A friend of Laura's sister Carrie was responsible for the housecleaning. Later she regretted her role. She called on Aubrey Sherwood at his newspaper office, mourning that "I've done something terrible, letting those things go. We should have saved those things." Written history of De Smet's first residents was tossed out. A few seemingly worthless items were saved by neighbors: a book, a shawl, a container of cloves, and a single volume of Mary's embossed-print Bible.

Laura's sister Carrie Ingalls Swanzey died in Rapid City, South Dakota, just weeks before the family home in De Smet was emptied. Her own home in Keystone, a few miles from Mount Rushmore, was chockablock with family keepsakes and letters. In the nick of time, before Carrie's attorney ordered her house cleared, a friend intervened. She gathered up a random sampling of historic gems: old photographs, clothing, jewelry, knickknacks, and letters. These treasures are now exhibited by the Laura Ingalls Wilder Memorial Society in De Smet and the Keystone Area Historical Society.

In 1957 Rose Wilder Lane presided over her mother's final days in the farmhouse at Rocky Ridge Farm. Laura died on February 10, three days after her ninetieth birthday. The long strain left Rose devastated and exhausted. She was seventy, the last link to the pioneering Ingalls family. She wandered through the chilly farmhouse on Rocky Ridge, confronting a lifetime of possessions. She found thousands of letters from Little House readers and boxes of foreign postcards she had sent to her parents during her worldwide travels. There were reams of typed letters she had sent home from diverse places. There were folders of personal and editorial correspondence, and piles of yellowing paper. Rose was overwhelmed by the tangible evidence of her mother's rich, multifaceted life.

Rose's initial response was to burn the papers she readily found. She destroyed numerous letters she had written to her parents. Little of the correspondence that Rose sent home after 1939 now survives, though her letters had continued unabated. Rose tossed handfuls of paper into the fireplace flames, and the smoke curled into the winter sky. Luckily, Rose overlooked six of the original Little House manuscripts. These were penciled proof that the books were extensively revised before their publication. "I thought I had personally disposed of all papers in the house," Rose said in retrospect. Fortunately, for history, her purge was spotty. "I was out of my mind at the time," she admitted, "all shaky inside, my mind quivery, too."

But then Rose's burden and bewilderment—deciding what to do with her parents' possessions—was alleviated. Mansfield citizens formed an ad hoc committee determined to preserve the Wilder home as a memorial. Rose agreed to the fledgling plan. When she closed the door at Rocky Ridge for the final time, she left the contents of the house essentially undisturbed from then on.

At her home in Danbury, Rose destroyed many of her mother's letters to her, particularly those written during the 1940s and 1950s. Between 1936 and 1949, when Rose was completely absent from Rocky Ridge Farm, her mother's affectionate letters still flowed regularly. The gap in documentation from 1940 until 1956 is regrettable.

Following Rose's death, Roger MacBride explored the cartons of letters stored in her cedar-lined attic. As he read the correspondence, he understood that Rose had left proof of her role in creating the Little House books. She always adamantly denied such involvement. But there is no doubt that the books were, as one scholar dubbed them, "rose-colored classics."

Laura and Rose's mother-daughter collaboration was enormously fruitful. The Little House books became staples in libraries, schools, bookstores, and homes around the world. Reader response to the books was overwhelming. Fan mail filled the Wilders' rural route mailbox with each delivery. Some days brought Laura twenty-five letters, others fifty or more pieces of mail. "I never came to visit but what Mrs. Wilder was answering her fan mail," a friend remembered. Her dining table was usually spread with letters, stationery, and postage stamps.

Laura devised a method to respond to admirers. She jotted notes on envelopes, citing particular questions the letter writer asked. These she incorporated into gracious responses, telling the fates of her family members, gently promoting her eight books, and returning her love and best wishes.

For fans, Laura's replies were exciting events when received. The letters, always in neat longhand, were displayed in classrooms and libraries, reported by the local press, and saved as family treasures. Those who received them often felt compelled to write again.

A librarian from Topeka wrote: "I wish you might have been there to see the boys and girls who were delighted with your sweet note."

A mother from New York described her children's awe: "I wish you could have seen the excitement your letter created here. . . . Richard, our little boy, met the postmaster and came tearing in the house shouting, 'Mother, Mother! Look what we've got.' Ruth's eyes nearly popped out of her head."

A classroom in Kansas wrote back: "We were happy to get your nice letter. It made us feel like we really know you."

A correspondent from Tarrytown, New York, replied during the era of World War II rationing: "It was more than kind of you to take the time to answer my letter. The children could hardly believe I had heard from the real Laura. . . . I want so strongly to do something for you. I am enclosing a sugar stamp. Perhaps your sugar allotment is not sufficient to permit you to make Mr. Wilder gingerbread or pie or cake as often as you would like to."

A mother from Wisconsin described her child's pleasure when Laura's letter arrived: "You will never realize, Mrs. Wilder, how happy you made our little boy, James, by writing him after he'd sent you a little card and letter. I'll never forget the sparkle in those little

black eyes of his when he read your letter. He will keep that letter—
forever he said."

On into the twenty-first century, the warm, friendly feeling toward Laura Ingalls Wilder still persists. Back in 1950, a reader apologized for addressing her as "Dear Laura"—too familiarly, she feared.

The answer was genuine, as one might expect from Laura Ingalls
Wilder:

"Certainly you may call me Laura. I am glad you feel like doing so."

# A NOTE ON EDITING

Laura Ingalls Wilder's letters appear in this book essentially as she wrote them, leaving intact occasional antiquated language, usage of the era, and style. Spelling errors have been silently corrected. Incorrect dates have also been remedied. In some cases, the contents of the letters contain redundant information. These sentences have been removed and are indicated with ellipses, or italicized summaries of the excised passages.

To avoid unneeded repetition in these pages, return addresses have been deleted from most of the letters. Unless otherwise indicated, the reader may assume that the bulk of the letters were written from Rocky Ridge Farm, in Mansfield, Missouri. Laura's dating system has been regularized. Throughout the book, the use of the familiar "Laura" is used in place of the more scholarly "Wilder." This was an editorial decision, and it seems a valid choice.

# A LAURA INGALLS WILDER CHRONOLOGY

| | |
|---|---|
| 1836 | January 10: Charles Phillip Ingalls born. |
| 1839 | December 12: Caroline Lake Quiner born. |
| 1857 | February 13: Almanzo James Wilder born. |
| 1860 | February 1: Charles Ingalls and Caroline Quiner marry. |
| 1863 | September 22: Charles Ingalls and Caroline's brother, Henry Quiner, jointly purchase 160 acres in Pepin Township, Wisconsin. |
| 1865 | January 10: Mary Amelia Ingalls born. |
| 1867 | February 7: Laura Elizabeth Ingalls born. |
| 1868 | April 28: The Ingalls-Quiner farm is sold. |
| 1870 | Ingalls family lives in Montgomery County, Kansas. Caroline Celestia Ingalls is born on August 3. |
| 1871 | Ingalls family returns to their farm near Pepin, Wisconsin, after the buyer defaults on payment. |
| 1873 | October 28: Charles Ingalls sells his farm a second time. |

1874        Ingalls family settles along Plum Creek near Walnut
            Grove, Minnesota.

1875        November 1: Charles Frederick Ingalls born.

1876        July 10: Charles Phillip Ingalls sells the Plum Creek
            farm.
            August 27: Charles Frederick dies near South Troy,
            Minnesota.

1876–1877   Ingalls family lives in Burr Oak, Iowa. Grace Pearl
            Ingalls is born on May 23, 1877.

1878        Ingalls family returns to Walnut Grove.

1879        Mary Ingalls loses eyesight. Ingalls family moves to
            Dakota Territory.

1880        Ingalls family settles in De Smet, living in town and on
            their homestead.

1881        Mary Ingalls enrolls in the Iowa College for the Blind.

1884–1885   Laura Ingalls teaches the Bouchie, Perry, and Wilkin
            schools.

1885        August 25: Laura Ingalls and Almanzo Wilder marry.

1886        December 5: Rose Wilder born.

1889        August: Infant son of the Wilders born and died;
            Wilder home burns.

1890        Laura, Almanzo ("Manly"), and Rose live with Wilder
            family in Spring Valley, Minnesota.

1891–1892   Laura, Manly, and Rose live near Westville, Florida.

1892–1894   Laura, Manly, and Rose live in De Smet.

1894    July: Laura, Manly, and Rose leave for Missouri.
        September: Laura, Manly, and Rose settle on Rocky
        Ridge Farm.

1898    Laura, Manly, and Rose move to Mansfield.

1901    October 16: Grace Ingalls and Nathan Dow marry.

1902    June 8: Charles Ingalls dies in De Smet.

1903–1904 Rose Wilder spends the school year in Crowley,
        Louisiana, living with Eliza Jane Wilder Thayer.

1905–1906 Rose learns telegraphy at Mansfield's railroad depot;
        works in Kansas City as a telegraph operator, where
        Laura visits.

1909    March 24: Rose marries Claire Gillette Lane in San
        Francisco.
        November: Rose delivers a premature baby in Salt Lake
        City; the infant boy does not survive.

1910    Laura writes agricultural articles for the *St. Louis Star-
        Farmer*.
        June: Laura and Manly sell the house in Mansfield and
        resettle on Rocky Ridge to try full-scale farming.

1911    Laura publishes her first article in the *Missouri Ruralist*,
        the start of a thirteen-year association.

1912    August 1: Carrie Ingalls and David Swanzey marry in
        Rapid City.

1913    Completion of the Rocky Ridge farmhouse.

1915    August–October: Laura visits Rose in San Francisco.
        She writes about the Panama-Pacific International
        Exposition for the *Missouri Ruralist*.

1917    Laura takes a job as secretary-treasurer of the
        Mansfield Farm Loan Association.

1918    Rose launches a career as a freelance writer after
        working as a staff writer for the *San Francisco Bulletin*.
        Her divorce from Gillette Lane is finalized.

1920    Rose accepts a publicist position with the American
        Red Cross office in Paris; she works and travels abroad
        for three years.

1924    April 20: Caroline Ingalls dies in De Smet.
        Rose lives on Rocky Ridge Farm, publishing books,
        magazine serials, short stories, and articles; Laura
        ceases writing for the *Missouri Ruralist*.

1925    September–October: Laura, Rose, and Helen Boylston
        travel to California.

1926–1928  Rose and Helen Boylston travel in Europe and live in
        Tirana, Albania.

1928    October 17: Mary Ingalls dies.
        Rose and Helen return to live at Rocky Ridge. Rose has
        a rock house built for Laura and Manly; in December
        they move in.

1930    Laura writes her autobiography, *Pioneer Girl*.

1931    Laura and Manly revisit South Dakota.

1932    *Little House in the Big Woods* is published.

1933    *Farmer Boy* is published; Rose's *Let the Hurricane Roar* is
        published. John Turner, an orphan, is taken in by Rose
        at Rocky Ridge. He is later joined by his brother Al.

1935     *Little House on the Prairie* is published; Rose's *Old Home Town* is published.

1936     Rose's *Give Me Liberty* is published; she leaves Rocky Ridge Farm permanently; Laura and Manly return to the Rocky Ridge farmhouse.

1937     *On the Banks of Plum Creek* is published.

1938     Laura and Manly visit the Pacific Northwest and South Dakota; Rose's *Free Land* is published and she establishes a home in Danbury, Connecticut.

1939     *By the Shores of Silver Lake* is published; Laura and Manly visit South Dakota and Colorado.

1940     *The Long Winter* is published.

1941     November 10: Grace Ingalls Dow dies. *Little Town on the Prairie* is published.

1943     *These Happy Golden Years* is published; Rose's *The Discovery of Freedom* is published.

1946     June 2: Carrie Ingalls Swanzey dies.

1949     October 23: Almanzo Wilder dies.

1954     The Laura Ingalls Wilder Award is established by the American Library Association; Laura is the first recipient.

1957     February 10: Laura Ingalls Wilder dies at Rocky Ridge Farm.

1968     October 30: Rose Wilder Lane dies in Danbury, Connecticut.

# PART
# I

PART
1

# THE FARMER'S WIFE
## (1894–1920)

Laura, circa 1917. "Mrs. Wilder is a woman of delightful personality."
—*The Missouri Ruralist*
(*Herbert Hoover Presidential Library*)

*Laura Ingalls Wilder's early life was shaped by the Homestead Act of 1862 and the adage repeated by her parents: "It is better farther on." She was born in a Wisconsin log cabin in 1867, near Pepin, seven miles from the dividing line between east and west: the Mississippi River. Her parents, Charles and Caroline Ingalls, were among those who felt the post–Civil War hunger for the open plains. For a decade, from 1869 to 1879, the Ingalls family was on the move, seeking a home. They endured nearly every challenge of pioneer life, and failed to find much success. Laura wrote, "With*

my parents and sisters, I traveled by prairie schooner across Minnesota, Iowa, Missouri and Kansas and into Indian Territory. . . .
Then traveling back to western Minnesota we lived for several
years. . . . From there we went West again. . . . We lived in De Smet
[Dakota Territory] and I married Almanzo Wilder."

There were four Ingalls daughters: Mary, Laura, Carrie, and
Grace. An infant son died. Mary lost her eyesight at age fourteen;
the family was never the same thereafter. Settling down in De
Smet, South Dakota, was due to Caroline Ingalls's "no further"
edict. Laura dutifully taught three terms of school as a young teen,
adding income to the struggling family's budget. In 1885 she became
Almanzo Wilder's bride. They were a companionable couple,
known to each other as Bess and Manly.

With good prospects for success, the couple homesteaded near
De Smet, but a cycle of bad luck dogged them during their first
years together. There were fires, crop failures, illness, debt, and the
death of an infant son. Their first child, Rose, was born in 1886.
After the fiasco of homesteading, the Wilders sought a new life in
the Missouri Ozarks. In 1894, Manly, Laura, and Rose bade fare-
well to family and friends, and left the prairies.

Rocky Ridge Farm, a mile from Mansfield, Missouri, became
the permanent family home.

## As I am going away

At twenty-seven and thirty-seven, Laura and Manly were starting
over, with a $100 bill saved to buy new land. As they prepared for
the 650-mile journey to Missouri, Laura wrote this note to the
Bethlehem chapter of the Order of the Eastern Star in De Smet, a
Masonic society to which the Wilders belonged. This is the earliest
known example of her letter writing.

De Smet
JULY 9, 1894
Mrs. Seeley.
Secretary Eastern Star Chapter No. 13

As I am going away I would like the Chapter to grant me a demit. Enclosed please find 75 cents which I believe is the amount of my dues.

Yours fraternally,
Laura Wilder

## *It is a continual picnic*

*"Manly Wilder started for Missouri last Monday and will make the trip in company with Mr. [Frank] Cooley. Mr. Wilder has been a resident of De Smet for several years and he is one of those men we dislike to see move away."* The Kingsbury County Independent *neglected to mention that Mr. Wilder was accompanied by his wife and their seven-year-old daughter, Rose. Frank Cooley's wife, Emma, and their two young sons were also part of the caravan. Laura Wilder kept a daily journal during the six-week trek to Missouri. As the trip neared its end, she wrote a travel letter to the* De Smet News and Leader. *The paper's editor, Carter Sherwood, printed Laura's description. By default he became her first publisher. Years later she noted on the penciled column: "First I ever had published."*

AUGUST 23, 1894

Ed. NEWS & LEADER: Thinking that our friends in De Smet might like to hear how we are progressing on our journey, I will send you a short account of it so far.

We reached Yankton in just a week from the time we started,

crossed the Missouri river on a ferry and bade good-bye to Dakota. The crops that far were about the same as they were around De Smet.

The next town of importance we saw was Schuyler, Nebraska, where we stayed a few hours for Mr. Cooley's people to visit friends. We went through Lincoln and saw the capitol buildings, the court house and a great deal of the city; then to Beatrice, which is a nice city. The crops of wheat and oats through eastern Nebraska were good. Corn was damaged by the drought.

We saw the capitol in Topeka, famous for the legislative war. [The "war" was a heated 1893 dispute for supremacy between the Republican and Populist parties.] It is a grand building. From Topeka we went to Ottawa and from there to Fort Scott, which is a lovely place. Coal crops out of the ground all through the country around Fort Scott, and at the mines it is only two feet below the surface. It is worth $1.00 per ton at the mines or $1.25 delivered. Crops through eastern Kansas are fair. It is a grand sight to see hundreds of acres of corn in one field.

We have had a very pleasant trip so far, no bad weather to delay us, having had only a few light showers, and those in the night. Our camping places have been delightful. We camped on the Jim river in Dakota, and on the Blue in Kansas and nearly every night beside we have camped on creeks, among the trees. It is a continual picnic for the children to wade in the creeks and play in the woods, and sometimes we all think we are children and do likewise.

We have eaten apples, grapes, plums and melons until we actually do not care for any more, and to satisfy a Dakota appetite for such things is truly something wonderful.

There are hazelnuts, hickory nuts and walnuts along the road, but they are green yet. Country is full of emigrants traveling in every direction.

Our horses are in good condition and our wagons are whole yet, having had no accidents. We are near Lamar, Missouri, now and expect to be on the road a week longer before we reach the land of promise.

Laura Wilder

## *We each and severally sell and convey*

*In the beginning, Rocky Ridge Farm could not sustain the family of three, so the Wilders rented a little frame house in Mansfield, to be closer to work opportunities. They lived there from 1898 to 1910. Manly was the town drayman and delivered products for Waters Pierce Oil Company. The Wilders received an economic boost when Manly's parents purchased the rented house for them; later they received funds from the elder Wilders' estate. Laura penned this receipt.*

DECEMBER 2, 1903

For ($500) Five Hundred Dollars to us in hand paid we each and severally sell and convey to Mrs. E.J.W. [Eliza Jane Wilder] Thayer, widow of Thomas Thayer, deceased, interests in the estate of our Father James Wilder, deceased.

Almanzo J. Wilder

Laura E. Wilder

## *Postcards to Rose*

*Rose Wilder was a bookish, unconventional teen. Farm life and small-town mores bored her. She joined the ranks of early twentieth-century bachelor girls, eager to be self-supporting, ambitious to experience big-city life. By 1908 Rose was a telegrapher in San Francisco. She reported to her parents that "I go to work at Fairmont, largest hotel here, tomorrow. Everything fine. Will write you heaps on typewriter at office. Hurrah! Rose." The popular penny postcard of the era, including an illustration or photograph provided by the sender, was a means of communication frequently used by the Wilder family.*

**AUGUST 30, 1908**

Out by Williams Cave, with Mrs. Quigley and Ava. That is Manly's foot, not mine. Notice Shep [the family dog]. Look at us with a magnifying glass.

Bess

**AUGUST 31, 1908**

Dear Rose,

How does this look to you? School began today & made me think of you & wish you were trotting along with the crowd.

Mama Bess

*As the family's finances improved, Laura indulged in travel. In 1902 she returned to De Smet at the time of her father's death; in 1906 she visited Rose, who was then a telegrapher in Kansas City. In 1908 she traveled by train to Sedalia, Missouri, as a guest of Mrs. John Quigley. Mr. Quigley had boarded with the Wilders while he superintended the building of the Bluebird Railroad spur from Mansfield to Ava, Missouri, in 1908. On each jaunt she updated Manly on her well-being and activities.*

*Having a fine time*

Sedalia

**OCTOBER 4, 1908**

Arrived last night. Am feeling good & having a fine time.

Bessie

Dear Manly—
   I'm in on the ground floor and having a fine time.
   Bessie

## *Sending you the rewritten poultry article*

*To supplement the farm's income, Bessie Wilder—as she was known in Mansfield—embarked on a career as a country journalist. Her first submission to the Missouri Ruralist was in 1911; it was the start of a thirteen-year association with the publication. Wilder's editor, John Case, relied on her for feature stories, interviews, poetry, and op-ed columns. "I am bursting with congratulations," Rose wrote when she read her mother's first published writing.*

MARCH 17, 1915
Mr. John Case
Kansas City
Dear Mr. Case:
   I am sending you the rewritten poultry article, as you requested, and I think it is about what the other was. Sorry you had the trouble of searching and trust this will meet your approval.
   Yours sincerely,
   Mrs. A. J. Wilder

---

*The Wilder farm, with its showplace house, became known as a unique example of successful agriculture in the Ozarks. This unidentified clipping dates to circa 1910.*

### MRS. A. J. WILDER

   Several farmers, and particularly those interested in poultry, have inquired who Mrs. A. J. Wilder is. This question was asked again by Rev. David Long, who lives in the eastern portion of the county and who in company with several gentlemen called on the Republican last week [unidentified newspaper]. Mrs. A. J. Wilder and her husband reside on Rocky Ridge Farm, one mile east of Mansfield. Mrs. Wilder has for some years been a contributor to various state publications. At present she is editor of the poultry department of the Star Farmer. She also contributes to the Missouri Ruralist and is on the staff of the Globe Democrat, as well as several eastern papers. A visit to Rocky Ridge Farm would probably give the inquirer a better insight to poultry raising than could be obtained in any other section of South Missouri. Mr. Wilder is a model farmer and can not only exhibit fine poultry but can undoubtedly show a greater percent of actual profit than anyone we know. Profit is the main thing and Mr. Wilder being in poultry raising for the money, has as a result of experiment, arrived at a knowledge of how to care for poultry, which would be beneficial to farmers of this section. An hour spent on Rocky Ridge Farm would, in our opinion, be more beneficial than to spend a week at any state poultry farm where the desire is to know how to raise poultry at a profit.

## All the time I am wishing for you

In 1915, Laura and Rose were publishing regularly. Laura's audience was the farm family; her scope, regional. Rose, who married Claire Gillette Lane, known as Gillette Lane, in 1909, was a staff writer for the San Francisco Bulletin. Her career flourished, but her six-year marriage to Gillette crumbled. She longed to show her mother the splendors of the world's fair—officially named the

*Panama-Pacific International Exposition. Laura traveled by train to California. For two months she wandered through the fair, visited local beauty spots, and worked with Rose to improve her writing. Laura wrote Manly often; the full collection of letters was published in 1974 as* West from Home *(edited by Roger Lea MacBride, Harper & Row). Excerpts printed here demonstrate Laura's expertise in describing the people, places, and events she encountered.*

AUGUST 25, 1915

Manly Dear,

I wish you were here. Half the fun I lose because all the time I am wishing for you.

We passed through the most desolate country this morning—the first desert I've seen. The mountains were around the edges and as the sun rose they showed the most beautiful soft colors. There were miles and miles and miles of sand dunes without a spear of grass or a green thing, only now and then where there was a tiny ranch and a ditch of water from the river. We are climbing up out of the desert now through the encircling rim of mountains. They are simply frightful. Huge masses and ramparts of rock, just bare rock in every fantastic shape imaginable. They are not like I thought. I had supposed there were forests among the rocky peaks, but there is only once in a great ways a stunted pine. The mountains look like those pictures of old castles in Austria we were looking at, and such wonderful fortified places they would make—such castles could be made on them!

## *I have washed my feet in the Pacific Ocean*

San Francisco
AUGUST 29, 1915
Manly Dear,

I arrived safely in San Francisco. As I walked down the walk from the train toward the ferry, Rose stepped out from the crowd and seized me.

On the ferry we sat on the upper deck and well in front, but a fog covered the water so I did not see much of the bay except the lights around it. . . . Gillette met us as we stepped off the ferry and we took a streetcar nearly home and climbed a hill the rest of the way.

. . . Yesterday afternoon I went with Rose and Gillette down to the beach. At Land's End I had my first view of the Pacific Ocean. To say it is beautiful does not half express it. . . . The water is such a deep wonderful blue and the sound of the waves breaking on the beach and their whisper as they flow back is something to dream about. . . . We walked from Land's End around the point of land and came to the Cliff House and Seal Rocks but the seals would not show themselves.

. . . I wanted to wade. Rose said she never had but she would, so we took off our shoes and stockings and left them on the warm sand with Gillette to guard them and went out to meet the waves. . . . The Salt water tingled my feet and made them feel so good all the rest of the day. . . . In other words, I have washed my feet in the Pacific Ocean.


## *One simply gets satiated with beauty*

SEPTEMBER 4, 1915
Manly Dear,

. . . Gillette and I went to the Fairgrounds in the afternoon while Rose wrote on her story. Then Rose came down in time for the illumination and fireworks and we stayed until twelve o'clock. One simply gets satiated with beauty. . . .

The coloring is so soft and wonderful. Blues and reds and greens and yellows and browns and grays are all blended together into one perfect whole without a jar anywhere. It is a fairyland. We went through a large entrance gate and were in the Zone, which is a long street of attractions like the side shows in a circus. . . .

The buildings are built like those of a city and the streets and the four corners of streets form the courts. One goes through beautiful archways in the buildings into the courts where fountains splash and lovely flowers and green things are growing. There are life-like statues and figures of animals and birds. The foundation color of the buildings is soft gray and as it rises it is changed to the soft yellows picked out in places by blue and red and green and the eye is carried up and up by the architecture, spires and things, to the beautiful blue sky above. I have never imagined anything so beautiful.

I saw the Southern Pacific Railroad exhibit in their building which is a life-like reproduction of California scenes, even to the waterfalls and the blossoming orchards in the Santa Clara Valley.

We went into the Navajo Indian village, regular cliff dwellings. It is built to be a rocky cliff and one climbs up by steps cut in the solid rock all along the way. After you get up the cliff, there are holes dug into the rock, smaller or larger where the Indians live, making baskets and pottery and weaving rugs. . . . The Indians are very friendly and good-natured.

We went back to the Zone and went to the Samoan Village. . . . There were several girls and men dressed, or rather undressed, in their native costume. . . .

## *Rose and I went downtown in the morning*

SEPTEMBER 8, 1915

Manly Dear,

... Rose and I went downtown in the morning and Rose turned in her copy at the *Bulletin* office. We had a few errands to do and then we had a cup of tea and some muffins at "The Pig 'n Whistle"—a tea room. ... After that we walked to the top of "Telegraph Hill."

... From the top of Telegraph Hill we looked down on the bay and boats and ships of all kinds going in every direction. ... Across the bay we could see some of the cities of Oakland and Berkeley. In other directions we could see nothing but water. When we tired of this we went down the hill on the other side of the waterfront, among the docks. ... This is a wonderful harbor, so large and quiet, with room for so many ships to anchor safely, and such a narrow, well-protected entrance: the Golden Gate.

## *Honest fact, I'm homesick*

SEPTEMBER 13, 1915

Manly Dear,

... Honest fact, I'm homesick, but there are so many interesting things still to be seen ... that I feel I must see some more of them before I leave. Then I do want to do a little writing with Rose to get the hang of it a little better so I can write something that perhaps I can sell. ... I am going to do the things I absolutely must do before I come home. There are a few you know, such as going over my copy with Rose and going out to the Fair a couple of times. ... I am anxious to get back and take charge of the hens again. Believe me, there is no place like the country to live that would lead me to give up Rocky

Ridge for any other place. . . . Gee! It will be good to get busy again on my job.

## It was simply glorious

SEPTEMBER 21, 1915
Manly Dear,
  . . . I have had a trip on the bay out into the sunset. It was wonderful and the more the boat rolled on the waves the better I liked it. I did not get dizzy at all. We went out to the highest fort in the world and around by the quarantine station on Angel Island and then back to the anchorage. The fog rolled up and came down on us and we could not see the land in any direction. The ocean swell came in through the Golden Gate and rocked the boat. . . . It was just a little steam yacht we were on and Rose and I stood up in the very front and let the spray and the mist beat into our faces and the wind blow our hair and clothes and the boat roll under our feet and it was simply glorious.

## Postcard

[Exhibit Palace, Carnation Milk Condensery, Panama-Pacific International Exposition, San Francisco]

SEPTEMBER 29, 1915
  I'll tell you all how they condense milk when I come. Was shown all over this very particularly.
  Bessie

## *Almost without breathing, listening*

OCTOBER 14, 1915

Manly Dear,

... Rose and I went over to Berkeley to hear Fritz Kreisler, the Austrian, play the violin. This you know meant a trip across the bay, which is always such a pleasure, then a streetcar ride through Oakland, for this time we landed at the Oakland pier, then a walk across the campus ... to the Greek Theater.

It was wonderfully beautiful at night. The lights were lit until the people were seated. . . . The stage and walls behind, like wings of a theater, are white marble and the tops of the tall pines and eucalyptus trees showed above it. The hills rise around the amphitheater so that the seats as they rise one above the other have the solid hillside behind them. . . . The moon shone just above the stage and it was all so beautiful that when Kreisler's violin began to sing it made one's throat ache. . . . We sat for two hours, almost without breathing, listening to it. [Kreisler (1875–1962) is considered by many to have been one of the greatest violinists of all time. He concertized widely, mostly in Europe and America, where he finally settled. His records were among those in the Wilders' music collection at Rocky Ridge.]

## *I will have my hands full*

OCTOBER 22, 1915

Manly Dear,

... At last I have a letter from the Ruralist with orders for copy and recommendations that give me passes into the Fair and throws the whole Missouri part of it wide open to me. The men in charge of the Missouri exhibits want me to persuade the Ruralist to issue a special edition at the P.P.I.E. and I have wired them about it. If they tell me to go ahead with it I will have my hands full for a few days getting out the copy for the whole paper. I expect to hear from them tomorrow. If I do the special edition I will not be able to start for home before ten days. . . .

Do take care of yourself and Inky [the family dog] and whisper to him that I will be there before long. I have so many nice things planned to do when I get home and I am sure the woods are beautiful, but I would not give one Ozark hill for all the rest of the state that I have seen. Oh, by the way, Missouri has SHOWN THEM at the P.P.I.E. Carried off more prizes than any other state except California and beat California on mines. . . .

*Laura wrote two feature stories for the* Ruralist *based on her San Francisco experiences: "Magic in Plain Foods," published on November 20, 1915, plus "And Missouri Showed Them," which appeared on December 5, 1915.*

## SURPRISE PARTY

*With no relatives near, Laura and Manly savored gatherings of friends in their spacious parlor. On January 5, 1917, just as the proceedings of the Eastern Star meeting started in the lodge chambers in Mansfield, the couple announced an unexpected party at Rocky Ridge. Everyone headed to the Wilder home. The* Mansfield Mirror *reported on the party with the headline "An Enjoyable Occasion."*

One of the most enjoyable of affairs took place Friday night. Mansfield Chapter, Order of Eastern Star, while in session in their hall were surprised by an invitation to adjourn to the home of A. J. Wilder and wife. The usual order of things was reversed . . . the invitation was a complete surprise to the chapter members, who had only expected the regular meeting. Three cars conveyed the merry crowd to

Rocky Ridge Farm, where the oak paneled, oak beamed living room was alight from the fire in the large fireplace and the glow of rose shaded lamps from the dining room. Delicious and unique refreshments were served during the evening, The table decorations were in The Star colors, the centerpiece being the regular Star emblem of the Order in the correct colors. The edibles served on each plate were also in the proper colors and design of the Star. After lunch, the guests gathered in the firelight and listened to the wonderful violin music of Fritz Kreisler, Elman, selections from well-known operas, Victor Herbert's orchestra and Hawaiian stringed instrumentals. The music was furnished by a Victrola, the Christmas gift of Rose Wilder Lane of San Francisco, daughter of the hosts. With music and conversation the time passed without a dull moment and the guests departed, regretting that the evening had been so short.

## *I am sure you will be pleased with the terms*

*In 1917 eight farmers founded the Mansfield Farm Loan Association, a branch of the Federal Loan Bank. Laura was elected secretary-treasurer, and served as a director. She held the position for over a decade, working at home and in office space on the town square, processing loans and recording minutes at meetings.*

FEBRUARY 24, 1920
Mr. Ira Young
Mansfield, Missouri
Dear Sir:

Mr. N. J. Craig has asked me to give you information about our Mansfield National Farm Loan Association.

If you want to get a loan at 5½% interest, with time [to pay] any-where from five years to 35 years, I am sure you will be pleased with the terms the Farm Loan Association can give you. If you take the loan for 35 years it practically pays itself out, but it can be paid off at any time you wish to pay it.

Mr. Wilder and I will be glad to show you all particulars about making the loan and I will make out the application for you if you decide to have it made, if you will come to our place. Come any time but if it is convenient it might be a good idea to telephone us you are coming so that we will be sure to be at home. . . .

### One hesitates to make enemies

MARCH 26, 1920
Hon. Alexander M. Dockery
Third Assistant Postmaster General
Washington
Dear Sir:

Our rural mail carrier is in the habit, whenever the weather is bad, of going part of the way on his route and then cutting across back to town leaving off this end of the route. There are eighteen boxes thus left without service and this has been done two days, and at one time three days in succession.

There is, I believe, a creek where he usually abandons his route. At times the water in this creek is high but there has been nothing at any time to prevent him from starting to town on this end of the route and going one and a half miles, and in this distance he would pass the eighteen mail boxes.

It would not matter so much to me if it were only my private mail but I am Secretary-Treasurer of the Mansfield National Farm Loan Association and the way our carrier has been doing interferes seriously with the handling of that part of the business of the Federal Land Bank which passes through my hands.

Complaints to the postmaster have done no good. Complaints of the manner of conducting the post office at Mansfield have been made to the post office Inspector at Springfield and I have been told that these letters of complaint have been sent to the postmaster here and no other action taken. For this reason I am writing to you instead.

When living in a small community like this, one hesitates to make enemies and if it is possible I hope this letter will be considered confidential, and that someone, other than the Inspector at Springfield, may be sent to investigate conditions at this post office, especially in the overseeing of the rural mail carriers.

About nine months ago, our carrier lost or broke his key to the mail boxes. My box is some distance from and entirely out of sight from the house, and I cannot trust the valuable papers that go to and from The Federal Loan Bank in it without locking. I have asked several times that another key be gotten for the carrier but so far it has not been done and it is impossible for me to have the proper use of my mail box until he does. . . .

Please do what you can for us so that the Mansfield post office will give its patrons the service it should. We will appreciate it very much. If an inspector comes and it is possible to do so, I would like to have a talk with him and explain more fully than it is possible to do in a letter.

Very truly yours,
Mrs. A. J. Wilder

*The interest is 5½%*

*Friends and neighbors recalled that Laura was a persistent ambassador for the Farm Loan Association.*

APRIL 14, 1920
Mr. O. S. Patterson
Hartville [Missouri]
Dear Sir:

I have waited a few days before answering your letter so I could get these little books to send you for they explain [the loan process] in a letter. You see the interest is 5½%. The payment is made twice a year, which makes it easier than paying the full amount at one time. I am sending you a blank application and if you want to apply for a loan, fill out the application and send to me with $10 membership fee. . . .

*Mr. Wilder and I can hold our own in all arguments . . .*

SEPTEMBER 9, 1920
Hon. Thomas L. Ruby
Lebanon [Missouri]
Dear Sir:

We would like some information on the present tariff laws such as affect the farmers and not knowing where to ask for it, are imposing once more on your good nature.

Republicans here are saying that because the Democratic administration removed the tariff on meat animals enormous numbers of them are being shipped into this country from Argentina. Answer: Elect the Republicans and raise the price of livestock. I'll admit I am weak on the tariff and I would like to know if the laws have been changed in that respect since Republican rule and if so, when and how.

Mr. Wilder and I can hold our own in all arguments so far except this one of tariff on livestock and we will be very glad of any information you can send us about it.

Yours very truly,
Mrs. A. J. Wilder

## *Vote for Mr. N. J. Craig*

> *Noah Jefferson Craig and his family were among the Wilders' clos-*
> *est friends. During his bachelor days, Craig boarded with the*
> *Wilders. When he founded the Farmers and Merchants Bank,*
> *they were among his first customers. Later, Rose Wilder Lane used*
> *Craig's life story as the basis for her 1926 novel,* Hill-Billy. *Laura's*
> *involvement in Democratic politics included stumping for Craig.*

OCTOBER 18, 1920
Mr. Robert Kinser
Hartville [Missouri]
Dear Sir:

I do not know what your politics are but I am writing to ask you to vote for Mr. N. J. Craig for prosecuting attorney if you can possibly do so. Mr. Craig has been a great help to us in our Farm Loan Association. There is no doubt that without his help we would not have had the Association, and so I think we ought to show our appreciation by giving him our votes.

Mr. Craig will make a good prosecuting attorney. We know this from his past record and his reputation. If you are a Democrat I'm sure you will vote for him and if you are a Republican I hope you will put his name on your ticket.

## *My sensibilities were somewhat bruised*

> *By 1920 Laura's column "The Farm Home" had been published for*
> *two years in the* Ruralist. *Her friendly rapport with her editor was*
> *briefly ruffled in late 1920. The misunderstanding was settled, and*
> *Laura's submissions continued unabated. Her column was re-*
> *named; it became "As a Farm Woman Thinks."*

DECEMBER 8, 1920

Dear Mr. Case:

My sensibilities were somewhat bruised by the December 5th issue of the Ruralist. I see that I am no longer Farm Home editor but that Mrs. Migliario has taken my honors as well as the name of my department.

Does this mean that I am not to do any more editorial work? It looked so interesting to me that I am sorry to give it up. I am writing personal letters to all the women who wrote to me in the contest . . . but under the circumstances perhaps I would better not send them.

I am sure it was not your intention that I should be humiliated before the Ruralist readers. But I feel it in that way, to be put off the editorial staff in just the way it has been done. It seems to me that the Ruralist does not need two Farm Home departments. . . .

## After dinner we sat by the fire

*Laura and Manly spent a cozy Christmas together in 1920, alone on Rocky Ridge. Rose was in Paris, working as a publicist for the American Red Cross; she telegraphed warm greetings to her parents. In a surviving letter fragment, Laura describes the holiday for her family in De Smet. Laura's sister Grace, and her husband, Nate Dow, were living with Caroline and Mary Ingalls in the family home.*

DECEMBER 27, 1920

Dear Mother and Sisters:

We were glad to get your letter Grace. It came on Christmas day. Manly and I spent the day by ourselves, with roast chicken and dressing, mashed Irish potato, baked sweet potato, brown bread, white bread, blackberry jelly, doughnuts, sweet potato pie (in place of pumpkin pie), cheese and coffee, for dinner. After dinner we sat by the fire in the fireplace and read and looked at our Christmas cards and letters. Then later we popped corn over the fire and ate apples and walnuts and corn.

We did not give each other presents of any value. I had made Manly a scrap book of clippings he was particularly fond of. . . .

# CHAPTER 2

# THE EMERGING WRITER
## (1921–1930)

Rose, Laura, and Isabelle, the Buick, in the Tennessee Pass,
Colorado, 1925. (*Herbert Hoover Presidential Library*)

*As America entered the 1920s, Rocky Ridge remained a quiet,
isolated country home. Laura and Manly found it increasingly
difficult to maintain the place. Rose abhorred her parents' relent-
less workload, and gave them a yearly $500 subsidy, enabling
them to reduce their labors. Rose's writing career flourished as she
continued her travels through Europe and the Middle East. At
last, in 1923, she returned to Rocky Ridge, vowing to spend time
at home.*

*The 1920s' new technology, cultural changes, booming economy,
and added leisure time influenced the Wilders' lives. A media
boom enabled Rose to sell her writings for high fees. With the*

proceeds, she bought her parents their first car. Rose spent freely on credit, her confidence bolstered as her stock market portfolio grew. Laura and Manly likewise invested their own small savings. When Rose felt assured that her parents were comfortable, she left the farm in 1926 to travel with her friend Helen Boylston, a nurse and sometimes writer. The women first settled in Paris, then moved on to Albania, where they lived until 1928.

Flush with selling a magazine serial for $10,000, Rose built a new house on Rocky Ridge for her parents' retirement home. The Rock House, as it was called, was a monument to 1920s consumerism. Rose symbolically presented the house to Laura and Manly as a 1928 Christmas gift. Next she customized the farmhouse to fit her own tastes. Electricity and central heating were added. Helen Boylston, supported by an annuity, continued as Rose's housemate in the original Rocky Ridge Farmhouse. In October 1929, less than a year after the Rock House was completed, the stock market collapsed. Rose was burdened with two expensive households to support, a dwindling market for her magazine stories, depleted savings, and a plummeting stock market account.

Laura was retired from the Missouri Ruralist and her farm loan job. Rocky Ridge was no longer a working farm; it provided only garden stuff, milk, and eggs. During this era of personal and national economic emergency, Laura resumed writing. In the modern Rock House, she pondered over the frontier times she knew, and drafted an autobiography. It was titled Pioneer Girl. It was the prelude to writing her Little House books.

## Dear Farm Women

Agricultural products were in high demand during World War I, but the inevitable postwar demand left farmers disgruntled. Returning soldiers abandoned the farm; cities lured them with better *wages and shorter work hours. The* Missouri Ruralist *invited the female readership to share views on the problem. Laura was gratified with the response; her note to readers was published in the* Ruralist's *first issue of 1921.*

JANUARY 5, 1921

Dear Farm Women,

For several years I have been talking and talking, hearing no reply, until I came to feel no one was listening to me. And to find that you are really there and will answer back is truly delightful.

Mrs. A. J. Wilder

## *I'm so hungry to see you*

*Laura enclosed a letter from* Ruralist *editor George Jordan when she wrote Rose, who was in Paris. Jordan said he "wanted to let you know that with your stories the pleasure of reading them compensates for the hatred I have of editing. . . . Frankly Mrs. Wilder, I like you and your stories better than anything that reaches us." Laura's letter alludes to Rose's continued financial support. Rose urged Laura and Manly to semiretire. She advised: "Think of Rocky Ridge as a country home, and not as a farm . . . there is so much that is fun to do on a farm, when you aren't killing yourselves trying to make a living on it."*

[CIRCA APRIL 1921]

Dear Rose,

Here is a letter I want you to read but I hate to send it to you for I like to read it over now and then. It gives me such a warm, comfortable feeling around in my interior decorations but I have decided that pleasure of sharing it with you is greater than that of keeping it. I have never seen Mr. Jordan you know; he is associate editor of the Ruralist.

Please do not lose the letter if it is not too much trouble to keep it and some day perhaps I may warm my feet again by reading it over.

Funny about the [lost] bags. Manly swears it's the same story but I'm glad as glad if it isn't [a reference to missing gifts sent by Rose]. A collar from Switzerland should have come with the hat, I suppose that was from Peggy [Peggy Marquis, a photographer and Rose's frequent travel companion on magazine assignments]. But the box was torn up and the collar and a box of Paris candy lost out. Later she sent Manly some ties and me some candy and a little powder box. I haven't heard from her since. It will be nice for you to have the old crowd in Paris.

I want to send Berta something [likely a gift for the artist Berta Hoerner Hader, whose son had been born in March] but I haven't the faintest idea what her address is and can't send it in care of Betty [Bessie Beatty] if she has resigned from McCalls, that is the only address I know for her. That's what Berta gets for not sending me a Christmas card. I wish Betty would not go into Russia. There is no doubt that it is a very unpleasant place. . . .

I do hope you are back from your Constantinople and beyond trip by now [this trip was canceled; it would occur in 1922] and that you are well and rested. I'm feeling fine and the weather is beautiful; indications are that we will have a dry summer and spring seems to be a month ahead of time. Planted the early potatoes yesterday—dark of the moon you know—had to plant 'em!

There isn't any news to write you. I haven't been to town to see anyone for so long except to the Farm Loan Association and then I was tied up all afternoon in the hall handling business. [Laura's office was in the Odd Fellows Hall on Mansfield's square.] Our colored member was there and when he was introduced to me I shook hands with him which nearly paralyzed some of the others. But if we have him for president, why not treat the colored brother kindly? [A reference to rumors that President Warren Harding had African ancestry; she was egalitarian in her views on race and nationality, and abhorred sexism, child labor, and the inappropriate use of power.]

I'm a hero worshiper, you know, and likewise a bitter ender and almost all the other foolish things you can think of.

Supreme Court has declared the Farm Loan Act constitutional so we'll begin business again as soon as the business can be put in shape. I'll be one busy person then, for I think everyone wants a loan.

I'm so hungry to see you Honeybug, my little Busybee. Write when you can find time and are not too tired and I will not let there be such a gap in my letters again.

Loving you so much,

Mama Bess

## Treated like visiting princesses

*When Rose's employment with the American Red Cross termi-nated, she was hired by Near East Relief to do similar publicity work. The new job sent her on fact-finding missions as she wrote about the organization's humanitarian efforts. In this letter frag-ment, Laura shares news of Rose with her aged mother, Caroline Ingalls.*

[CIRCA SEPTEMBER 1922]

A letter from Rose yesterday, so I can tell you the good news that she is about five miles from Constantinople and she says we are not to worry about her for they are treated like visiting princesses and no one will harm them. They are both with the Near East Relief people, you know, Rose writing and Peggy taking the pictures. Her letter was written on ship board on the Black Sea and dated September 2. She says that they would be in Batumi the next Sunday. The Black Sea ports were closed so they would go the whole 585 miles from

Constantinople without a stop. They will take a trip through Armenia, Georgia, Azerbaijan, and northern Persia, then back to Constantinople. After that, Palestine, Mesopotamia, Egypt and possibly, Arabia.

## *Just live on the Ozark climate and views*

> *Meroe Andrews and Ed Stanton made their wedding plans while they picnicked at Rocky Ridge Farm on July 4, 1915. When the couple moved to Florida, Manly supervised the loading of their possessions onto one end of a railroad emigrant car. The other end was reserved for the Stantons' livestock, which Manly tended on the trip to Florida. On visits to Missouri, the Stantons and their five children never failed to call on the Wilders.*

DECEMBER 17, 1924

My Dear Meroe:

You will likely be surprised to hear from me after so long a time, but if you knew how often I have planned to write to you "tomorrow" and how busy I have been, you would forgive me the delay in answering your letter.

We often speak of you and wonder how you all are and if you still like Florida. There is no prospect yet of our leaving here, but sometimes we wish we were loose from everything for a little while anyway.

We are well as usual and have cut down our farming until we really don't do any. Just live on the Ozark climate and views.

The State Highway runs just north of the house now, just far enough away that the dust does not reach us. It is only now open to travel. People say it has added $1000 in value to our farm, but we don't see it that way. We get tramps now and people who want to stay all night or borrow things to fix their cars and all that. It is a nuisance.

Rose is in New York now. She was with us nearly a year and will be back again in January. It is lonesome with her gone and we will be glad when she is with us again. . . .

And now I will get my little bit of business out of the way. The Federal Land Bank has made a new ruling that stickers like the enclosed one must be attached to canceled certificates after this, and they asked that we get them signed and attach them wherever we could to those transferred before the ruling (meaning unclear; possibly a bureaucratic technique to validate loan documents). . . . I will appreciate it very much if you will sign it and return it to me at once so I can get my books in shape as soon as possible.

Mr. Timberlake and I were talking over the phone this morning. He said they were both "fine as silk." I haven't seen Mrs. Timberlake for ages, nor any of the Quigleys. . . . They come out to see us whenever they come to see Sophie's mother. Sophie has her hair bobbed now. I wonder if you have bobbed your beautiful hair, some way I hope not.

How I would like to see you and the kids, I can't believe you are grown up and with such a houseful of children. Give my regards to Ed. And we wish you all a Merry Christmas and a very happy New Year.

Lovingly your friend,

Mrs. A. J. Wilder

*A few words to the voters*

*In March 1925, Laura made her sole bid for political office. She ran for tax collector of Pleasant Valley Township, which paid an annual salary of $300. She claimed the independent farmer's ticket, though she was well known as a Democrat. She roundly lost the election, but Rose remarked that "thank goodness Mama Bess doesn't awfully mind." Laura's statement to voters leaned heavily on her Farm Loan Association work.*

I have been asked to place my name before the voters of Pleasant Valley Township as candidate for the office of Collector in the election of March 31, 1925.

Mr. Wilder and I came to Wright County thirty years ago and bought the farm east of Mansfield where we now live. My character is known to neighbors and friends throughout the county. I have been a busy farm woman and have not had time to do as much for the community as I would have liked to do, but wherever possible I have done my best.

Seven years ago, with eight other farmers, I organized the Mansfield National Farm Loan Association, which I have served ever since as Secretary-Treasurer. The Association now has 54 members. . . . I have been entrusted with $102,675 . . . government money, which the Association has loaned to farmers in this community at 5½% interest. I believe that this amount of money . . . has increased our prosperity . . . and has been of direct or indirect value to us all.

I have personally handled all the details of these loans and been responsible for the money. Federal bank examiners certify that I have attended promptly to the business and that my records are always accurate and in order. I believe the members of the Farm Loan Association who receive an 8% dividend on their stock every year will testify that my work has been satisfactory to them.

After these seven years of experience I am confident that I can perform the duties of Collector of Pleasant Valley township. . . .

I am not a politician and have no thought of entering politics, but I appreciate very much the compliment of being asked to be candidate for this office. . . .

Mrs. A. J. Wilder

## Wonderful for the family to have such a record

*Laura's last regular column in the* Ruralist *was printed in December 1924. Rose had returned to Rocky Ridge from her travels and was living there. Her articles and short stories were published regularly in* Country Gentleman *and other mainstream magazines. She urged Laura to submit to* Country Gentleman, *assisting her in placing two articles in 1925: "My Ozark Kitchen" and "The Farm Dining Room." Laura thought of her pioneer heritage as possible writing grist. She wrote her elderly aunt Martha Quiner Carpenter in Pepin, Wisconsin, asking for family lore. This letter indicates her first tentative resolve to write about frontier times.*

JUNE 22, 1925

Dear Aunt Martha,

Mary [Ingalls] writes that you have not had the circular yet and so I am cutting across the corner and writing you direct. [Quiner-Ingalls relatives maintained a continuing circulating letter that shared family news for many decades.]

I have been wondering how you are standing the hot summer, for I suppose it is warm weather there as well as here. We have been having a very dry season as well as hot and are needing rain very badly now. We are not doing much farming but would be glad to have rain on meadows and pastures.

Rose is still here and busy on a new book. I don't know what the title is nor how soon it will be finished. It is a story of the Ozarks. [The book became *Hill-Billy.*] Her friend Helen Boylston from New Hampshire is still here with her. [Rose met Boylston, a nurse, in Europe. She became a semipermanent guest on Rocky Ridge, and Rose's traveling companion.]

We are all usually well just now but I have had a very serious sickness, very near to nervous prostration. It is good to be well again, though I am not very strong. . . . [Wilder's illness prompted Rose's return to the farm in January; she referred to her mother's illness as indeterminate exhaustion, brought on by overwork.]

The Ladies Home Journal is wanting me to write an article for them on our grandmother's cooking, brought down to date, and I am thinking that you could give me some old recipes for dishes that your mother or yourself used to cook. . . . I would like to cook them for myself as well as write about them.

Mother used to make what she called "Vanity Cakes." . . . They were mostly egg and they were friend in deep fat. When done they were simply bubbles, usually with a hollow center and they were crisp around the edges. Perhaps you know how to make them. I would so much like to have the recipe.

There was something I wanted the girls to do for me, but they never got around to it and Mother herself was not able. I wanted all the stories she could remember of the early days in Wisconsin when you were all children and young people. Now it is too late to ever get them from her [Caroline Ingalls died in 1924], but I think as I thought then it would be wonderful for the family to have such a record.

I want them principally for that, but I think too that Rose could make some stories from such a record, for publication and that would be fine too.

Could you, I wonder, tell the story of those days. . . . Just tell it in your own words . . . if only you could talk to me.

If you will do it, I will be glad to pay the stenographer for taking it down for me and I want lots of it, pages and pages of things you remember. As you begin to tell it so many things will come back to you about the little everyday happenings and what you and Mother and Aunt Eliza and Uncle Tom and Uncle Henry did as children and young folks, going to parties and sleigh rides and spelling schools and dancing school, if you did, or whatever young folks did do then. About your work and school too. Also about way back when Grandma

[Charlotte Tucker Quiner] was left a widow and the Indians used to share their game with her and the children. . . .

We have thought about going up to see you and talk about these things but I am not able to make such a trip. . . .

Please Aunt Martha, do tell these stories for us all . . . I can make a copy . . . and pass them on to the rest of the cousins.

I am very busy these days with my writing, though I do not pretend to write anything like Rose. Still I have no trouble in having the little things I do write published. Keeping house does not leave much time for other things as you know.

What do you do to pass the time away? You read a good deal, I know, and that is such a pleasure. I have gotten so that I would rather sit in a rocking chair and travel with a book than to make the exertion of going anywhere.

Rose still wants to travel and after a long rest at home she plans to go to Europe again and wander around for a time.

Give my love to all the cousins that are within reach. Tell them I often think of them all. With much love to you,

Your niece,

Laura Ingalls Wilder

### *I had forgotten what sunset and starlight was like on the prairie*

*Accustomed to naming horses and other farm animals, the Wilders' dubbed their Buick "Isabelle." Rose taught both her parents to drive, but Manly became the chauffeur. In September 1925 Laura, Rose, and their peppy houseguest Helen Boylston drove from Rocky Ridge to California. Manly stayed at home to tend the farm, and he received regular postcards and letters from the three women as they journeyed through Kansas, Colorado, Nevada, and California. The trip, with some nearly impassable roads en route, was considered adventurous for three women traveling without a male escort.*

Hotel Lassen
Wichita, Kansas
SEPTEMBER 18, 1925
Dear Manly,

We got to Wichita last night. We had to detour all over the state of Kansas because they were working on the highway so we did not get here until the sun had set and the stars came out, but we were in time for a late supper. It had been a hard day, so we are staying over a day to rest. The hotel is nice and comfortable and Isabelle has behaved well all the time so far.

I had forgotten what sunset and starlight was like on the prairie and the girls had never seen anything like it, or rather Rose did not remember, and Helen had never seen it. The wind of course blows all the time in the regular old way and everything is blowing on the street. I am glad we are in Missouri for I could not stand it to live in the wind.

Dodge City is the next stop and an easy drive, they say.

I hope everything is all right and that you are keeping comfortable. Rose is talking of getting you one of the new style Fords, but I don't know what she will do, of course....

There isn't anything to write for nothing happens, we just drive over the roads and stop at the usual hotel. Everyone has been very kind and helpful and the hotels make special efforts for tourists.

Lots of love,
Bessie

*Please do remember to be careful about the fires*

Lakin, Kansas
SEPTEMBER 21, 1925
Dear Manly,

We were held up yesterday in western Kansas by a bad storm and frightful roads. Spent the night in this little country town hotel kept by people who came here from Missouri 19 years ago. The storm is over this morning and the wind is drying the roads so that we expect to start on again in about an hour.

Thirty five miles more and we will be out of the state of Kansas and on good roads. The roads are good all through Colorado we are told and the passes are still open. Depends on the weather. If there is any danger of bad weather in the mountains we will turn south and take the southern route but we think we are in time to get through.

It is strange to see the plains again with nothing to break the view in any direction as far as we can see. We are now on the old Santa Fe trail along the Arkansas river. The country is still full of buffalo grass and houses are miles and miles apart. Land can be bought for $10 an acre and they think this is a great country if people would only try to farm instead of running to town all the time. A good crop of corn is 19 bushels to the acre. The only people who are making good are those who are keeping cows and selling cream. The woman here at the hotel says they cannot get along unless they do.

It is cold here this morning and I have on my high shoes and a sweater. Your warm underclothes are in your sock box in the closet. I don't know whether I told you or not.

Please do remember to be careful about the fires.

We expect to be making better time from now on because we do not get tired riding anymore and once we get across the mountains we will have good roads. We all have a feeling that the state of Kansas put a hoodoo on us [a traditional African American term meaning a run of bad luck] trying to keep us in the state. We feel we must make a special effort to get out of the state of Kansas. We expect to do that and much more today if all goes well. The girls will be along soon and I must fix the suitcases and be ready.

Take good care of yourself. The girls have promised if the trip drags out too long they will send me home on the train, but I do want to see the Painted Desert on the way home if possible.

Saw one of the new Fords yesterday. It is a beauty. The man said it is going to make the old Fords awful cheap. They would have to about give them away, so don't do anything reckless because you think it is a bargain.

Lots of love,

Bessie

## Postcards to Manly

[Postmarked from Grand Junction, Colorado]
*Some of the dates on Laura's letters and cards are incorrect. She*
*obviously sent small bunches of mail to Manly when she had access*
*to a post office.*

SEPTEMBER 22, 1925

All day we have driven among the mountains with snow on the tops but have not been cold. We are now past danger in the passes from snow. Are staying tonight in Glenwood Springs and tomorrow going to Grand Junction. Everything fine.

Bessie

SEPTEMBER 22, 1925

Buena Vista is a beautiful town in a valley with snow topped mountains all around. The air is wonderful and so is the water. It was very warm in the valley but the air was so fresh from the snow on the mountains.

## We all like eastern Colorado

The Antlers Hotel
Colorado Springs, Colorado
SEPTEMBER 22, 1925
Dear Manly,

We got into Colorado Springs last night and we are stopping at this beautiful hotel. The girls have gone downtown to have Isabelle repacked and gone over a little for the trip to Denver and over the pass.

We expect to have an early lunch and start before long for Denver. The car is running beautifully, the engine just purring along. I do believe that barring accidents it will make the trip and be as good as ever. We have had good luck in finding Buick garages all along the way to give us oil and gas and look the car over to see that it is all right. Helen is proving to be a careful driver and we do not go as fast as some because she will not slam the car over rough places nor take any chances. I think you can rest perfectly easy about that. Colorado roads are good and the whole feeling of the state is different than Kansas. Everyone we meet hates Kansas.

Yesterday we came through the melon growing district, melons and alfalfa and honey to be sold by the truck load. Rocky Ford is a beautiful small city. We got cantaloupe and a Dew Drop melon being packed in crates at packing sheds beside the road for miles. We could not stop to get the seeds [for you] for we were going to be late getting here, but I will mail them tomorrow.

It is cold here and the air and water are splendid. The sky was lighted last night by the glow from the smelters etc. It was a weird looking light.

We saw potatoes piled in the fields yesterday and dozens & dozens of Shetland ponies and little colts. The horses are nice too, and children are riding them to school. We all like eastern Colorado.

I wrote you yesterday from our last stop in Kansas, but it was such a funny little place I feel like you might not get the letter. We are all well, but I am rather dreading to have my ears pop when I go over the pass.

The people are so nice through here, the regular old western type. I thought it has disappeared, but it is the same as it used to be. Made me feel queer as though I had gone back years and years.

Tell you what—let's sell the farm, pack our suitcases, take Isabelle with her nice heater and go wandering for awhile before we settle down again.

Helen is some surprised at the size of the U.S. Says she knew it was six days by train to San Francisco but it didn't mean much to her. She had no idea it was so far and was sort of overwhelmed by the prairies.

Rose is already planning her next novel, but I am intent on moving the trip along, to see as much as possible but to get home as soon as we can. [Rose noted her mother's uneasiness and eagerness to return home.]

We will not stop in Denver as we planned but will go on. Take good care of yourself and we will be home before long so you can take your trip South.

Lots of love,
Bessie

## *Postcards to Manly*

[Postmarked from Buena Vista, Colorado]

SEPTEMBER 26, 1925

We went through this pass on the road from Colorado Springs. Buena Vista is 7980 foot high. We are leaving this morning to cross the mountains through Tennessee Pass. By night we will be past danger of snow in the passes. Will not go through Denver because of storms that way. Saved 300 miles by this route.

Bessie

## *"This world . . . she's sure a whopper"*

Hotel Utah
Salt Lake City, Utah
SEPTEMBER 28, 1925
Dear Manly,

As you see, we have reached Salt Lake City. Got here at 4 p.m. yesterday.

I have not written you a letter since we were in Lakin, Kansas, because I would be tired when we got in and there were no writing materials in our rooms. Then in the morning we would try for an early start. So I have been sending you just postcards. Hope you got the crate of Rocky Ford melons all right, that ought to be enough seeds.

I am afraid to mail the Honey Dew melon seeds. They are so wonderful. . . . I shall bring them home safely.

From Lakin we got an early start and were out of Kansas and at Holly, Colorado at lunch time. We were all glad to see the last of Kansas. . . . The drive from Dodge City to Lakin was so short but we were two hours getting over 20 miles of road. Of course we could have dashed on and wrecked Isabelle and maybe ourselves but we wanted to go the rest of the way.

As soon as we struck Colorado the roads were good, though rather awful among the mountains and over the deserts. We drove from Lakin to Colorado Springs in one day through wonderful mountain scenery and gorges and streams. Colorado Springs is a nice place among the mountain tops. We passed Pike's Peak on our way out the next morning, went through the Ute Pass and traveled all day within sight of snow covered mountain peaks. Stopped at Buena Vista that night and there is a really wonderful place! A little city in a hollow among mountains. The air was cold at night so that I put my coat on my bed for extra cover. In the morning the sun shone warm and all around the town snow covered mountain peaks rose high into the air. The air was wonderful to breathe. I've never smelled any like it before. It was warm . . . and so wonderfully fresh and pure. The water came down from the mountains and bubbled in drinking fountains on the streets. It was of course cold and soft.

We drove most of the next day in sight of snow and there had been a sprinkle on the roads. . . . Between Colorado Springs and Glenwood Springs we stopped for lunch at Leadville, where we sent the cantaloupe. It is a mining town, but quite a nice city. Glenwood Springs was the next stop, a summer resort, just closed. The mountains shut in so close around, that the air seemed stale and damp.

From Glenwood Springs we traveled through more mountains the character of which changed until they were desert mountains, altogether different from the eastern slope of the Rockies. We passed through a tunnel three miles long, instead of going through Independent Pass. The tunnel route was shorter, with better roads.

We stopped at Grand Junction over night and next morning soon were out of the desert. It was not a sand desert, more silt and dirt which drifted into piles and mounds, then became set and caked. Sagebrush and cactus grew here and there for awhile and then, even that stopped and there was nothing but the awful baked, queer looking earth.

We were told at Grand Junction that there had been floods in Utah and bad washouts on the desert. . . . Bridges were out . . . we had to go through the washes because the bridges were not rebuilt. Believe me, Isabelle with Helen driving can point her nose straight up and climb out of a wash. I think she could climb the side of a house!

We had lunch at Green River, which is a hot desert town. We all wore goggles to protect our eyes and Helen and Rose wore green eye-shades when driving, besides the goggles.

After Green River the desert was worse and worse. Hot. We passed through the oil field where the government gets the gas for their air ships, the kind that will not set them on fire. We got across the desert safely and stopped at Price, Utah at night, which made for an easy run into Salt Lake City yesterday.

There is a desert dry farmer just the other side of Green River, who came there because he was tired of cities. He is a good mechanic and he has three automobiles that people abandoned, giving up the drive in despair, and taking the train out. The mechanic easily fixed the cars.

We passed two men at a washout on the desert. One was from Mexico and lay asleep or drunk in the shade of the bank. The other man sat on the running board of the car, watching the road. They were loaded down with weapons, guns, and knives. We sailed merrily by them.

From Price we went through mountains again, range after range of desert mountains, no timber on them, just rocks and very low bushes that are red, yellow, brown and some green. We came through these mountains into the Salt Lake valley.

We are staying at Salt Lake City to have Isabelle gone over, oiled and washed and polished up for her body's sake. There is, I believe, a little tightening to be done here and there. The engine is running like a watch, brakes held beautifully, but we want to be *sure* everything is right about her for the rest of the trip. We expect to be here two days, and then four days should put us into San Francisco.

The girls are out looking at the city and buying some clothes while I write you. Everyone has been as nice as possible to us. I believe we will all be glad to get home again, for "if this world is as big in other directions as it is in this, she's sure a whopper."

Helen is some astonished. She had never seen anything like the country we have gone through and I think she thought it didn't amount to much west of Buffalo, New York, except for California.

I am sending you a sprig of sagebrush. Smell it! Also sending some maps under separate cover, which shows our route.

I am enjoying the trip, but times I wish I was home, for after all, I do get tired, and "there is no place like home." We are getting anxious to hear from you and expect to do so in San Francisco. Don't have any worry about us.... I do hope everything is all right at home and that it is still warm there.

Love from us all,

Bessie

## Postcards to Manly

Tonopah, Nevada

OCTOBER 2, 1925

Dear Manly,

This house was built of empty green bottles laid in plaster. Relics of the old days. Our journey will soon be over now with good luck and we will be on the way back.

Love,

Bessie

OCTOBER 2, 1925

Tonopah, Nevada is a pretty mountain hometown, the home of the Comstock Lode, richest in the world. The vein of ore 60–70 feet wide, much of it pure enough to go direct to the smelter. Silver and gold. The finding of this mine won the Civil War for the North, and riches.

*An unearthed $400 million in silver from the Comstock Lode did indeed help finance the North's defeat of the Confederacy.*

*It has been a wonderful trip*

The Palace Hotel
San Francisco
OCTOBER 4, 1925
Manly Dear,

We got into San Francisco this noon and are settled in this hotel for the few days we will stay. Rose had intended to stay two weeks but has cut the time to one week, for which I am more than glad. I am homesick. (Please don't ever tell Rose.)

We found your letters waiting for us with a big bunch of other mail for the girls. I don't see how other people make the trip to California and back so quickly. It must be hard on their cars to say nothing of themselves. . . . Someway I cannot believe them at least if they go the way we have. It has been a wonderful trip and I am glad I have seen it but I would not take it again for anything. I have had all the mountain travel I want and I think Rose has too. Helen is a very careful driver in really bad places like Tioga Pass, and she has been very easy on the car. The engine is running like a watch and everything in good order except that the body is dusty and travel stained but a cleaning and paint will fix that.

Manly I have thought how long you have been tied to the farm and when I get home you *are going* somewhere for a trip if for no other reason than to make you glad to get back home again. It is really doing me lots of good. You know how tired it made me to ride only a little way in the car and now I ride 250 or 300 miles and am not a bit dizzy at night, and my head is clearer than it has been for years.

I had gotten so at home that I went through everything in a sort of daze and felt as though I was all tied up with everything. It has done me good to break away for a little and you shall do it too. You need it. Then, as I said before I left, we can take hold of things on

Rocky Ridge with some pleasure in it and with our little income we ought to be able to have a good time, too.

I had thought of the trip north that Mrs. Aubert [unidentified] told you about and I think it would be a nice trip, but if we can't sell the farm we will use Isabelle to run around with. Sometimes I am like you in thinking that I can't bear to give up Rocky Ridge for as you say, you have made it all with your own hands. I am sure we can have a good time there if we can only break away a little from the work.

I haven't written you very often because we have started as early as we could get started in the morning and I was dead tired every night when we got in. I have written a bit of a diary every day to read and talk over with you when I get back but it is just scribbled while the car was going so nobody could read it but me.

I haven't seen any place that I think either of us would really want to come to. It seems that where the land is level there is always something else wrong with it. There are places in eastern Colorado where they raise the melons and honey that looked nice to work, but it gets awfully cold there in winter. There are places to raise sheep and cattle where I think we might like it, if we were younger, but they are so far away from every place, and we are not strong enough to do it now.

There is government land in Nevada where we could take desert claims and I believe it will be a wonderful country some day. For I feel sure we could take desert claims . . . someday for they will get the water on it. It is level of course and the soil is rich as rich but it is desert now and will be for years to come and we are too old to help make any more new countries. The valley here in California is of course level and rich . . . but the land is too high priced as it was before. [During her 1915 visit to California, Laura had also explored the possibility of moving west.]

I think if we find a place any better than Rocky Ridge you will have to be the one to find it. I can't.

I do like the western people though. It sounds good to hear again the hearty, western "You bet I will!" and have the waiter call me "dear" instead of "honey" as they do at the small hotels where we sometimes have to stop.

The day we left Salt Lake City we traveled down the valley and out of it through sage brush hills and across deserts and over desert mountains and stopped at a little town called Beaver. Next day we crossed more sagebrush hills and across deserts and over desert mountains to Ely, Nevada. It is a mining town built all up and down a gulch in the mountains. We did not get in until after dark but we had to keep going because there was nowhere else to stop. Ate supper at a Chinese restaurant and slept in a very comfortable hotel in old Ely. The new town was full. I heard the blasts going off in the night and it was really a western mining town.

The next day we climbed over mountains and across more desert. Right in the middle of the desert miles from anywhere we found three men building a filling station. They seemed awfully glad to have a chance to talk to us. The little frame store and lunch room and filling station were combined and the piping of water to it from the mountains cost them $10,000. It cost them $25 a thousand to get lumber hauled in and $9 a day for carpenters to build it. Gasoline cost us 50 cents a gallon, and we were glad to get it.

I am tired. We drove 100 miles this morning to get here and I've been busy since.

Lovingly,

Bessie

## We had good roads all through Colorado

OCTOBER 6, 1925

Manly Dear,

Another letter from you came a little bit ago.

We had to change our plans and not go to Denver because of storms and snow in the mountains that caused us to turn south and go through Tennessee Pass. We had good roads all through Colorado and they were rained on and washed out in Utah deserts.

The girls came in to get ready for the dinner they are going to. They had been out getting their faces and hair fixed up. They each bought a new evening dress for the occasion and look stunning.

I am sorry I am not there to talk about buying the mules but of course by now you have used your own judgment about it. So would I rather get money from the cream than the farm loan business. You don't know how tired I am of the work and responsibility of that secretary business, but you know I have tried to do my part of the cream work . . . so we would get the money for both. But I think I will not have to do [the farm loan business] any longer for John Brentlinger is right, we will not make any more loans if we have to send a larger fee to the Federal Loan Bank.

So after you have your vacation we will sell cream. [Manly planned to visit his siblings in Louisiana.] I think you are doing wonderfully well to get $4 a week off the cream. You see the milk is not so much disturbed as it is when I am home.

Don't worry about cleaning up the house. Let it go until I get back, only take good care of yourself and the dogs. Poor Judy [a farm dog]. Don't pet Nero more than you do her, and make her feel badly.

I hope John [a neighboring farmer] does make them pay for the corn the cow gets into.

Oh, you see we could not tell you the towns ahead [of us] for we knew our way depended on the weather. We might have had to beat it south and come in by the southern route. As it was we came through the Tennessee Pass just ahead of the snow and as we left Nevada over the mountains we were just ahead of another storm that would have made the roads impassable, but we wanted to see that country on the way over, for we can see the other coming back. There will be no snow to stop us or kill us by slipping off some mountain. . . .

Let me see—I left our trip at Mono Lake in the other letter. The wind blew all night and was still blowing in the morning so hard that

Isabelle could hardly face it. We got an early start, so early we had to get the first garage man out of bed to give us gas. Mono Lake was simply covered with ducks when we woke . . . and began to climb the mountains to get to Tioga Pass. [A tense moment on the pass caused Rose to abandon the wheel to Helen, and limit all future driving.] We climbed and climbed up one rise and then the next until we got in among the peaks where the wind did not hit us. At first there were houses in the valleys and little farms. Then we came to a national forest reserve and there were ranger cabins here and there. Then we found ourselves on the mountainside. . . .

To climb the mountain the road bends back on itself twice to ascend. We climbed into the sky among the snow peaks and saw frozen waterfalls below us. Never again will I climb over the mountains unless I have to do so.

Rose and Helen exclaimed over the scenery and smoked cigarettes but I could only pinch myself to keep from screaming and look for the end of the climb. Please don't tell anyone this.

At last we passed the summit and soon came to where Uncle Sam had a cable stretched across the road and a little house at one side [this was the entrance to Yosemite]. A big sign said "Stop!" "Blow your horn!" We did so and a man came out and asked us if we were intending to go straight through, if we had any firearms or any dogs or cats. No dogs or cats are allowed to go into Yosemite National Park, no one is allowed to take in any firearms and the park was closed to campers. We were late, you see, but as we were going straight through the [park ranger] lowered the cable and let us pass after we had paid $5 for a permit.

Then we came into a wonderful place, a lake, creeks and rivers and the blessed woods again. You see all those awful mountains on the west slope of the Rockies and the east slope of the Sierra Nevadas are not timbered but now we were among giant pines and cedars and hemlocks and redwoods and quivering, beautiful aspens. There were nice big, clean boulders and grassy meadows. We passed a lake whose

Indian name means Lake of the Shining Rocks and the mountains around it sparkled and shone where the rocks were. We passed through Wildcat Canyon and White Wolf Meadows and then began to climb again. It seemed as though the top was a depression or hollow down into which we went and up again out.

I saw a deer among the boulders on a hill. Oh, it was the most beautiful thing. I got one good look at it with its beautiful antlers . . . then it disappeared. The girls didn't see it at all.

There was another cable across the road on the other side of the park and another guard who also took the number of our car, where we were from, and where we were going . . . and let us go on. Then we were in another forest reserve and the beautiful woods. Had lunch at Carl Inn, a summer resort. All the way we saw camps of forest rangers here and there. We passed Bret Harte's old house. [Harte (1836–1902) specialized in fiction of the Old West and the California Gold Rush, literature favored by the Wilders.]

And then we came to the road down off the mountains, corresponding to the road up in Tioga Pass, though not such a steep descent. . . . This wind down the mountain was 6½ miles long. Plenty long enough.

It got dark while we were going down . . . and at last we struck the cement road and went on into Oakdale where we stayed all night. Next morning we followed the cement road 90 some miles into Oakland. Then across the bay on the ferry into San Francisco. We had lunch on the ferry as we were crossing.

When we got settled into the Palace Hotel in San Francisco, Rose had to buy some shoes, get the mail, read it, and write answers. Then we walked through Chinatown to Little Italy for 7 o'clock dinner. We ate and listened to the music and watched the dancing, then went to a movie and back to the hotel.

Imagine me doing that all in one day!

Today Rose and Helen shopped, and Rose had interviews and callers and phone calls. I have been touching up my hair a little and resting and helping Rose now and then. Tomorrow they will both be wrecks, after tonight. And it is time I was in bed myself. Good night.

Lovingly,

Bessie

## *A delightful quaint foreign looking place*

OCTOBER 8, 1925

Dear Manly,

Rose and Helen are out to dinner again tonight. We leave the Palace Hotel tomorrow to go to the Older ranch for Friday, Saturday and Sunday. [Fremont Older was the editor of the *San Francisco Bulletin* and Rose's mentor during her early journalistic career. Older and his wife, Cora, became Rose's valued friends.]

I dread going out to the Olders' and meeting a crowd of strangers but I've got to pretend to like it for Rose's sake. She certainly is popular in California.

Monday Rose has to go to Berkley to see a friend and we expect to start for home on Tuesday if nothing happens. . . . Rose has been so rushed since we got here. Met people she knew before we registered in the hotel and it has been one continual seeing of people and accepting and refusing invitations ever since. We all admitted tonight that we would be glad to be on the road again. We have bought a small trunk and are shipping most of our things home in it, so don't be surprised when it comes. The car was so full that it was crowded and now there are more things . . . we are going to ship everything except what we can get along with on the way home.

I haven't been around San Francisco much. Up on Telegraph Hill and to some of the stores and the restaurant Rose told about in her book. [The book was *He Was a Man,* a fictional biography of Jack London with a San Francisco setting, published by Harper & Brothers in September 1925.]

The Italian who runs the restaurant and his wife, the Coppas, knew Rose and came rushing to greet her. They took extra pains that we should have a good dinner and when we tried to pay, they would not let us. The waiter talked a stream of Italian when Rose asked for the check and bowed and smiled and spread his hands and said "You are welcome." And the woman, "Mama Coppa" came and visited with us and she and "Papa Coppa" shook hands and bowed us out. It was a delightful quaint foreign looking place.

I think when Rose is in Berkley Helen and I will roam around a little.

Lovingly,

Bessie

## Postcard to Manly

[Los Angeles]

OCTOBER 17, 1925

Got here last night. This is a beautiful as well as comfortable hotel. [While in Los Angeles, the ladies stayed at the Biltmore Hotel.] Rose has to see a friend here today and we expect to go on this afternoon.

Love,

Bessie

## We got into the traffic at Hollywood . . . and it is frightful

[Los Angeles]

OCTOBER 17, 1925

Dear Manly,

We are spending part of the day here. Grant Carpenter, the writer, will show us the motion picture studios at Hollywood. [Carpenter, a friend of Rose's, was a San Francisco newspaperman, novelist, and Hollywood scriptwriter.]

We have to look up the best route and roads from here home. There are several ways we can go, all about the same distance. . . . We want to find a road that will bring us home without crossing the high mountains again, because I do not like them with a car. We think this southern route will be the one we want.

It seems to me you must be able to hear the roar of the city when you open this letter. I think less of cities than ever before and you know I did not like them ever . . . this will be the last stop in a large city.

It will hardly be worthwhile for me to write you again because we will be following so closely if we have good luck and it seems a pity to spend the time writing about things when I will so soon be able to tell you much better.

We are all well. Rose and I each have gained four pounds and Helen has lost four. It is a hard job, this cross country driving. We got into the traffic at Hollywood last night and it is frightful. There and here the traffic policeman keeps hurrying the cars to drive faster.

We expect to leave for home this afternoon.

Love,

Bessie

## We often think of you and your visit here

Rose first met Guy Moyston, a newspaperman, in San Francisco. She later encountered him in Europe. Through the 1920s they carried on a mostly long-distance romance, while careers and residences kept them apart. In 1924 Moyston spent three months on Rocky Ridge, collaborating with Rose on a play and a magazine serial. Rose rebuffed Moyston's marriage proposal, disappointing her parents, who were fond of him. In 1926 when Laura wrote to

*Moyston, Rose and Helen were in Paris studying languages at the Berlitz school.*

JUNE 28, 1926

Dear Mr. Moyston,

Mr. Wilder and I were glad to hear from you, for we often think of you and your visit here. You may be interested to know that the Jersey cow is just as mean as ever, but Nero [the Airedale terrier] drives her up to the barn now. Nero has grown to be a wonderful dog.

Yes, isn't this a curious summer. It is a very cold season here but from what we hear. I think it is not so cold as in the east. I suppose you have read the forecast that next summer is to be colder still.

A motor trip to Canada sounds delightful even if the weather was cold, but I am sorry you were disappointed in your vacation plans.

It seems impossible for Mr. Wilder and myself to get away from the farm this summer. We had planned a trip to the Grand Canyon but can find no one with whom we can safely leave the place and the animals.

We are both well as usual.

Wouldn't it be funny if Rose and Troub [Helen Boylston] should get their languages mixed? What a confusion of tongues it would be.

Thanks for the interest check. [Rose's finances were occasionally entangled with Moyston's. Ever mindful of her parents' needs, she arranged for Moyston to forward some interest proceeds to the Wilders, as payment of a debt to her.]

Best regards from us both.

Sincerely,

Mrs. A. J. Wilder

## We hope you'll be on hand

Rocky Ridge Farm was known for its hospitality. Costume parties were held there, as were dances, candlelit suppers, club meetings, and card parties. An "heirloom" birthday celebration was planned as Laura turned sixty-one on February 7, 1928. She composed her own rhyming invitation. Though Rose's name was included, she was not present. At the time, Rose and Helen Boylston were en route home from Albania.

JANUARY 28, 1928

> No doubt you have an heirloom
> A scarf, a book, a shawl,
> A picture or a platter, that good old days recall,
> So an heirloom birthday party
> for special friends we've planned
> With old, treasured heirlooms,
> We hope you'll be on hand
> And tell us of their birthdays,
> So we will understand.
> Laura Ingalls Wilder
> Rose Wilder Lane
> Promptly at 8 p.m.
> February 7, 1928

## Can it be 50 years ago?

The fiftieth anniversary of De Smet's founding was the theme of the town's Old Settlers Day in 1930. Aubrey Sherwood, the energetic publisher of the De Smet News, was passionate about his

*community's story. His relatives, the Masters and Sherwood fami-*
*lies, were linked with the Ingalls family for generations. Aubrey*
*continued to nurture a friendly rapport with the Ingalls daughters.*
*Laura, Carrie, and Grace each contributed their memories to the*
*golden anniversary edition of the De Smet News. Laura sent her*
*recollections to G. E. Mallery, a De Smet druggist. She also con-*
*tributed a poem for publication in the* News.

MARCH 12, 1930
Dear Sir,

My sister Mrs. D. N. Swanzey [Carrie Ingalls] sent your letter to
me asking me to write you what I knew of some of the happenings in
the early days of De Smet.

As my father and family were the very first settlers of De Smet, I
should be able to tell you all the things you wish to know, but being
only a girl I did not pay much attention to some of them. . . .

My father with his family drove from Tracy, Minnesota, the end
of the railroad track, to where Brookings is now located. He was a
bookkeeper and timekeeper at the railroad construction camp there.

Later in the summer as construction work moved west, we drove
from Brookings to the railroad camp on the banks of Silver Lake,
which was then a wild, beautiful little body of water, a resting place
for the wild birds of all kinds. There were many varieties of ducks,
wild geese, swans and pelicans.

In the late fall when the work on the grade stopped, Father was
put in charge of the railroad property left on the ground, which included the house built for the railroad surveyors on the bank of the
lake. We moved into the house and lived there during the winter of
1879–1880.

At Christmas time Mr. and Mrs. Boast arrived and lived in a little
house within a few steps of us. It was there that Mr. and Mrs. Boast
entertained the population of De Smet and Lake Preston at a New
Year's dinner. Our family was De Smet; Lake Preston's population at

that time was one lone, single man named Walter Ogden. He was present and that was the whole of the crowd.

The first church services in Kingsbury County were held in our house, or rather the railroad house in which we were living. That was the last of February [1880]. . . . The Congregational Home Missionary, E. H. Alden [a descendant of the *Mayflower's* John Alden and the Ingalls family's minister in Walnut Grove], with another preacher . . . drove up one night after dark, to our surprise. They stayed a few days and held church services before driving on west. Besides our family and Mr. Boast's, there were present only several other men who were traveling through.

About a week later Reverend Alden and his friend came again, stayed overnight, and held another service before going on east, promising to return later in the spring. These were the only church services held in this house.

The house was later moved from the banks of the lake to the eastern part of town and converted into a section house.

Church services were held in the depot as soon as it was built, by Reverend Woodworth, a retired minister who was the station agent. . . . Father and Mother were very active in the organization of the church and Sunday School during the spring and summer.

Father may be said to have kept the first hotel in De Smet, for ours was the only place one could stop between Brookings and Huron, and when loads of travelers drove up cold and hungry, he took them in and we did the best we could for them.

As soon as Father was relieved from charge of the railroad property we moved into a building he had built on the corner where Couse's Hardware Store stood [at Main and Second Streets]. After selling that location to Mr. Couse, Father put up a building on the [opposite] corner which he later sold to Mr. Carroll for his bank.

I know he was the first Justice of the Peace. His office was in the front room of the building on the Carroll corner, while we lived in the back rooms.

My husband lived on his homestead, north of De Smet, in the fall of 1879 but went out to civilization for the winter and we did not meet until sometime later. We were all there through the winter of 1880–1881, known to all the old timers as the Hard Winter.

Mr. Wilder and myself are planning on being with you people on June 10th and if so, Mr. Wilder can tell you tales of that winter that will present to your imagination the lives we lived at that time. [The Wilders did not travel to De Smet until 1931.] Mr. Wilder can tell the story better than anything I can write about the Hard Winter. Can it be 50 years ago?

Sincerely,

Laura Ingalls Wilder

CHAPTER 3

# A NEW ENTERPRISE
## (1931–1936)

Laura and Manly with their dog, Nero, on the terrace of the
Rock House, September 1929. (*Laura Ingalls Wilder Home Association*)

*Of her emergence as a children's author Laura wrote: "For years I
had thought that the stories my father once told me should be passed
on to other children. I felt they were much too good to be lost. And
so I wrote* Little House in the Big Woods."

*Although* Pioneer Girl *failed to find a publishing home, writing about Laura's childhood was not abandoned. Through her old
friends the author-illustrators Berta and Elmer Hader, Rose met a
children's book editor who was smitten with the idea of a book
based on Laura's frontier memories. Piecing stories together from*

Pioneer Girl, *Laura produced a new manuscript. The book was an account of a year in the life of the Ingalls family in early 1870s Wisconsin. Ultimately, it came to the attention of Harper & Brothers, and was accepted for publication.*

Little House in the Big Woods *was well received when published in 1932, but the deepening Depression limited the market for new books. Sales were respectable enough to encourage Laura to write a second book, this one about Almanzo Wilder's boyhood on a farm in upstate New York.* Farmer Boy *was published in 1933.*

*"My mail was full of letters begging for still another book," Laura said. "The children were still crying, 'Please tell me another story!' My answer was* Little House on the Prairie, *being some more adventures of Pa and Ma, Mary, Laura and Baby Carrie. . . . I have gotten the idea that children like old fashioned stories."*

*By the time* On the Banks of Plum Creek *was under way in 1936, Laura Ingalls Wilder was well launched as one of America's most important children's writers.*

## Postcards to Rose

*In 1931 Laura and Manly packed the Buick for a return trip to South Dakota. Manly had not seen the prairies since 1894; Laura's last visit had been in 1902. With their Airedale, Nero, riding on the running boards, the Wilders reversed the route of their 1894 journey from De Smet to Mansfield. They drove through heat and blistering winds, observing drought conditions as they traveled through north Missouri, Kansas, Nebraska, and into South Dakota. Along the way, Laura kept a journal for Rose to read (published in* A Little House Traveler *in 2006 by Harper Collins.)*

*The Wilders found their arrival in De Smet to be both perplexing and nostalgic: the town was modernized, therefore unfamiliar.*

*Friends and family were gone. The sole relative who remained was*
*Laura's sister Grace. With her husband, Nate Dow, she lived in*
*Manchester, seven miles west of De Smet. Both Dows were as de-*
*pleted physically as their burned-out farmland was. Laura wrote*
*that a day spent in De Smet was "stupid, tiresome and hot." She*
*and Grace made a bittersweet visit to the Ingalls home, now a*
*rental property. There the sisters examined "Ma and Mary's things*
*that had been stored in one room." Laura and Grace discovered*
*that "everything of value has disappeared." Manly drove past his*
*old farms and Laura wrote that no buildings remained, only a*
*grain field and acres of grassland.*

JUNE 8, 1931
Came cross lots from Eureka to Highway 81. Wonderful roads.
On 81 headed north for De Smet, all the way on 81.
Love,
M. B. & A. J.

Belleville, Kansas
JUNE 9, 1931
Just to let you know everything is fine. Car running like a top. In
Belleville, only a few miles from Nebraska state line. 9:30.
Mama Bess

Howard, South Dakota
JUNE 11, 1931
Here at 8 a.m. 26 miles from De Smet. Everything fine. Had
breakfast and about ready to go on.
Love,
Mama Bess

Manchester, South Dakota
JUNE 12, 1931
Rose Dearest,

Am sending you notes made along the way. Please keep them for me. Everything is fine. Nero good as can be. Both of us feeling well.

Will stay a few days longer and then go on to the Black Hills. Will write more later. Lots of love,

Mama Bess

Manchester, South Dakota
JUNE 14, 1931
Rose Dearest,

"So this is De Smet, not London" and here we are. The width of the streets is something beautiful.

Lots of love,

Mama Bess

*The trip west continued to South Dakota's Black Hills. In Keystone there was a reunion with Laura's sister Carrie, who had married David Swanzey, a mine owner. Together they visited Mount Rushmore, where only Washington's face was complete on the mountainside. Sounds of jackhammers and dynamite blasts echoed through the hills as Thomas Jefferson's face was being etched into the granite. Laura and Manly toured the Black Hills, driving through tunnels and forests, past rock formations, and visiting tourist attractions. They were assailed with intense heat on the return trip home, and overcome with an aura of dissatisfaction. Laura thought the feeling was the loss of their youth. When they drove into the yard of the Rock House, under the shade of the walnut trees, Laura commented, "East, west, home is best."*

*Circa 1931*

*Very little written material remains to trace the evolution of* Little House in the Big Woods. *Laura and Rose obviously discussed the book manuscript during visits or over the telephone. This letter fragment indicates that Laura was aware of literary process. She understood that characterization included an accurate depiction of the characters' speech patterns.*

Don't give either Pa nor Ma any dialect. I never heard Pa swear; never anything stronger than "Gosh all hemlock, Well I'll be *darned* or Great Gehosophat."

But of course a lady like Ma would never use such expressions. Her language was rather precise and a great deal better language than I have ever used. She was a school teacher and well educated for her time and place, rather above Pa socially.

Mary and Carrie were like her. Grace and I were more like Pa, using an expletive now and then as we grew older and inclined to laugh and joke and sing.

On page 12—you have Ma say "she vowed she didn't believe these young ones were *ever* going to sleep."

Never in the world would she have said [that]. Many times she said "Charles I don't believe those *children* will ever go to sleep."

Neither of them ever did or would have thought of calling us "young ones"—we were always children and "I vow" was something Ma would never have said, being a lady and a school teacher.

*I feel lucky too*

*A procession of Rose's literary friends visited Rocky Ridge, and Laura met them all. Genevieve Parkhurst, a magazine editor and author, was a houseguest several times. Laura informed her of the publication of* Little House in the Big Woods.

FEBRUARY 16, 1932

My Dear Genevieve,

Hurrah! And congratulations!

Rose has just told me your good news and I am so glad.

I am sure it is not too late to wish you a happy new year in your work and every other way.

Perhaps you have heard of my little book which Harpers is publishing in April. So I feel lucky too.

I have missed having you in for tea this winter. We have all been very quiet this winter. I have played what we call bridge only once.

Best regards,

Laura Ingalls Wilder

## Postcard to Carrie

*During his retirement from farming, Manly raised goats, gardened, and harvested walnuts and pecans on Rocky Ridge. Several fruit trees remained from the former orchard, enough to share fruit with friends and family. Shipments were sent to Laura's sisters in South Dakota.*

SEPTEMBER 24, 1932

Dear Carrie,

Manly is sending the pears today by express to Hill City. Hope they reach you all right. They must stand awhile before they are good to eat, but cook all right now. Will answer your letter soon.

Laura

## *I hope you will like it*

*Ida Louise Raymond was Laura's editor when* Farmer Boy *was being written.*

MARCH 3, 1933

Dear Ida Louise Raymond,

I am sorry to have been later than expected in sending you the revised manuscript of Farmer Boy. Because of sickness in the family I have been unable to finish it sooner. You will see that I followed your suggestion of adding incident and tightening up the plot. I hope you will like it in its latest form.

If it is still too long, the chapter "Breaking Roads" could be cut entirely without injuring the thread of the story, as could also "Breaking the Calves" though I think both add interest to the winter life on a farm. They show also the great contrast between those days and now. But if the story must be shortened still more, it will be all right with me to cut them out.

Yours sincerely,

Laura Ingalls Wilder

## *Your frank opinion of Farmer Boy*

MARCH 21, 1933

Dear Ida Louise Raymond,

Indeed I am very grateful to you for giving me your frank opinion of Farmer Boy.

An honest opinion even though not favorable is much more to be desired than one more flattering if insincere.

Yes! George Bye is my agent. All business arrangements must be made with him and such agreements will, of course have my approval.

Since sending you Farmer Boy, I have been planning my next story. It will tell of my childhood experiences in Indian Territory [now Oklahoma] when my father's family was the only white one living there among the Indians. [The locale of the Ingalls cabin in Indian Territory was actually in the Osage ceded lands of southeast Kansas. Not until the 1960s was the cabin site thoroughly researched and located.]

The surroundings, the country and events have an altogether different character than Little House, but in my memory they have the same glamour as the Wisconsin woods. I am sure the story will be as good as, if not better than Little House, and much shorter than Farmer Boy.

I work slowly and it takes a long time to bring such old memories to the surface of my mind and verify the facts. But the more I remember of Mary and Laura in those days; of the wild range cattle and the wolves; and prairie fires and huge watermelons; of the wild panther that screamed in the creek bottoms—the more impatient I grow to begin writing it.

I am sorry you have been ill and hope you are quite recovered by now. Again thanking you for your kindly criticisms, I remain,

Yours sincerely,

Laura Ingalls Wilder

## *An old daguerreotype of my Father and Mother*

*Laura loaned a 1860 image of her parents to the illustrator Helen Sewell, who duplicated it for the opening page of* Little House in the Big Woods. *Miss Phillips is unidentified, but she was likely a librarian or a teacher. The following letter fragment was a portion of Laura's reply.*

APRIL 19, 1933

Dear Miss Phillips,

Thank you so much for writing me and for the kind things you say about my little book. I appreciate them all the more as coming from you, who are doing good work yourself.

It makes me very happy that you felt the spirit of those days which were so happy for it assures me that I did not fail in my attempt to make it live again.

You may be interested to know that the first picture in the book, the little oval on one of the first leaves, is a very good copy of an old daguerreotype of my Father and Mother, Ma and Pa in the story. . . .

## A good contract for "Farmer Boy"

*In addition to being the literary agent for Rose and Laura, George T. Bye represented prominent writers including Rebecca West, Heywood Broun, Alexander Woollcott, and Charles A. Lindbergh. Bye was also First Lady Eleanor Roosevelt's agent, encouraging her to write her newspaper column "My Day."*

APRIL 26, 1933

Dear Mr. Bye,

Am returning contracts for revision as suggested in your telegram. Your efforts in securing a good contract for "Farmer Boy" are appreciated.

Yours sincerely,

Laura Ingalls Wilder

*You know a great deal about the history of the Indians*

*Before* Farmer Boy *was published, Laura began her third book,*
*Little House on the Prairie. Her memory was sometimes vague*
*about her family's interlude in Kansas. She and Rose made a road*
*trip to the general vicinity, near Independence. Since the Osage*
*Indians were significant in the story, historical research was re-*
*quired. This letter fragment indicates Laura's search for data.*

JUNE 26, 1933
Dear Sir,

Mr. and Mrs. Lyn have told me about your wonderful collection of
Indian relics and that you know a great deal about the history of the
Indians in your part of the country. So I thought perhaps you could
tell me the name of an Indian chief that I have forgotten. I do not
know even the tribe of which he was chief but the time was the years
of 1870 and 1871. . . .

*I shall appreciate the honor*

JULY 8, 1933
Floyd S. Shoemaker, Secy.
Missouri State Historical Soc.
Dear Sir:

In reply to your letter of June 26, about the middle of October I
will have a shipment of books from my publisher and will send you
for your Missouri Authors collection a copy each of my children's
books, Little House in the Big Woods and Farmer Boy. I shall appreciate the honor of having them preserved in the collection of the
Missouri Historical Society.

Sincerely,
Laura Ingalls Wilder

*I did enjoy the letters from your pupils*

> *Soon after* Little House in the Big Woods *was published, Laura received letters from readers praising the book. Her earliest responses to reader mail were lengthy and detailed, as is this letter to students from Tipton, Iowa.*

Fourth Grade
Tipton Consolidated School
Alfarata Allen, Teacher
SEPTEMBER 26, 1933
Dear Miss Allen,

Perhaps your pupils of the spring are with you again this fall and would be interested to know that my new book "Farmer Boy" will be published by Harper & Brothers on October 12th. I feel sure they would enjoy the story, both the boys and the girls.

Please tell Jack Fields that I have been a long time answering his question about "Little House in the Big Woods." But here is the answer. I never went to the town [Pepin] again while I was a child. When I was 23 years old I went back from South Dakota and took my own little girl to the town of Pepin. [They were visiting Laura's aunt, Martha Quiner Carpenter.]

I did enjoy the letters from your pupils so much and if they are still with you or have passed to a higher grade, will you please give them all my love and best wishes.

With kindest regards I am yours sincerely,
(Mrs.) Laura Ingalls Wilder

*The Tipton students wrote again.*

DECEMBER 19, 1933

Dear Fourth Grade Teacher & Pupils,

It pleased me very much to hear from Tipton School's Fourth Grade again and I am so glad you liked my "Little House in the Big Woods."

It was a tiny house in a great *Big* Woods, Hilda as you say and it was a very nice home as you said Nadine Jane.

Yes Donald! I made candles when I was little, or I should say, I *helped* make candles. We made them just as Almanzo did in "Farmer Boy," only not so many.

Richard! You and Donald must like to have bad boys punished, for you both were pleased with the story of the bees stinging Charley. Well he did deserve it I think.

I haven't another pioneer book published yet Eloise, but I am writing one for next year all about Mary and Laura when they lived where there were many Indians in Indian Territory, which is now Oklahoma [the actual location was southeastern Kansas] in your geography.

Marilyn! I am glad you found "Little House in the Big Woods" so interesting.

I thank you for all your nice letters and hope you will all like Farmer Boy. The farmer boy was my husband, Mr. Wilder, when he was a boy and he did . . . all the things I have told about in the story.

Dear Miss Masden, I appreciate your letter too and am sorry not to write a separate letter to each one of you. But I am not very strong and writing letters is a task for me just now.

Please give my regards to last year's Fourth Graders and tell them they must keep right on climbing up to higher places. Wishing you all a Merry Christmas and a very Happy New Year, I remain

Sincerely,

Laura Ingalls Wilder

## We would like to drive again to De Smet

*In this letter Laura mentions Rose's nervous breakdown to Aubrey Sherwood, but not its actual cause. Rose felt trapped by rural isolation on the farm and felt far removed from stimulating companions. Her money woes were never ending. Plagued by physical ills and mental depression, she spent an unproductive year, struggling for equanimity.*

JANUARY 15, 1934

Dear Mr. Sherwood,

Your letter came as a pleasant surprise. Mr. Wilder and I often talk of our visit to De Smet and we never seem to be able to get over a homesickness for the old home, or perhaps it is more for the old ways.

Once in a while I have a clipping of your paper from Carrie or Grace and have been intending to write you thanking you for your kindness in mentioning Rose and myself as you have done. But the days slip by so fast and are so full of many things.

Rose hasn't been at all well for a year now, a nervous breakdown caused by an attack of the flu. Which will account for her neglecting to reply to your letter.

In regard to her book "Let the Hurricane Roar" I think there is nothing particular to say. [In reality Laura was greatly offended by the novel, which was originally a 1932 serial in the *Saturday Evening Post*. She resented the use of family names and history, which she planned to utilize in her own writing.] It is of course fiction with incident and anecdotes gathered here and there and some purely imaginary. But you know what fiction writing is.

The publisher is Longmans, Green and Company, New York.

Mr. Wilder and I are about as usual only we do grow a year older every year.

We often say we would like to drive again to De Smet as we have always felt our visit there [1931] was cut short. And one of these days we may do so. [They made two more South Dakota trips, in 1938 and 1939.]

The Ozarks are well worth seeing and I am sure you would enjoy a trip over them. Later, when our National Forest is located and put in order, they will be even more beautiful.

With best regards I remain

Sincerely,

Laura Ingalls Wilder

*I cannot be of much help in tracing relationship*

FEBRUARY 6, 1934

My dear Mrs. Dalphin,

Your letter was a pleasant surprise, but I am afraid I cannot be of much help in tracing relationship.

My father was Charles Philip Ingalls and he was born in New York State, but I have no idea of the county. Neither do I remember what my Grandfather Ingalls was named.

I have heard my father tell the same story as you do of the three brothers who came from England, so no doubt we have those remote ancestors in common. [Laura referred to Jonathan Ingalls's three sons: Samuel, David, and Jonathan. Samuel was Laura's great-grandfather.]

There are Ingalls relatives somewhere in New York, who have the history of the Ingalls family from the time of the three brothers from England down to the present time so far as they have been able to trace the descendants. But unfortunately I do not know the names or address.

They came to see my father after I left home and though Father wrote me of their visit I have forgotten all except they were bringing the family down to that time and had come west looking up connections.

My sister might be able to give you their address if you care to write to her. Her address is: Mrs. D. N. Swanzey, Keystone, South Dakota.

Father's brothers were named James, Peter and George. [A fourth brother was Hiram.]

My father's children are three daughters, Carrie Ingalls Swanzey, Grace Ingalls Dow (Mrs. N. W. Dow, Manchester, South Dakota) and myself. The oldest sister, Mary Ingalls, died several years ago.

My sisters have no children and I have only one, Rose Wilder Lane, of whom you may have heard as she is a writer of some prominence.

My father's brothers married and there were numerous children, but I have not kept any trace of them and do not know how many or where they are.

With sincere regards, I am

Laura Ingalls Wilder

### *An all too small income*

*Ida Louise Raymond forwarded copies of reviews, explained lagging book sales due to the Depression, and commiserated over Farmer Boy's skimpy royalty rate. Her letter of March 12, 1934, mentions that "I can't tell you how eager I am to see who has followed this time in the foot-steps of Laura and Almanzo."*

MARCH 16, 1934

Dear Ida Louise Raymond,

Many thanks for the clippings on Farmer Boy, just received. They seem to me very good.

Will you please let me know how the book is selling and also if Little House in the Big Woods is still selling well. I am anxious to know how they are going, both as a matter of sinful pride and as a hope of addition to an all too small income.

Your assurance of a better contract for my next book is gratifying, for, frankly, I am not at all pleased with the one for Farmer Boy.

The new book is ready for the final typing before sending it to you. Like the others it is a true story. I think I will name three of the titles I am considering for it and leave the rest to your imagination until you see it. They are—Indian Country, (On) the High Prairie and Pioneering in Indian Land.

Yours sincerely,

Laura Ingalls Wilder

## *Your letter was a regular budget of good cheer*

*Excerpts from Little House books were reprinted in elementary reading texts and anthologies, generating extra income and readers.* Child Life *and* St. Nicholas *magazines published lightly rewritten chapters from* Farmer Boy, Little House on the Prairie, *and* On the Banks of Plum Creek. *Use of Laura's stories became entrenched in elementary education; this use has continued into the twenty-first century.*

JUNE 23, 1934

Dear Ida Louise Raymond,

Your letter regarding Scribner's reprint of parts of Little House in the Big Woods has been received and I do thank you for the trouble you have taken. Will try to get a copy of "Childhood Reader."

I am certainly pleased that you have had other requests for selections. Your letter was a regular budget of good cheer.

I hope Farmer Boy may be as popular. Many good short selections could be made from that book also. There are several chapters that would make good short stories if used separately.

Anyway, Hurrah for Little House, may its sales increase.

Again thanking you, I remain

Yours sincerely,

Laura Ingalls Wilder


## *I do hope you will like the story*

JULY 2, 1934

Dear Ida Louise Raymond,

I am sending you, by express today, the manuscript of my book. Not being able to decide on the title I am enclosing a list of several so you may make the choice. [See the list in Laura's March 16, 1934, letter.]

Like the Little House in the Big Woods and Farmer Boy, it is all true and like "The Little House"—it is written from my own memories of what happened to us and how we lived, three miles over the line from Kansas, in Indian Territory in the years 1870 and 1871.

I do hope you will like the story.

With best regards, I am

Sincerely,

Laura Ingalls Wilder


## *I would like to have a report*

AUGUST 14, 1934

Dear Ida Louise Raymond,

I hope you will not think I am too impatient but I would like to have a report on my manuscript.

My next story, On the Banks of Plum Creek, is beginning to shape itself and as it is quite different in setting and incident, it bothers me not to have my mind free from "Indian Country." ...

## Making me safe from complications

> The use of song lyrics in Little House on the Prairie prompted Laura's agent, George Bye, to secure releases prior to finalizing the book's contract. Bye suggested: "Why should I not obtain from Harpers a statement that they have looked up the [song] titles ... and that they are satisfied that these are all in the public domain ...?"

NOVEMBER 23, 1934

Dear Mr. Bye,

Please secure for me from Harpers, release of responsibility in copyright of songs used in Little House on the Prairie, as suggested by you in your letter of the 20th. It is a fine idea for making me safe from complications.

Very sincerely,

Laura Ingalls Wilder

## Much larger than the bulldogs I see now

JANUARY 14, 1935

Dear Miss Raymond,

The dog in L. H. on the Prairie is the same dog that was in The Little House in the Big Woods.

Pa always called him a bulldog and I remember he looked like one but was much larger than the bulldogs I see now. He was so large that I used to ride him when I was four years old if I was going with Pa and Jack and it was too far for me to walk. So he must have been a large dog but he had all the characteristics of a bulldog and looked like one.

Perhaps the breed was larger sixty years ago. I am glad the illustrations promise so well but of course they will be beautiful if Miss Sewell does them.

Sincerely,

L. I. Wilder

## I am sure you will like Little House on the Prairie

*Tipton, Iowa, children anticipated new Little House books. Early in 1935, their teacher inquired about the publication of Little House on the Prairie. "My pupils are interested in you personally," she said. "They ask dozens of questions. . . ."*

FEBRUARY 12, 1935

Dear Mrs. Walsh & Sixth Grade Pupils:

It was a pleasure to have all your letters and to know that you liked Farmer Boy.

Yes, Almanzo grew to be a very good farmer. Has been a farmer all the years since his father gave him Starlight and he has always loved horses.

As you have heard the letter I wrote to the 4th grade, you already have most of your questions answered.

Someday soon I will write a story about when Laura and Almanzo met away out on the frontier in Dakota Territory before it was divided into two states. But before that time many interesting things happened to Laura.

After you read Little House on the Prairie, I hope to have another book ready for you. I think I shall call it On the Banks of Plum Creek. Would you like that? I am sure you will like Little House on the

Prairie which will be published early next fall. I am sorry it will not be so large as Farmer Boy.

Perhaps you will be interested to see the enclosed snapshot of Laura, Almanzo and their Airedale, Nero. This was taken five years ago but it is the only one I have. We haven't changed except that my hair is whiter. No, we are not shamed of anything. We are just looking down at Nero trying to keep him still and we were snapped unexpectedly before we could look up. We are standing on the terrace by our rock house where we live, just the two of us with our dog Nero.

Rose Wilder Lane, our daughter lives on the other end of the farm in a larger house. You may have read some of her stories for she writes a great many for the different magazines, often the Saturday Evening Post.

Very best regards to you all,
Laura Ingalls Wilder

## *I have already written another book for the children*

*Children and adults realized that the books were about real people, and many of their letters inquired about the characters.*

[NO DATE, 1935]
My dear Miss Pettis,

It was a pleasure to have your kind letter and of course I will answer the children's question.

The Aunt Eliza of Little House in the Big Woods was not Eliza Jane of Farmer Boy. The only relationship between the characters of the two books is that when Laura and Almanzo grew up, they met, away out in South Dakota. They married and "lived happily ever after." Laura was myself when I was a little girl and Mr. Wilder was Almanzo.

I have already written another book for the children which will probably be published next fall. It is a story of pioneering among Indians and wolves. Mary and Laura are there, and I feel sure the children will like it.

With best regards to you and your pupils, I remain,

Yours sincerely,

Laura Ingalls Wilder

## I am sure we will get a good review

*John Neihardt, the author of* Black Elk Speaks, *settled in Branson, Missouri, in 1930. Among his interests was pioneer migration, which explains Laura's determination that he receive review copies of her books.*

APRIL 22, 1935

Dear Miss Raymond,

I have just learned of Mr. John Neihardt, book reviewer for the St. Louis Post-Dispatch. He carries a lot of weight in Midwestern book trade and is intensely interested in pioneer things and in Indians. He has never seen any of my books.

If you will send me a copy of Little House in the Big Woods I will personally place it in his family and with the way thus prepared I am sure we will get a good review for Little House on the Prairie when it comes out.

Please be sure to see, when the new book comes out, that a copy of it goes, for review, to Mr. John G. Neihardt, Branson, Missouri. . . .

## It is a wonderful book

*Laura and Manly took short trips through picturesque areas in Missouri to celebrate their fiftieth anniversary on August 25, 1935. After sightseeing in the Lake Taneycomo area and the resort towns*

*of Hollister and Branson, they arrived home to discover the first
copies of* Little House on the Prairie *in the mail.*

SEPTEMBER 26, 1935
Dear Miss Raymond,

Your letter of the 11th and the copies of Little House on the Prairie are at hand. They came while I was away from home which explains my delay in writing you.

I am glad that you are pleased with the latest Little House and I think, myself, that with Miss Sewell's illustrations and the makeup and all it is a wonderful book. It surely does take Helen Sewell to bring my stories to life. [Sewell received a flat fee of $200 for the art used in the book.]

Please send me three more copies of Little House on the Prairie and charge to my account.

Thanking you for your good wishes, I remain
Sincerely,
Laura Ingalls Wilder

## *It was dear of you*

*Virginia Kirkus (1893–1980) accepted* Little House in the Big Woods *for publication, but left Harper & Brothers when the children's book department she created was placed on economic hiatus. She went on to found the influential magazine* Kirkus Reviews. *Her support of the Little House books continued unabated with each volume published.*

NOVEMBER 30, 1935
Dear Miss Raymond,

Thanks so much for the Times review and Virginia Kirkus' review of L. H. on the Prairie. It was dear of you to send them.

The two books ordered arrived today.

With kindest regards,

Laura Ingalls Wilder

## Altogether too good to be lost

*Alvilda Myre Sorenson knew members of the Ingalls family well. She passed their house going to school, chatting with the blind Mary as she sat on the porch. After college, Alvilda married Hans Sorenson. They endured the tragedy of their daughter Nancy's deafness, teaching her to speak and function successfully in school. Reading was important to Nancy, including each new Little House book. The Sorensons treasured their autographed copies.*

DECEMBER 13, 1935

Dear Mrs. Sorenson,

It was a pleasure to have your very interesting letter today and I hasten to reply.

I have ordered The Little House in the Big Woods for little Emily Ann [a playmate of Nancy Sorenson's] and as soon as received will autograph it and send it to you.

As we have no bookstore here I was obliged to order from Harpers and it will be some time for the book to reach you. We live in the country on a rural route and time is lost between mails, but I will be as soon as I can.

If you ordered a book from Harpers and asked them to forward it to me to be autographed I feel sure they would do so. I would autograph it and send it to you. That, I think would be the simplest way to handle the copies you may want to get.

I am delighted that you and your club like my little stories.

I began writing them because they seemed to me altogether too good to be lost. You must have a fine club. Our study club died a few years ago and was born again as a bridge club. Not nearly so interesting to me.

I am in very good company in your list of Kingsbury County's artists although I am a very humble member of the group. Thanking you for your letter I am

Sincerely,

Laura Ingalls Wilder

P.S. Please excuse the tablet paper and matching envelop. I seem to be out of stamps for sending anything else. L.I.W.

---

## THE BOYS OF ROCKY RIDGE

On a rainy September day in 1933, a fourteen-year-old orphan, John Turner, rapped on the door at Rocky Ridge. He asked for work. Rose was skeptical, but she was touched by the sight of the bedraggled boy. He weeded the garden, which earned him a meal and a bed for the night. The unhappy boy had lived with his older brother Al at an uncle's home fifteen miles from Mansfield. The uncle, impoverished by the Depression, could not keep the boys properly attired for school attendance. John ran away.

Rose's generous nature prevailed; she invited both boys to live with her and attend high school in Mansfield. For the first time, the farmhouse was filled with the youthful activities of high schoolers. Rose taught a French class for the Turners and their friends. She arranged dances, birthday celebrations, and costume parties. She rooted for the boys' athletic teams and worried about their health, their grades, their grammar, and their girlfriends.

In 1935 "the Clubhouse" was built for John and Al. It became a gathering place for Mansfield teens, with a basketball court nearby. The brothers had workbenches there; both were fascinated by electronics. They had a newspaper route, stoked the furnace, milked the cow, did dishes, and assisted in the house and yard. "Mrs. Lane kept us busy," said Al. While the boys were in school, Rose worked at her typewriter, writing to support her enlarged household. "Am I crazy," Rose wondered, "thinking that youngsters are one of the most infinitely varied, amusing, unexpected, never monotonous, entertaining interests in the world?"

When Rose left Rocky Ridge for long intervals in 1935 and 1936, the Turners remained on the farm. They finished high school, and Rose encouraged them in their goal to attend college. Both Turners served in World War II; their connection with Rose was by then diminished. She wrote Al in 1942: "The first thing is to protect our country; that's got to be done. And afterward I hope your generation will get the country back to its revolutionary principle of personal freedom and every individual's right to live his own life in his own way"

Both Turner boys achieved successful careers in the postwar years, and they credited Rose for her motherly nurture during their youth. John wrote Rose: "You have been everything to me that my mother never had a chance to be."

## I don't know what to do

*Rose was ensconced in the Tiger Hotel in Columbia, Missouri (160 miles from Rocky Ridge), in 1936. She did intense research at the University of Missouri for a book project. In absentia Rose also assisted in the preparation of Laura's* On the Banks of Plum Creek. *She left her Mansfield friends Corinne and Jack Murray in charge of the farmhouse and the Turner boys. The situation was far from ideal. The boys salvaged tires from an abandoned hulk of a car they found near Rocky Ridge, and eventually their prank was discovered. Without Rose to sort out the problem, Laura and Manly became embroiled. The following letter shows Laura's dissatisfaction with the Murrays' presence, but not that she hoped to*

*return to her old home after seven years in the Rock House. Soon*
*after the Murrays left, Laura and Manly returned to the old farm-*
*house.*

JUNE 25, 1936

Rose Dearest,

Your letter just came and I am going to answer it plainly.

I have the title to the car from Secretary of State to Todd White. The description as to the make and name is correct. The numbers of course I do not know. The title is assigned by Todd White to Geo. Baker, city marshal here, the man I settled with. The title is legal, so the car could not have been stolen. Did you see yourself that the number had been removed from the engine? If you did not, I do not believe it. There is no way of checking on it, for the road workers have hauled the carcass away to some junk pile.

The title shows a mortgage on the car to National Brokerage Co. of Springfield for $27.50. But the transfer to Baker shows it was cleared.

Bruce Prock says the tires were in good shape when Al took them. [Bruce Prock and his wife rented the Wilders' tenant house on the farm; Bruce served as a handyman and farm caretaker for the Wilders.] They were worn only a very little, and new would have cost $9 apiece. . . . Bruce says, and so does Al, that Al took only three of them.

Bruce does not know what became of the other tire, and Al says he does not know. . . . If the tires were worth that much, the price asked in settlement was reasonable and we got off darned lucky, which I don't think Al appreciates.

Baker is the kind of officer who is sure you see his badge and the sight of it on him makes me want to knock his head off. I don't know why.

But Jones is different. He is a rough specimen but seems to want to be fair. He owns five good farms, besides the part of the old

McNaul farm where he lives and has been bailing fine clover hay for sale. He has a herd of good white-faced cows and altogether is not in a position where he needs or would spend time fooling with a small steal off a boy.

I think Baker is the kind who would, which was why I wrote you telling Al to be careful.

I hope you will not be a crazy nut and seem to take Al's part too much. He will be all right if he goes carefully, which he should do for your sake if not for his own.

Jones told Bruce that Al phoned him that he wanted to buy the parts of the car. This was after you were here and told him to do so.

But Jones also said he asked Al to come in and see him so they could talk it over, and Al never did. Bruce thinks Jones knew then who the owner was and Al could have settled it then if he would have gone to see Jones.

I hope you don't give Al the tires and let him get off without anything to make him remember. If he gets off too easy, he might think he got away with that all right and you would help him out again, and he could try something else. This I do think.

Bruce did think for Al's sake he should pay for taking those tires in some way, slowly perhaps, but some way. Otherwise he would not realize what he had done.

Oh Damn! I don't know what to do.

Bruce was here yesterday, to see Manly. He told me he hoped you would not be too hard on Al. That the boys hadn't any chance after you went away. He said Corinne would have had them arrested. . . . Bruce said the boys actually went hungry because Corinne did not cook for them. He was at the house once when John was complaining that he was hungry and said they hadn't had a meal for a month, nothing only what they could pick up. "And what," said Bruce, "could you expect of boys left that way."

Bruce said he thought the best thing you could do for Al would be to help put him through next year's school at Ava, where his uncle could look after him. You could pay what of his expenses you wanted to, and his uncle could watch over him. Bruce said also that the uncle was in a hard place himself, with children of his own, his wife dead and losing nearly everything he had in the bank mess there, so perhaps he should be excused some if he did not do so well by Al as should have been done. But he thinks the uncle would do what he could.

Bruce also offered to go see the uncle if you wanted him to do so, and talk to him. Anything he could do to help you out, just let him know, he said.

Oh yes! Bruce said too that Al should have a chance for his last year in high school, for Bruce missed getting jobs because he hadn't a high school education.

How can we show the boys that such doings do not pay and at the same time keep Corinne and Jack on the place when the boys know what they both done, and know that we know it?

Bruce told me yesterday that he had found out why Corinne was always out of water when she made such a fuss about his not pumping any water for them, and all the fuss about the pump. He said his wife had told him at the time, but he wouldn't believe it could be so. But now he has seen it himself while he has been working in the garden.

Jack is hauling water from there to the laundry in big cans in his truck.

There is no shortage of water in town, so it is not necessary. But he is using your electricity and wear and tear on your pump to save his water bill.

In other words, Jack is stealing water.

Now if we keep the Murrays on, Al will naturally think, "What is all this talk about stealing anyway? Just look."

I am going to take back all I said about letting the Murrays stay on the place and say as I did before, let's get rid of them. I asked Bruce what he thought of his being able to watch the place and keep the house from being broken into.

He said he thought it would be safe. That he could fix the place so it could be locked up and fastened securely. That he would get a good watch dog and shut him up there nights. He said he would do his best to keep everything safe. . . .

He said also, that if the Murrays were leaving someone should be there to see what they took away.

Bruce also said, if you stopped paying their bills and they were on the place, they would find no reason to stay. I am sure if we keep them on, they and Bruce will be fighting again and it seems like I can't stand it.

If we take the boys away and leave them in possession, it will be just what they have been trying to get done. And that gets my goat. . . . I would like not to have any trouble or row with them. It might be reasonable that you want to close the place, cut out telephone, gas, electricity. I can take over the electric bills you know. . . .

They could rent a room in town. They saved their dishes and a rug and some chairs, etc. They could furnish one room. I would help if necessary. Tell them you want the place closed and locked so you will not have to think about it. On many sober second thoughts I again say, send Al away and close the house. I believe it would have a better effect on the boys than anything you could do or say about not stealing. I feel sure Bruce and we could keep your things safer than with the Murrays there.

Lots of love,
Mama Bess

## But of course you know best

*A week after Laura vented about the farm situation, she was engrossed with her writing. She wrote Rose in detail about Minnesota blizzards, grasshoppers, and cattle, all features of* On the Banks of Plum Creek.

JULY 2, 1936

Rose Dearest,

Perhaps it would be all right to have Ma see the cloud and go to the stable before the blizzard struck. . . . And I thought the suddenness of the storm striking so unexpectedly was more dramatic.

However, if Laura must get to the stable there is no other way that I can see [the action]. . . . That Ma should see the cloud and remembering how quickly the storm came when she was in town, thought she would have the chores done before Pa got there. But she would not have milked at noon. Chores were always a little late winter mornings and there would have been no milk the cow would have given as soon as noon. Pa was expected for late noon dinner. . . .

It might be that Laura could follow Ma into the barn and doing the chores with her imagination, having seen Pa do the chores, she would know how they would be done and how the animals would act.

She would know how Ma would cling to the rope with one hand all the way and how she would shut the stable door carefully . . . for Pa had followed the line and done the chores in blizzards before.

Are you sure the transition as I have written it would not do? But of course you know best.

The blizzards came this way:

At first they were a black streak on the horizon around the northwest corner. As a child I always had the impression that they did actually circle a corner. The day was usually rather warm, always clear, no clouds in sight and the sun shining brightly.

As the cloud rose, the sky was overcast on that corner and when high in the sky the upper edge was lighter and the cloud seemed to roll. They always came swiftly but there was a difference in the speed and fury with which they struck, though they always came quickly enough to catch people unprepared.

No one measured the speed of the wind in those days, but it surely was as fast as hurricane speed. And the sun shone brightly in the one part of the sky until the whole black cloud reached and blotted it out.

It in no sense changed to a cloudy day before the blizzard struck. It doesn't threaten, you see, to give Ma the idea she has time to do the chores.

All the milk would blow out of the pail if it were not sheltered as much as possible. I don't remember of its ever being frozen.

They would be tired and breathless and Laura's legs would ache, but not sore as if beaten.

About how long it would take to go from the stable to the house, I suppose about five minutes. . . .

Whichever direction one goes [in a blizzard] he goes against the wind, a wind so strong that one leans into it, not walking upright. It buffets one on every side at the same time and sucks the breath away. One is sightless of course, for the eyes are full of the fine icy snow particles, and there is a feeling of confusion and helplessness.

[Here Laura switches to a discussion of the cattle runaway, told of in *On the Banks of Plum Creek*.]

I suppose you are right about the cattle. But children weren't raised to be helpless cowards in those days.

The real truth is that Pa did send us and it would have been perfectly all right except for the fact that someone had set a dog on them and he had bitten off the end of one cow's tail. The stump was bleeding and you know how cattle act when they smell blood. Pa didn't know about the dog or he never in the world would have sent us. But if the cattle must all be in one day, have Laura say after the runaway that she didn't like cattle. And Pa say that he'd had enough of them himself and was going to have some horses someday before long or know the reason why.

Handle the cattle as you think best, also the storm, only don't weaken nor change the character of the storm.

[Next the letter shifts to a discussion of grasshoppers.]

Grasshoppers do *not* turn green from eating. The young, just hatched, grasshoppers were green, but only for a few days.

The idea of grasshoppers "burrowing into the ground" and

disappearing . . . I think I wrote plainly how they did. I remember them sitting with their hind part in the ground laying their eggs. . . .

[Laura concludes this letter with local and personal news.]

Our paper says Roosevelt is losing the colored vote and the women's vote. I will write you a letter soon, but now I must catch the mail with this.

Manly is in town at the Thursday [livestock] sale. Ben [the bulldog] and I are alone and very comfortable, thank you.

We had a wonderful rain night before last, nearly two inches. It was *good* and again the air is fit to breathe.

Paul and Dessie Cooley were here a few minutes yesterday. They had a week vacation and spent most of it in Springfield with Ethel Burney Morris. Mrs. Cooley [Paul's mother] from here went up and stayed at Ethel's with them. [Paul Cooley traveled with his family and the Wilders from South Dakota to Missouri in 1894. Dessie was his wife, Odessa.]

Dessie is sweet as she can be and Paul is natural as life, a Roosevelt man, but I am sure Dessie does not approve, so there may be hope.

They say to tell you they were so sorry you were not here and that they enjoyed so much having you drop in on them.

I must run.

Lots of love,

Mama Bess

*Laura wrote again on the following day. She was not satisfied that Rose comprehended the setting of the Ingalls farm along Plum Creek.*

JULY 3, 1936

Rose Dearest,

I hope the map will help you understand Plum Creek better. The swimming hole was actually . . . a deep hole with the creek coming in and going out. I suppose it was gouged out by high water at some time, really a pond in the creek.

The creek was a prairie creek, running between grass grown banks, deeper where the banks narrowed and spreading out shallower where the banks set back. The creek water was low in the hot weather.

Because of the bend in the creek, the water was thrown against the bank under the dugout door and foamed and roared as it went around. The plank was across the creek when we came. I suppose it was there so the man before us could go quickly to the other part of the farm.

Pa always took the oxen and then the horses to water, down the slope of the high bank to where we played in the creek, never down by the plank across it.

I have an awful suspicion that we drank plain creek water, in the raw, without boiling or whatever. But that would make the reader think we were dirty, which we were not. So I said there was a spring . . . as it is located in my imagination, you may put it where it is most convenient.

The west bank might be higher, but we must be above it as we sat at the dugout door. The steep steps did go down from the earthen shelf in front of the dugout door, but Laura did go back up the steps, up the path past the dugout and along the top of the bank, just back of the dugout roof, then down the slope to the tableland until she came to the creek where Pa watered the oxen.

We never went just along the water's edge from the plank to the place where the oxen were watered. I think it was a muddy, slippery bank at the very edge of the water. Anyway, it was only by the path from the stable along the grassy slope to the lower bank and the creek.

The creek was rather shallow where it came into the swimming hole. There it widened and deepened. Willows and plum trees grew thick on the western side, making a little grove. From the swimming hole the creek narrowed again and became shallow, making a place to wade and play on the edge of the little round meadow.

It ran narrower still, and deeper around the dugout and then away among plum trees and willows where I never followed it. I saw it at the other end of the plum thicket where I waded in the mud and got the bloodsuckers. When I waded into the dimness of that plum thicket I was going up creek toward the dugout. The banks were mud.

When the creek came from there out into the sunshine it ran over the sandy pebbly bottom where we waded and played so much after we lived in the new house. There was a little patch of sandy, gravelly beach right there. Just below the banks were muddy again and willows and plum trees grew again.

The first tree was a big willow. One end of the footbridge was fastened to it. The other end was fastened in the mud bank and from there the path went to Nelson's. Below the footbridge was another pond-like place in the creek where big fish lived. The creek ran away among the plums and willows and I never followed it. Never saw it any farther along except where we crossed it to go to town.

There it was out in the sunny prairie, shallow and rather wide, with a gravelly bottom. The water sparkled and rippled and looked altogether different than the dark water in the shadow of the willows and plum trees between the muddy banks.

After all I was only six and very busy about my affairs. What I remember is of course only a series of pictures.

Manly is waiting for this to go to town. When he is gone I will write you another letter.

Hurrah for the Glorious Fourth of July!

Much love,

Mama Bess

## *Believe me I <u>screamed</u>*

*A flurry of letters were exchanged between Rocky Ridge and the Tiger Hotel, as Laura and Rose worked through the* Plum Creek *writing process. It was their first long-distance collaboration. Letters like the following one indicate Laura's contributions to the critique sessions as she and Rose discussed plot, characterization, and technique.*

[CIRCA JULY 1936]
Rose Dearest,

I think I have straightened out the difficulties about the willows etc. in the copy and that it is ready to be typed except for the last bit with note attached.

I don't like the cattle at the stacks on the same day as the runaway of the cattle on the wagon. How would it be if Pa said the herd boy must be asleep and sent Laura and Mary to find and wake him so he would drive the cattle? Then let them, of their own notion, drive the cattle when they couldn't find the boy. Would that not clear Pa's character?

Do as you think best after considering. We could leave it out altogether. Just the runaway on the day in town.

Hope you could get the map straightened out. I see the pictures so plainly that I guess I failed to paint them as I should.

We had some excitement that I guess Corinne wrote you about.

Night before last the electric wires gave an awful pop and our lights went out. I called up and they were out in town and at the other house [the farmhouse] so we waited awhile and Manly went to bed. Ben had barked when the wires popped and he kept barking and I thought he was just nervous. I went to the back door to lock it and stepped out on the porch. And there was a fire back of the garage down toward the barn.

Believe me I *screamed*. I thought the barn and hay and sheds and all were afire. I managed to make Manly understand and then I ran for the barn to turn the kids and the calf loose. Ben went with me. Around the garage, I saw it wasn't the barn burning, but the woods, back of the garage . . .

So I came back to the phone for help and the phone didn't ring right and no one answered. I dropped the receiver and ran with a bucket of water and Manly came, without his pants or socks, just his shirt and shoes. We left Ben in the house and he kept barking.

The fire hadn't so much of a start and we had it mostly out when Corinne and Mrs. McCormack drove in. Then in a little Jack and Al and Tom [Tom Carnall, a friend of the Turner brothers]. Corinne heard Ben barking over the phone and felt sure something was wrong. So they came. Nice of them and good to have them.

We got Hyberger and his man out and they found our transmitter had blown up and scattered stuff around that caught on fire from the wires someway. I do not understand it yet. I don't know what caused it, but it was all over town and on the telephone lines too. . . .

[An additional two pages added to this letter returned to the *Plum Creek* manuscript.]

I am stumped about Ma in the stable.

I can't see how Laura can go to the stable with her. Laura couldn't reach the clothesline [a guide between the house and the stable during blizzards].

The storm came suddenly you know and was enough to lose Pa. It would be something Ma would never do to let Laura go out in it, worse than sending her to drive cattle. The only way Laura could get to the stable and back would be to cling to Ma.

Ma had both hands full with the rope and the milk pail and all she could do to go through the storm herself. We can't have the storm let up so soon after starting. They never, never did. It is unreasonable that Ma should let her go when there was no need for it.

I don't know how to handle it.

Seeing the inside of that stable and how Ma did the chores seems rather necessary to the interest of the whole thing. But how?

I'm beat!

*A stream-of-consciousness technique was devised, in which Laura constructed Ma's every move from house to stable, and her activities while tending the livestock.*

## *Grasshoppers coming one summer . . . going away the next*

AUGUST 6, 1936

Rose Dearest

The central idea is that field of wheat which was going to make them rich. It took both banks of Plum Creek [life in a dugout on the east bank of the creek, and later experiences in the new frame house on the west bank] and three years and the wheat wasn't raised yet, but the inference in the last chapter is that it was raised in the fourth.

We can't have the blizzard the year of the Christmas tree, for that awful winter was the beginning of the wet seasons that kept the grasshoppers down and put them out. The winter . . . was so bad that no one would have gone out to a Christmas tree. It was an open winter that permitted them all [the Ingalls family] to go so far to [Walnut Grove for] Christmas.

The last winter was one bad storm after another as I have written it, unsafe to leave home. It caught Pa and Ma at the first [told in the chapter "Keeping House" in *On the Banks of Plum Creek*].

No, I think that last winter must be left as it is more or less or we spoil the effect as well as not being correct as to conditions in the grasshopper times.

Cut out the dog fight. [The episode was a fierce battle between the Ingalls dog and the Nelson dog.]

On page 62 let the chapter end with the words "The smell of the air was different and the sky was not so sharply blue."

Cut the chapter "Gathering Plums." That will gain a little space and nothing lost.

At the last of Page 96 say, "Where Pa had broken the prairie sod for the wheat field the ground lay black and wet." Pa looked at it and said, etc.

Cut out the town party. Let the girls come out on Saturday afternoon to play on the banks of Plum Creek. Nellie . . . can be snooty just the same. That will keep the action closer to the banks of Plum Creek.

Cut out the prairie fire and the Nelsons altogether except for what has been said. Cut the whole chapter "Straw stack" if you wish.

Pare going to school down as small as possible. . . . That will let the action stay on the creek more.

The chapter about the Christmas tree is all that is needed about that winter.

I have no copy of the thing here that I can go over. If I should try to use the first scraps of scribbling I would get us all confused for I changed it so much from then. This makes it hard for me to tell you where to cut. . . .

Christmas tree for one winter, blizzards for the next, the hard, last winter.

Grasshoppers coming one summer, hatching and going away the next.

The wheat is what they are working and waiting for. The banks of Plum Creek are the stage setting where all these things happen while waiting for the wheat. Would it not be possible to make the chapter shorter? Couldn't Pa's coming home and the Christmas tree make one chapter? Couldn't Pa's boots be in the church chapter. I mean shorten both and combine in one. . . .

## *Very much pleased*

*The New Deal's Wisconsin Works Progress Administration (WPA) created employment by transcribing books into Braille. The Wisconsin School for the Blind compiled a list of requested book titles; several hundred women assembled Braille editions.*

AUGUST 17, 1936
George T. Bye
New York
Dear Mr. Bye,

I have yours of the 13th and am very much pleased that the Wisconsin School for the Blind is going to transcribe Little House on the Prairie into Braille.

Certainly you have my permission and I am glad you did not wait to hear from me before giving it.

With kindest regards, I remain
Yours sincerely,
Laura Ingalls Wilder

## *My position is that Harpers should now give me their best terms*

*The small royalty percentage on Farmer Boy still rankled Laura and Rose when On the Banks of Plum Creek was submitted. Rose wrote George Bye that "this is the fourth book in a series of seven. The first four are paying my mother around $1,200 a year . . .*

*we met Harper's unheard-of low terms on FARMER BOY . . . a*
*flat 5% royalty. Harpers can now come across with a fair contract*
*for an absolutely certain best-seller juvenile, part of a series that is*
*a permanent gold-mine for them. If they do not want this book, we*
*can go to another publisher with the whole series."*

SEPTEMBER 24, 1936

Dear Mr. Bye,

This is the manuscript of On the Banks of Plum Creek, a sequel to my former juveniles published by Harpers.

Ida Louise Raymond of Harpers is expecting this manuscript. She has written me that she will give me better terms on this book than on the previous ones.

I know that Little, Brown and Co. give an advance of royalties and a sliding scale of royalties, reaching 15 per cent at 3,000 [sold] for juveniles by unknown writers.

I would like an advance on this book and a royalty of 12½ per cent. The sales on my former books have been excellent and Harpers published one of them at a royalty of 5 per cent.

My position is that Harpers should now give me their best terms for juvenile fiction.

I believe your office can get better terms for this book than I have had before, without difficulty because Ida Louise Raymond has herself suggested them.

Yours sincerely,

Laura Ingalls Wilder

## My "books are very popular"

*Laura sent Ida Louise Raymond essentially the same letter she mailed*
*to George Bye. When her request for an increased royalty was stated,*
*she concluded with friendly news about the Little House books.*

. . . At last we are enjoying cool weather and rain and are about re-covered from our heat prostration which lasted all summer.

Among other pleasant things came a letter from the librarian of Los Angeles Public Library which is very nicely making a display of my book. She wanted my photo to use in the display and "any bits of per-sonal information that would interest the children" among whom my "books are very popular." I have sent picture etc. [Laura posed for a dignified photo to be used for the exhibit, but she was unsatisfied with it; it was never again used for publicity.]

I am very glad that the Wisconsin School for the Blind printed Little House on the Prairie in Braille. Sister Mary lost her eyesight when she was 13 years old and read her small library with her fin-gers. She would be pleased that L.H. on the P. was printed for the blind to read. [Mary was actually fourteen when she became blind in 1879.]

I hope you will be interested in Laura's adventures on the banks of Plum Creek. . . .


## Rose insists that I must carry the story on

*Ursula Nordstrom was hired as Ida Louise Raymond's assistant in Harper's children's book department. She was awestruck when read-ing the manuscript for On the Banks of Plum Creek. "The Wilder books required no editing," she recalled. "Not any." One of her first job tasks was writing jacket copy for On the Banks of Plum Creek. She approached the job as if dealing with the Holy Grail.*


OCTOBER 26, 1936
Dear Miss Raymond,

I am so pleased that you like On the Banks of Plum Creek so much. It is very dear to me for I lived it all over again as I wrote it.

Your terms are satisfactory, a royalty of 10% to 3000 [copies sold],

12½% to 6000 and 15% thereafter, with an advance of $500 payable half at signing of contract and half on publication.

I will be willing that it shall be published early in October, 1937 if you will give all my previous books a generous publicity this fall and especially for the Christmas holidays.

If there is to be nothing coming in from the new book, it is rather necessary for me that the old ones should continue selling.

I am sorry I was so late in getting the manuscript of Plum Creek to you, but it was impossible to work faster this summer. I shall begin to work soon on the next [book] and perhaps I will not be so long with it.

Rose insists that I must carry the story on until Laura married Farmer Boy. And so I suppose I will.

I am sorry you have been ill and hope you are quite recovered.

With kindest regards, I am

Sincerely yours,

Laura Ingalls Wilder

## The best of the lot

*Alvilda Sorenson's work among farm communities during South Dakota's drought years allowed her to recommend the Little House books to families she met.*

DECEMBER 8, 1936

Dear Mrs. Sorenson,

Many thanks for your kind words about my little books and recommending them to others.

The next of the series On the Banks of Plum Creek has just been accepted by Harpers who were kind enough to say it is the best of the lot. It will not be published until next fall.

On the Banks of Plum Creek carries the story on from where it is left off in Little House on the Prairie.

I am planning the next one telling of when we first went to Dakota ahead of the railroad.

Your work must be very interesting also. Though I know very little about it. [Mrs. Sorenson worked with the Farm Home Bureau, an agency created to help farm families.]

Hoping you will be pleased with my autographs and wishing you and yours a very Merry Christmas,

I am sincerely,

Laura Ingalls Wilder

# PART
## II

# CHAPTER 4

# STAR OF THE CHILDREN'S DEPARTMENT
## (1937–1943)

> Rocky Ridge Farm
> May, 23, 1939
>
> Rose Dearest
>     I might have known you
> would fix things!
>     We are delighted that my business
> with Harpers can be done so
> speedily.
>     May I send you "The Hard
> Winter" now?   I would rather
> you had it so if anything
> should happen on our trip
> you could finish it. Shall
> I send it to New York or
> will you be in Connecticut?

Most of Laura's correspondence to Rose was written with pen and ink
on the same lined paper she used to draft her book manuscripts.
*(Herbert Hoover Presidential Library)*

*Laura's nostalgic wish to honor her pioneer father and preserve his
tales morphed into a mission. As a story keeper of pioneer life, she
became the storyteller for children of the frontier era. Laura's speech
delivered at the Detroit Book Fair when* On the Banks of Plum
Creek *was published in 1937 explained the purpose for writing her
books:*

"*I began to think what a wonderful childhood I had had. How I had seen the whole frontier, the woods, the Indian country of the great plains, the frontier towns, the building of railroads in wild, unsettled country, homesteading and farmers coming in to take possession. I realized that I had seen and lived it all—all the successive phases of the frontier, first the frontiersman, then the pioneer, then the farmers, and the towns. Then I understood that in my own life I represented a whole period of American History. That the frontier was gone and agricultural settlements had taken its place when I married a farmer. It seemed to me that my childhood had been much richer and more interesting than that of children today, even with all the modern inventions and improvements.*

*I wanted the children now to understand more about the beginnings of things, to know what is behind the things they see—what it is that made America as they know it. Then I thought of writing the story of my childhood in several volumes—a seven volume historical novel for children covering every aspect of the American frontier.*

*After the work was well started, I was told that such a thing has never been done before; that a novel of several volumes was only for grownups. My daughter, Rose Wilder Lane, a writer and novelist, said it would be unique, that a seven volume novel for children had never been written. . . . Someone has to do a thing first; I would be the first to write a multi-volume novel for children.*"

# *I am having to live over those days with Pa and Ma*

FEBRUARY 5, 1937

Rose Dearest,

I am going to send you a day by day letter. There isn't enough in my head to make a letter, but every little bit, I think of something I want to say to you. The letter will be like the dictionary, "fine reading but the subject changes too often."

Looking through my desk yesterday, I found a book Ma made of writing paper. When I put it there I couldn't bear to read it, but I am having to live over those days with Pa and Ma anyway, so I did.

Ma had written some of her own poetry in it and copied some that she liked.

And Pa had written two songs. "The Blue Juniata" and "Mary of the Wild Moor." Any time you want them, I'll send you copies. He signed the songs and the date is 1860. The whole songs are there. "Blue Juniata" is not much like the printed one we had when I used it [in *Little House on the Prairie*] but it is as I remember hearing it. I have never seen or heard it anywhere else. So is the other but I have never seen nor heard it anywhere else.

"Oh father, dear father, come down and open the door. But watch dogs did howl and the village bells tolled and the winds blew across the wild moor."

I am going to write Grace about the wild flowers there and refresh our memories. I'll be able, I think, to sort out the later imported ones from the old timers. I'll send them to you when I get them.

Bruce was over yesterday. Drove over after his day's work was done, to see if we were all right and if we needed anything. Only stayed a minute for he had to hurry back to do his chores.

He asked me if I knew Al [Turner] was here. Said he hadn't seen him, but Mrs. Brentlinger saw him go up to the house. She thought she was sure it was Al. I have not heard anything from him and sort of hate to phone anyone and ask. I'd have to ask Hoover's [Dorothy Sue Hoover was a girlfriend of Al's].

Just wondered how come, if true.

You remember the old saying that "A man who won't steal from the R.R. co. ain't honest."

I am, at present, working on the R.R. story

And here is something I can't use in a child's story, but you could use it if you have a place for it.

On Uncle Hi's first contract he lost money. He had tried his best to make a profit, been careful of expense, worked three of his own teams for which he could draw no pay. In the settlement the R.R. cheated him in measuring the yards of dirt moved. The surveyors measured the finished grade and did the figuring. All goods for the camp, in the store, feed for the horses, tools, etc were furnished by the R.R. but charged to the contractor. The company overcharged Uncle Hi on those.

He was broke and more, but the company was good and kind and would give him another contract. I remember hearing him say, the only way to make anything was to go behind on a contract. The farther behind a man went, the more he would make.

So he took another contract. He worked his own teams but under other men's names so he could draw pay for them. The R.R. kept a team hauling oats out of the feed store away somewhere and selling them. They took them away at night. Contractors had the right to take goods out of their stores, but had to be a little careful. The family took more than they could use of dry groceries and goods. When camp broke up Aunt Docia took the three teams. She drove one, Lena drove one and Gene drove the other. The wagons were loaded with goods and tools. They went before the camp broke and Uncle Hi stayed for the settlement. He was away behind on the contract, but his pockets were full of money.

All the contractors did that way. "Old Stebbins" kept three teams working hauling oats, 100 pounds to a load, for a month. The oats were unloaded into a feed room 12x16 and after they had hauled for a month there were only a few oats in the room. Manly was one of the teamsters. I don't know where feed was hauled to sell. Perhaps sold to the R.R. to furnish another contractor. Must have been, there was no other market.

The letter from Grace came. She said:

"Flowers that used to grow here, some are here yet, but lots of kinds we don't see any more. The crocus came first in the spring— and the prairie used to be white with the blossoms of wild onions in the spring. Then there were violets, purple and yellow and such a lot of sheep sorrel with its pinkish blossoms. There were no sunflowers, goldenrod nor dandelions until much later. There were yellow but-tercups and white anemone, common name is wind flower. There were two kinds of wild peas blue and purple and wild parsley and wild clover bean. There were tiger lilies in low places.

"Forty years ago there were wild geraniums, white and red, around Manchester [seven miles from De Smet, where Grace and her hus-band, Nate Dow, farmed]. Never saw them around De Smet."

To think that I have forgotten all this which comes back to me now. That's why the sooner I write my stuff the better. You remember the roses of course and have heard us tell about them. [Rose was named for the wild prairie roses.]

Well my dear, I must get to work. It is nearly dinner time.

Every year, I think, I will remember Valentine's Day and be nice to people, but every year I forget until it is too late. Christmas and birthdays seem to be all I can manage. But it was delightful to have you remember us.

Don't you love the styles this spring? Had a catalogue from Bellas Hess, Kansas City—oh all the clothes are the prettiest for years and years. The only fault is that most of them have short sleeves. Likely I am prejudiced because my arms are not pretty any more, but there should be more long sleeves. I think the styles are beautiful, princess and swing skirts.

I am now re-reading Tros of Samothrace and Manly is reading it. Whoever gets it first in the evening reads it. The other has to put up with something else. [*Tros of Samonthrace* and Talbot Mundy's other historical adventure tales were favorites of Laura and Manly. Mundy was a friend of Rose's; *Tros of Samothrace* is dedicated to her.]

I can't work on my book in the evening, because if I do, I can't sleep. My brain goes right on remembering and it's H——.

Lots and lots of love my dear,

Mama Bess

TUESDAY MORNING
[SHEETS ADDED TO THE ABOVE LETTER]

There is snow over everything and prospect good for more to come.

Manly thought of an anecdote you will likely remember hearing him tell.

I don't know if you can use it, but it gives a sidelight on the spirit of those times and just to refresh your memory, here it is.

A Dr. Cameron, living in Sioux Falls, had a claim near Manly's [north of De Smet]. The hay on it was better than on Manly's or Roy's places and they wanted to put it up.

E. J. [Eliza Jane Wilder insisted on being called E. J.] wrote Dr. Cameron asking if they could cut it. But she forgot to put a stamp in the letter.

He answered, but all he wrote was "Where in Hell is your postage stamp?"

E. J. wrote underneath, "In the northwest corner by the furnace door. You will see it as you go in."

She mailed it back to him, still without a stamp for reply.

And the Dr. answered with a nice letter, saying they were welcome to all the hay they wanted to cut.

So much for that.

## "PART OF THE PRAISE OF THE BOOKS BELONGS TO YOU"

*Manly bought the largest mailbox allowed by the United States Post Office Department to accommodate Laura's fan mail. She shared some of the mail with Rose, including a 1937 letter from the Eagle family of Barrington, Illinois. She wrote Rose that "this is the picture of the little boy whose father wrote the letter. Barrington is a suburb of Chicago. Part of the praise of the books belongs to you, so I am sending it on."*

JANUARY 21, 1937

My dear Mrs. Wilder,

 The entire Eagle family has appreciated and enjoyed your books and your courtesy to us. My own mother as a little girl, lived in a log house made by her father near Aiken, Minnesota, "in the big woods." Their nearest neighbors were Sioux Indians. Your beautifully written stories are very similar to those that were told me as a little boy. I'm glad that Edward [the letter-writer's son] is having the pleasure of hearing your books read. He's been fascinated by them. Thank you so much for autographing the books for us. It makes them more than "just books."

 Sincerely,

 H. L. Eagle

## *God knows the farm is not self supporting*

*Rose considered the reelection of Franklin D. Roosevelt to be national approval of the New Deal. Laura and Manly shared Rose's dislike of the administration. In this letter Laura refers to Rose's*

*official residence as being at Rocky Ridge, claiming head of the*
*household status to reduce her income tax. Laura discusses this*
*situation, her own local anti–New Deal activities, and home news.*

MARCH 12, 1937
Rose Dearest,

Your letter enclosing Dewey Short's came this P.M. [Republican Dewey Short, who hailed from Missouri's Seventh Congressional District, was a member of the United States House of Representatives. He was a staunch opponent of the New Deal.]

Dewey Short is a grand person. He and Clark deserve a medal for valor. We were interested in his letter.

It is all right about those tax reports. If we work you for a handout, it is not your fault. I'll stay out of income tax as long as I can. You can contribute quite a bit to us, and still the figures won't amount to $2,500 and that is what I understand is the limit to keep us from paying tax on our income. So rest easy.

Damn everything anyway!

You can still be head of this household, and we can keep it up for you. God knows the farm is not self supporting. You have contributed to keeping it up for years. You don't have to pay rent; the farm house can just be your home, and if you pay to keep it up, that is supporting us and our home. . . . Who's the wiser?

Truman is a liar. I wrote to him on this tablet paper. [Harry S. Truman was elected as a Democratic senator from Missouri in 1934.] There is a petition being signed to send congressmen at Dennis's office. We keep talking, but I don't know how much good it does.

I will be in town tomorrow to see Aunt Daisy and to give her your message. I will stir around a little and see how many I can get to sign the Dennis petition. [Aunt Daisy was Daisy Bray Freeman, the second wife of George Freeman, organizer of the Bank of Mansfield and a prominent citizen.]

People drive me wild. They as a whole are getting just what they deserve. "What's the use?" they ask, "it won't do any good," they say. [Laura refers to political apathy.] I simply can't read it in the papers any more. It makes me sick, actually.

Well, I hasten to relieve your mind, when all the time the subject of greatest importance is my new spring suit. To say that I was flabbergasted when I opened the box is putting it mildly. Rose, honey, it is lovely and fits like new spring suits should fit. The color is exactly what I like too. I like the feel of the goods of my new suit. It feels like sugar and cream tastes.

But look what you have done to me!

Not a blouse did I have but what disgraced the suit and absolutely not a hat I have will go with it. So I have spent my tightly pinched pennies. I have ordered two blouses from Montgomery Ward's, one a lighter blue and one an eggshell. And then as a crowning extravagance I have ordered a dress, the exact blue of the suit, to wear with the top coat when I need it. It is acetylene silk, I know it but it is not spelled right. It is Acetate Crepe and cost $2.98. But I know it is a beauty. The blouses are silk. Haven't got them yet, just sent the order. Now I must get a hat.

Isn't it grand how John is doing? I'm tickled pink. [Rose sent John Turner to New Mexico Military Institute for the school year.]

Haven't heard anything from Corinne. She has no phone and I hesitate to have them call her down into the drug store [the Murrays, after vacating Rocky Ridge, moved into rooms above Fuson's Drug Store in Mansfield]. She could call me from somewhere, but never has since they moved. I haven't seen her. Have only been in town three times since they moved, or maybe four, and had so many other things to do. Didn't want to climb the stairs, either. I'm saving of my breath, you know, though it hasn't bothered me for some time. The house stands just as it did when Manly wrote you about it. I think Corinne is all right, or she couldn't do the things I hear of her doing. There is no need that you should worry about her.

Manly has made a garden this week. Planted potatoes, peas,

lettuce, radishes and turnips. It is lovely weather, makes an itching in my feet [to travel]. But! dust settled over us again.

I'll wear the grapes whenever possible. Just now, I am wearing the pearls day and night. I sort of forgot about 'em till one night they woke me up saying they were sick. I got them out next morning.

I think I have found the yarn to finish the rug, at Montgomery Ward's. Have ordered it and if it is not right can return it.

Manly likes so much to make rugs, I think I will let him work up all my old clothes into rugs like the pattern you drew.

I have so many clothes now, I'll never make over the old ones. As for giving them to anyone, they would go on relief before they'd make them over. Besides I'm fed up with giving things to people. So we'll put those lovely old things into rugs.

How wonderful for Talbot Mundy to be able to write "The Sayings of Taliesin" himself. They are so good. Do you know the book I have, "Queen Cleopatra" by Mundy, comes between "Tros" and "The Purple Pirate"? It is grand to have them both. Don't lose Tros.

We will try our best to keep the strawberries safe. Manly is doing something in the garden this afternoon. I don't know what, but seems unable to keep away from it.

We often talk of what you mention, there being no opportunities now. If we had had such opportunities when we were young we would have been rich. If we were only a little younger than we are, we would do something about them. Anyone who will half try can make money surprisingly now. How they can keep from it, I can't see. Nor what they do with the money they can't prevent themselves from making.

Bruce says he gets $20 a month from his three cows. He feeds them hay he put up himself. They eat the leavings from our goat's roughness. I mean, the cows eat what the goats won't eat, and a little grain. And still Bruce is always hard up. I use him for an example because I know his affairs. Everyone else is the same. Suppose it costs half of the $20 to feed Bruce's family, which it doesn't. What would $10 a month clear have meant to us when we came here [in 1894]? Besides Bruce works a great deal of the time at good wages. They don't seem to be extravagant. But what becomes of their money? Of course nobody else's business is any of mine. But I find my heart is getting harder. I can have no least sympathy for people who can do, and will only holler that there are no chances for them now.

I wish they all might have the opportunities we had when I was young and no more. Wouldn't it be fun to watch 'em?

My dear, I thank you so much for my new suit. It is lovely! Wish I could do something that would please you half as much.

I sent you a little loaf of "Sweet bread of Greece." Tell me how you like it.

I'll burn your letter and you burn mine.

Much love,

Mama Bess

## *Pa's old R.R. account book*

*In this undated letter, likely written in 1937, Laura refers to the notebook Charles Ingalls kept while operating the railroad company's store; the notebook revealed the prices the construction crew paid for goods. Laura may have thought that Rose could use these details in her current writing project, Free Land.*

[NO DATE, 1937]

Rose Dearest,

Looking over Pa's old R.R. account book to find some help for Silver Lake, I find the following items charged to one of the men:

1 pr. overalls $1.00 June 9, 1879
1 shirt .70 June 16
1 pr. boots 4.40 June

1 pr. suspenders .35 June 22
2¼ bu. corn .52
Board bill 4.80

There is another bill:

June 3, 1879
1 thousand feet lumber $13
20 lbs nails .80
50 lbs flour 1.50
3 shovels 3.75
2 scrapers 20.00
1 Big Plug tobacco .40

Still another:

June 1879
1 plug tobacco .10
1 rubber coat 3.00
1 hundred lbs. flour 2.75
1 lb tea 1.00
2 shirts 1.60
June 12, 1879
½ lb. smoking tobacco .20
1 pr. Boots .50
Must have been poor or second hand boots can't understand why
    they were so cheap.
1 sack Flour 3.10 Must have been 100 lbs.
2 pans .35
3 lbs butter .36
2 lbs. Meat .20
1 Loaf Bread .10

This is June 1879 at the Sioux River camp. Pa didn't go to Silver Lake camp until September. There was no butter to buy there.

Silver Lake camp broke up Dec. 1st. Everyone left but us and we moved into the Surveyors house.

Sorry I didn't find this when you asked the questions. We tried to remember. But these prices and dates were written down at the time. There is also a short account of the settling of De Smet. What a pity Pa didn't write about the Hard Winter.

The bill sent you by the Farmer's Exchange was for cow feed that Al got about the middle of last April . . . they say they sent you the bill several times to your address here, but heard nothing. . . . Likely Al will remember it with this to go on. [Rose kept a cow while living on the farm; the Turner boys were responsible for feeding and milking.]

A man came to look at Corinne's car. He didn't want it after he saw it because the engine is ruined. He showed Manly a crack in it about as long as his hand . . . said it must have been left full of water and frozen up and busted. . . . But in that case John cannot be blamed for the ruin of the car, nor Al either, for they were both long gone before cold weather. I just mention it in passing so your mind will be easy about it. . . .

Manly is in town for the day, having the car gone over thoroughly for the third and last free examination. It still runs sweetly and is satisfactory in every way. [The car was a 1936 Chrysler, which replaced Isabelle, the Buick.]

Have you noticed the increase in tax on gasoline? Darn it all! By the time we get a car that can go, we can't afford to buy the gasoline.

Well, anyway—"It's a great life if you don't weaken."

I am feeling so well lately. Can walk and walk and walk and still breathe. Won't it be grand if I've worn out the asthma?

I hope you are feeling well and that your work is going good. Did Dorothy Sue go to Columbia to visit Al?

I love you very much,

Mama Bess

P.S. In Pa's book is a day by day record of weather for Jan., Feb., March 1886. Would it be of any use to you?

## *"In the days of pioneers"*

*While Rose provided editorial suggestions for the Little House books, Laura offered historical data for her daughter's writings. In 1937 Rose researched* Free Land, *a novelized version of Almanzo Wilder's homesteading years. In this letter, Laura also recounted her family's trials prior to the era described in* By the Shores of Silver Lake.

MARCH 23, 1937

Rose Dearest,

I hope the letter Manly wrote you this A.M. will help you find out why we were so hard up in Dakota. Farming there was like the chicken business as you and Mrs. Quigley figured it out. We could get rich on paper—IF, but the "IF" was too big.

Already I see I forgot to tell you something you asked.

There were no Pullmans on trains west from Tracy [Minnesota]. There were only freights, a few freight cars with express and day coaches behind. We called them passenger trains because they were all the passenger trains we had.

The Land Agent at the Land Office might have come from Sioux Falls or Yankton [Dakota Territory], we never knew. We think they were appointed from the Land Office in Washington. . . . In that case it would likely be by political preferment. Indian agents were appointed from Washington, as you know.

If it is important to know for sure, you could likely find out by writing to someone in Yankton, perhaps the postmaster, and asking when the first trains came.

It was on the trip from New York to Spring Valley that Manly and Roy ate the crackers. [Almanzo and Royal farmed the Wilder land near Malone, New York, after their family moved to new land in Spring Valley, Minnesota, during the early 1870s. The brothers traveled overland to Minnesota.]

It was Richard Sears, not Harry. Manly always called him Dick. [Richard Sears, an acquaintance of Manly's, was a cofounder of Sears, Roebuck, and Company.]

The Doctor paid Manly and Roy $25 exactly to build the sod shanty on his son's claim. [Homestead land was often claimed on speculation by easterners. The government required that the homesteader erect a dwelling on the land. The Wilders built several shanties for themselves and their sister Eliza Jane.]

Manly had a bad toothache driving from Yankton to Sioux Falls. Roy stopped the horse where a sign said Dentist upstairs. Manly went up the stairs two at a time. A man there, supposed to be a dentist, said he'd pull the tooth. But he didn't know how and couldn't get the tooth out. He wouldn't let go . . . climbed up on Manly's shoulders with his knees and jerked Manly around. Finally the tooth came out.

Manly had backed him into a corner and was about to beat him up when the real dentist came in. The man who pulled the tooth was an apprentice, just beginning to learn the trade. So Manly left without paying his bill, "cussing them both out" as he left. A visit to the dentist. Visits to the dentist and such like should be included in the expense account of those times. But you notice no allowance for them was figured. How about this visit to the dentist, "in the days of pioneers." (How do you like that as a comprehensive name for my series?)

As to why my family was so hard up after selling the place on the banks of Plum Creek, it is all explained in the four years not included in the series. [The story of this era was told in the Wilder autobiography *Pioneer Girl*, which Rose was using as reference while writing *Free Land*.]

There was the trip to eastern Minnesota, where we stayed awhile

at Uncle Peter's because the little brother born on Plum Creek was
sick. There was the expense of his sickness and death [in August
1876].

I think we went out of our way to visit Uncle Peter and Aunt Eliza
because we were on the way to Burr Oak, Iowa. There Pa and Ma
worked as partners with the Steadmans in the hotel. Steadman handled the money and someway beat Pa out of his share. I don't suppose
there was much.

Then we were out of that [the hotel operation] with rent to pay
and doctor bills. Grace was born there [in 1877] and we all had mea-
sles. And we had to eat and buy clothes and school books.

Pa worked catchely here and there but never enough to pay expenses. When we left there was not enough money to pay the last
month's rent and feed us on the way back to Walnut Grove. There
Pa bought a lot and built a house just on his credit. "Old Man Masters," who used to own the hotel in Burr Oak, owned the land and
lumber yard. Pa bought from him. It was not all paid for when Pa
went to work on the railroad west from Tracy. He sent more back,
then made some kind of bargain and turned the property back to
Masters. As usual getting the worst of the bargain. But you can see
where it left him.

There was of course interest on the debt and I have a dim remembrance that the interest was all he had been able to pay and Masters
took the property back on the debt.

There were no jobs lying around to go begging while the government hired men as now. Interest was *high*. A man once in debt could
stand small chance of getting out.

I remember Pa worked for Masters at carpenter work. He worked
now and then a little bit on some farm. He worked a short time in a
tiny butcher shop in town. No refrigerator, no ice in the shop, and I
remember when meat would be getting to its last chance, Pa would
take some home on his wages, and we had plenty of meat.

Mary had some sort of spinal sickness. I am not sure if the Doctor named it. [It was spinal meningitis.] She was sick a long time [April through June 1879] but the Doctor finally did save her. She was para- lyzed and as she gradually recovered from her stroke her sight went. We learned later [1892] when Pa took her from De Smet to Chicago to a specialist that the nerves of her eyes were paralyzed and there was no hope.

You can see that all of this cost money. I would have no idea how much. I know Pa sent money home for doctor bills after he was work- ing for the railroad. But Pa was no businessman, He was a hunter and trapper, a musician and poet.

Manly is waiting, to take this letter as he goes by the mail box.

I'll finish writing to you after he is gone. I won't hold the letter now for you may need it in your work.

Lots of love,

Mama Bess

## *I talked over those times with Manly*

*This letter is not dated, but it was written in close sequence with that of March 23, 1937. The story of Almanzo, Royal, and Eliza Jane filing on homesteads in Yankton, and the horse's untimely death, was used in* Free Land.

[NO DATE, 1937]

Rose Dearest,

My eyes have been bothering me, so I talked over those times with Manly and told him to write it. He has read me his letter and I will complete the picture as I got it from him.

They drove from Marshall, Minnesota [home of Manly's sister Alice Wilder Baldwin], to Yankton in two days [by present roads, 170 miles]. They took oats for horse feed and eats for themselves . . . ex- pecting to stay overnight with some settler. But settlers were scarce, sometimes they drove 25 or 30 miles without seeing anything but the bare, wild prairie.

The second day at noon they had found no settler nor any water. Stopped at noon to eat their dry lunch. Manly says he has no idea what is was, but likely bread and butter, cake and pie, for that is what they would have had.

The horses were fed their noon oats. Roy said better let them go without their dinner, but Manly was sorry for them because they had been driven so hard and were hungry, so he fed them. They were his horses. After eating they hitched up and drove over a rise in the prairie about six miles, and there was a windmill pumping water, and a house.

Everybody drank. The horses were watered and they drove on. About five miles later, the horse was taken sick and died in a few minutes. Driving hard on dry oats, getting too hot, then drinking water and swelling 'em up. Manly has always blamed E. J. because she kept urging him to drive faster. The horse cost him $125 in the spring and he had refused $200 for her just before they started. That was *money* then.

The hurry was for fear others would find out that the railroad planned to make De Smet the end of the division. They made it at Huron, after all.

It was about 25 miles to Yankton when the horse died. It seemed too far to go back to the windmill for help when the hurry was to go on, so they went on with the one horse. They left the doctor [a Wilder family friend accompanied them] in Yankton and E. J. in Sioux Falls to lighten the load on the one horse going back, and took three days for the trip, sleeping two nights in the hack, with the horse picketed to eat grass. I hope they had the sense to take along a couple of jugs of water, for themselves and the horse, but Manly does not remember. They carried horse feed and lunches with them again.

The Land Office was a one story board structure with a false square front common in those days. Not even painted. The town of

Yankton was new and crude. The official in charge was called the Land Agent. Clerks waited on applicants (showing the sectional map on the counter behind which they stood). Any quarter section not marked X was still open to entry and could be filed on. A man "filed a claim" on a homestead or tree claim and got his "first papers" on it.

I never saw those papers and neither Manly nor I can remember what they were called legally. They were always spoken of as first papers. There was no especial crowd when Manly filed, just a few men standing around in the rather bare office.

I am using a mob scene at the land office when Pa files the next spring, so please don't use that. [This was one of the few purely fictitious scenes Laura created in her books. See her letter to Aubrey Sherwood of November 18, 1939.]

The Dr., Manly says, was with them, filed on a claim for his son, signing the son's name. He hired Manly and Roy, paying them then and there, to build a claim shanty on the claim and hang up some old clothes in it to be left there so it would look as though it had been occupied. The son never saw the land office nor the claim until the next spring. It was the law that a man must do his own filing. There was no opening time for settlement or filing. As soon as the country was surveyed it was open to homesteading. There was a small rush that fall and next spring, settlers following the R.R. survey and the new R.R.

Opening day, with everyone starting . . . at the gunshot, came later in Kansas and Oklahoma. Manly signed an application, filed on, and the first papers were given him. At "proving up" the homesteaders went to the land office with two witnesses to prove that for five years he had made a continued residence on his claim, never being away from his home (house) there for more than six months. That he had a house on it and ten acres of land under cultivation.

A homesteader proved up at the end of five years. The only expense was for making out and recording the "patent." But Manly does not know how much that was. It was a patent from the government, not a deed. If a man wanted to prove up, before the five years ended, he could do so by paying $1.25 an acre.

There were no sections of R.R. land. In Minnesota but not in Dakota. In Dakota the R.R. had only a "right of way," a strip of land 100 feet wide. On this they must have the tracks and all. Someone connected with the R.R. filed a homestead at the town site, proved up and sold the land for town lots.

As for getting Manly to tell what someone said— Have you heard of oysters? It is long ago. But you can imagine what E. J. would say to make him drive faster.

You must see the picture of the long, hard drive. 150 miles is a long way with a team, the dry noon lunch, the eager drinking at the windmill and all the rest. Picture the prairie with no settlement, no least sign of "human habitation" for mile after mile, the hope of good investment to urge them on, or perhaps a home, however you are working up to it.

Imagine the loss of such a valuable horse to a poor man making a start in the west and the courage and resourcefulness needed to go on and make a success in spite of "hell and high water." There was no whining in those days, no yelling for help. A man did what he could with what he had.

I hope this will help, I do hope it will. It doesn't seem like much but it is the best I can do. It was nice to have you ask me to help you and I am glad to do what I can. Will answer your letters soon. Just now no more.

Much love,

Mama Bess

P.S. I have mailed you a synopsis of Hard Winter and Prairie Girl today. It is the best I can do until I write them out. I am sure they will run to more chapters as I write them.

I hope you like the way I have planned to have all the characters in all the books sort of rounded up in the last one. Giving news of them. I think we do it naturally through Uncle Tom and Alice & Ella.

The Hard Winter is only one winter out of the whole story [the Little House series] and I think it adds to the feeling of it that the Ingalls family should be more of a solitary unit than they would have been with kinfolks around. People became numbed and dumb with the awfulness of those storms and terrible cold. There were only a few who kept normal and very much alive. Pa and the Wilder boys did. They were the only ones who would go to haul hay or hunt or anything. The others cowered in the house. Cap went with Manly because he would follow Manly and he was that kind though only a boy. I can't have relatives cluttering up Hard Winter.

By now you have my letter with list of characters. Think of them as you read the synopsis. You see I have cut a year out of Prairie Girl or rather crowded the incidents of the two years into a little more than one. I am plugging away at Hard Winter but I don't feel "first rate" and am interrupted all the time. Sorry I am not further ahead with these books. . . .

## *"I earned them"*

*The following letter is undated, but discusses economic pitfalls of homesteading and Manly's work ethic. He was characterized as David Beaton in* Free Land. *Why Laura consistently referred to her husband as an eighteen-year-old when he went to Dakota in 1879 is a mystery. Manly was twenty-two when he filed on his land claims.*

MONDAY P.M. [1937]

Rose Dearest,

Here is a bit that adds considerable points to the death of that horse on the trip to Yankton.

Manly was supposed to be 21 years old. To enter a homestead a man must be 21 or the head of a household (married). E. J. told later (she would) that he was only 18. Manly has never admitted it but as near as I can figure E. J. was right.

I asked Manly, last night, how an 18 year old boy happened to have a team of his own worth $400.

"I earned them," he told me.

After I insisted on the how, and pried the oyster open, this is what I found. As perhaps you know, Manly was doing all the one man work on his father's 100 acre farm at Spring Valley [Minnesota] when he was 13. There was help at harvest time and his father sowed the grain in the spring. Besides doing this work, Manly worked for the neighbors in his spare time. He worked one month for $15 but the work was so heavy, he was too small to do it.

One harvest time, after the harvest was done, a neighbor wanted Manly to pitch bundles of grain on the wagons in the field. He asked Manly if he could keep up to three teams. That means load fast enough so that no team would have to wait to be loaded when it came back empty from the stack.

Manly said he didn't know if he could but he would try it. The neighbor said, "If you can keep up to them, I will pay you $3 a day." Manly kept the three teams busy for several days until the stacking was finished. The money he earned was his own. Sometimes his father gave him some money and he kept part of it until he had enough of his own to buy a pony for $50. He kept the pony a year and sold it for $75.

With $30 of that money he bought a colt. Next spring he sold it for $100. With this and $25 of his own, Manly bought one of the horses that made the trip to Yankton. His father bought the other horse at the same price and gave Manly time to pay for it. Manly went to Marshall, Minn. with his team in the spring, worked them there all summer and was offered $200 just before he left, for the one that died on the trip.

Don't you know it took courage for an 18 year old boy to go on from there.

When they went west to build the claim shanties, as he wrote you, they went with Roy's teams.

After they were back in Spring Valley, Manly's father sold Manly one of his own horses, so Manly would have a team to work and all winter Manly hauled and sold cordwood at $4.00 a cord until the horse was paid for.

Then he had a team to go west to his homestead in the spring. It was two or three years before he got the dead horse paid for. Do you wonder that Manly hasn't much patience with the boys (?) of 20 to 25 who can't feed themselves?

I don't know if you can use any of this in the story you are writing. . . . But maybe you can use it sometime and I may never think of it again.

Imagine what it must have meant to Manly to lose that horse, not only that he was fond and proud of his first team, but that he would still have to pay for it. As I said, it took courage to go on from there.

Thanks for the pages from Pioneer Girl. They will help. All that time is rather dull to me now for some reason. Not exactly so vivid as when I wrote Pioneer Girl. But maybe I can struggle it out someway.

Lots of love,

Mama Bess

TUESDAY A.M.

P.S. When Manly told me the price of cordwood I found there was more to the story.

He and Roy bought the timber standing, paying what figured out to be 25 cents a cord. They paid $1.00 a cord for chopping it down and into cordwood.

Every two weeks the horse's shoes had to be reset, cost $2.00. Every six weeks they had to have new shoes on the horses that cost $4.00. Gloves wore out quickly handling wood and new ones must be bought. Manly says about every two weeks. Gloves cost from $1.50 to $2.00 a pair. He remembers he wore out his coat and had to buy a new one. Work coats, he thinks they called them, mackinaw coats, from $5 to $7.00.

The horses had to be well fed. That would cost 50 cents a day for oats and hay were cheap. You can see that the $4.00 a cord would be cut considerably when expenses were paid. It took all winter to pay for the horse.

It is *grand* about John's grades. He is one fine boy. Shame about his English teacher, but it will take more than one teacher to make John stop thinking. Thing he must learn is to keep such strong thinking to himself. When you write, tell him please, that I am proud of him.

There were, in the yard this morning at one time, two redbirds and a *bluebird*. A *bluebird* scratching around like chickens. And in a few minutes there were a pair of meadow larks busy as could be, scratching and picking. I don't know what it was they were finding but they stayed a long time. They are the first I've seen here, but Manly said a pair nested, last year, in the field across the road.

My eyes are better this morning. All they need is rest. I worked them on my writing and sewing all day and read most of the night all winter and they went on strike— Save the mark.

Lots of love,
Mama Bess

## MANLY'S VERSION

*Manly was a man of few words in a household of voluble women. He seldom wrote letters, but could be prodded to share his stories for his womenfolk to include in their books. Manly's spelling and mode of expression are preserved from his original letter.*

MARCH 25, 1937

Dear Rose,

A horse with colic bloats. As we were driving along I noticed she was bloating and pulled them down to a walk and
in a few minutes large drops of sweat came out all over and I
sed to Roy Cate is sick and said Whoa and she commenced
to lay down so I started them up to keep them from lying
down, hitched up and Roy got out and unhitched the other
horse and the sick one rolled and wood get up and lye down
at once and roll again. In about 10 minutes she lade down
and stratined out dead.

On the way home from Yankton we stade over nite with
a man who used to drive the pony express for the government carrying mail to California and he told us that if we
had had a little pulverized alum and gave the horse a spoon
full when we furst noticed her bloting we could have drove
rite on all right he said all the teamsters on the Pony express
had to carry alum in case of colic.

How I hapened to be at Marshall, Minn. was this way.
Sister Alice married a man that lived at Marshall on a farm
and there was a 160 acre farm join[ing] them that could be
got for a thousand dollars and I wanted it so mother bought
it because the man had to have the cash and mother sold it to
me on time. Then the next year when we could get homestead land I went and took land as I have already told you
and I let mother have the Marshall land back and throde in
the improve[ments]. I had broken up 4 acres and dug a well
put up a small barn and set some trees for shade and she sold
it in a year or to for fifteen hundred. We drove across to
Yankton because we could go quicker across by team and
cheaper. To go by train from Marshall you would have to go
east as far as Winona, Minn. then south to some point in
Iowa then west to Yankton. You see even now take a map

showing the railroads. They run east and west not many crossroads north & s. The Missouri River is south of Yankton. We did not cross the river. When you and I crossed the Missouri at Yankton [1894] we crossed on a steam ferry.

Yours truly

Bessie will ans. the rest.

*Again, Manly provided data for Rose's* Free Land.

Dear Rose,

You don't seem to think there is a lot of overhead expense in living. The first year, 1880, I worked on the railroad till the middle of July. When I quit the railroad I hired five acres broke on the homestead and five on the tree claim. Had to have that much to hold it.

When I quit the railroad I went down to Marshall, Minn. to harvest 25 acres of wheat. Help was scarce so I changed works with a neighbor to cut and bind my wheat, also to stack and thresh it. I had to pay 6 cents a bushel for threshing. I got 18 bushels per acre. It was 50 cents a bushel. I got 5 bushels ground into graham flour and changed 8 bushels into white flour and took 50 bushels to Dakota for seed.

That left 237 bushels to sell but they always dock off some for dirt and weed seed, so I got about $200. By that time I had left railroad work and was gone.

In 1881 I only had 5 acres for wheat. Had to put trees out on the tree claim. Had to get a breaking plow, $28. I traded my horses for a yoke of oxen so I could break more land, and broke about 50 acres before it got too dry.

I broke for O'Connell at $3 per acres to help out.

I had to hire my hay cut as I did not have a mowing machine.

I also hired my 5 acres of wheat cut. I got 175 bushels

> (35 bushels an acre) Kept 80 bushels for seed and sold the
> rest. Came to a little over $40 to live on for another year.

## For some time we have planned a western trip

Aubrey Sherwood inquired about visiting the Wilders at Rocky
Ridge. The western trip Laura alluded to was postponed until 1938.
At that time, Laura and Manly visited Sherwood at the De Smet
News.

APRIL 22, 1937
Dear Mr. Sherwood,

I am sorry, but neither Rose nor I will be at home to visitors this
summer.

For some time we have planned a western trip, that will take most
of the summer to make, and intend leaving here the last of this month,
or sooner if we can get ready.

Yours truly,

Mrs. A. J. Wilder

## Thank you for the box of candy

AUGUST 19, 1937
Rose Dearest,

In each letter I have written you lately, I have intended to thank
you for the box of candy. And each letter has been sent without my
doing so. Oh well, I would think after mailing one, I'll tell her next
letter how much we enjoy it.

In the meantime we eat and eat on it and soon it will be too late to
mention.

It is good and so nice of you to think of us. Many thanks my dear.

I have just discovered some notes I made years ago, thinking I would use them some time. I never will, I am sure, but perhaps you can use them as anecdotes or in some way, so I have copied them and here they are.

They were written when Wilson was president and are true. I saw the Mt. Zion and Mt. Pleasant meetings myself. Mrs. Frink told of the woman who wouldn't look in the glass. She knew of her and said it actually happened that way. [Laura's notes refer to stories of extreme fundamentalist religionists who lived deep in the isolated Ozark hills.]

I do hope you are resting better now. We have both had a summer flu, or cold that is going around but are recovering. Our winter's coal is in the basement. We think enough to last through. Corinne's stove is gone. She has not been able to get the dray or anyone to come for it. So when the dray was hauling coal, I called and asked her if I should send it in. And so I did.

Much love,
Mama Bess

## *How delightfully you would illustrate the verses*

*During Rose's San Francisco Bulletin days, she assisted with the children's page. Rose and Laura collaborated on verses for "The Tuck 'Em In Corner." Years later, Laura thought of recycling those 1915 poems, together with Berta Hader's illustrations. The verses were mediocre; the project never came to fruition.*

SEPTEMBER 11, 1937

My Dear Berta,

Looking over some old keep-sakes, I found the note you sent me when I was leaving San Francisco during the world's fair.

You wouldn't remember it but the weeping little girl you drew and the sweet note you wrote beneath her, have been among my treasures all these years.

Rose writes me that she has seen you and that you and your husband are very busy with your lovely work.

I am still writing my little books. The fourth in the series is out this fall and I have just completed the first draft of the next, which is already being asked for by the publishers.

Some time ago Rose sent you some of my children's verses and some of hers which were to be signed with my name if used.

Has anything been done about this book of children's verse? And do you intend to carry on with it when your season's rush is over?

I have a large field of readers because, as of course you know, my books have a large and increasing sale. I feel sure that my name will guarantee a good sale for the book of which some would undoubtedly be to readers unacquainted with your work. Your name would do as much for me. So I think a children's book carrying both our names will be sure of a satisfactory sale at least, and be valuable to us both in increasing sales of your other books and my other books.

What is your opinion of its probable publication?

Since finding your San Francisco note, I have been thinking how delightfully you would illustrate the verses of the fairies.

With kindest regards,

Laura Ingalls Wilder

## *I shall be very glad to make your acquaintance*

*Laura spoke at the Detroit Book Fair, held at J. L. Hudson Department Store in October 1937. Silas Seal, a Mansfield friend, drove Laura and Manly to Detroit in their new Chrysler. Rose was full of suggestions, plying Ida Louise Raymond with ideas for* Plum Creek *advertising posters. She coached Laura on author-editor* protocol. *She telegraphed: "Go at once to Springfield and have good photograph made. Send 6 glossy prints to J. L. Hudson Company. Love, Rose." She assured her mother, saying, "You will make a lovely lion."*

*Laura's letter to Miss Raymond was somewhat disingenuous. She had experienced large cities before and never considered herself a "hillbilly."*

OCTOBER 8, 1937

Dear Miss Raymond,

Copies of "On the Banks of Plum Creek" have arrived and I am pleased with their appearance.

Glad you like the book so well and think you will like the next one "The Shores of Silver Lake" even better.

I expect to arrive at the Statler [Hotel] in Detroit on the morning of the 16th and hope to meet you soon after.

Being unused to large hotels I feel rather timid about it all.

You see, after all, I am just a hillbilly and cities are places where I am not used to wandering.

I shall be very glad to make your acquaintance.

Sincerely,

Laura Ingalls Wilder

## *Almanzo seems to have made quite a hit*

*Laura's speech, describing her book series, was well received. In the audience was Alice Adams of Central State Teacher's College in Mount Pleasant, Michigan. Her students at the laboratory school were enthusiastic about the Little House books. When Miss Adams described meeting the actual Laura to her classroom, the children wrote letters to both Laura and Manly.*

NOVEMBER 2, 1937

Dear Miss Adams,

Indeed I am pleased with the letters from your school children and thank you for sending them just as they were written.

Almanzo seems to have made quite a hit with them. He was surprised and pleased that they wrote to him.

I am happy that you have all enjoyed my books and hope the later ones will please you as well.

Did I meet you in Detroit? I met so many pleasant people that of course I didn't remember any of their names.

Being so unused to crowds made me even dumber than usual that way.

With kindest regards, I am

Yours sincerely,

Laura Ingalls Wilder

## Rose is in New York

*Helen Stratte, a librarian at the School of the Ozarks, met Rose in 1935. Miss Stratte and her nephew Owen, a School of the Ozarks student, were entertained at Rocky Ridge. Owen and the Turner boys bonded. Helen Stratte later wrote from Macalester College to inquire about the Wilders and the Turners—and to request an autograph in* On the Banks of Plum Creek. *Laura's response was found among Stratte family papers in 1992.*

DECEMBER 22, 1937

Dear Helen Stratte,

The copy of Plum Creek for my autograph arrived today. It will go to Sallie and Halle on the first mail out, which will be tomorrow.

I am glad to autograph it for them.

Rose is in New York and we are living in the old house where she was when you were here. I do not know how long Rose will stay in New York, but I think for some time. She is very busy there and enjoying her contacts with editors, publishers and writers, old friends and new.

I am sorry you were not able to call when you were in the Ozarks and hope for better luck next time.

Your work must be very interesting. How I would love to know more of Scandinavian history and literature, especially that of Medieval times.

I shall be happy for you if you can make your trip to Norway next summer.

I will send your letter to Rose, for I know she will like to have news of you.

The boys are scattered. John is in Paris with a tutor. Al is in St. Louis working with radios.

Mr. Wilder remembers you with pleasure and sends his regards.

We are well and as busy as ever.

Wishing you a Merry Christmas and a very Happy New Year I am

Sincerely your friend,
Laura Ingalls Wilder

## *A story for grown-ups about the times I am writing of*

*After their Detroit meeting, Laura relaxed her letters to her editor in tone. Miss Raymond was addressed as Louise. The allusion to an adult novel was "The First Three Years and a Year of Grace." It was an account of Laura and Manly's early marriage. It remained unfinished, but it was posthumously published as* The First Four Years *(Harper & Row, 1971). "As to your doing a novel," Rose wrote, "there is no reason you shouldn't if you want to, but unless by wild chance it became a best seller, there is much more money in juveniles."*

DECEMBER 13, 1937

My Dear Louise,

It is pleasant news to hear the Plum Creek is going so well and I am looking forward to seeing the reviews.

Perhaps I can find something to loan for a window display with the next book. I will look around for something that may be interesting.

For some time I have had in mind to try a story for grown-ups about the times I am writing of in the Little House books.

I have the idea, but do not know if it will jell. If it does I shall be glad to let your Mr. Saxton see it.

Will try what I can do as soon as I get the next two books for you a little farther along. But you know I am slow and it will be some time.

With best regards and sincere wishes that you may have a Merry Christmas and a Happy New Year I remain your

Laura Ingalls Wilder

## *Thanks for your good wishes*

DECEMBER 24, 1937

Dear Mr. Bye,

"On the Banks of Plum Creek" seems to be going very well indeed. Thanks for your good wishes on its behalf.

Rose has written me how much she enjoyed a visit at your home and I am glad she has such pleasant friends.

Wishing you a merry holiday season and a very happy New Year I am

Yours sincerely,

Laura Ingalls Wilder

## *We had a very nice Christmas*

DECEMBER 29, 1937
Rose Dearest,

I am so glad about Al. He seemed so nice when he was here. It was so good to see him and I liked him so much that it made me wild to think I had been so mistaken in anyone. That he should take what didn't belong to him and fool me so completely. [Laura refers to the tire theft mentioned in her letter of June 25, 1936.]

I will write him and send him some little something for a late Christmas gift.

But I will mail the letter in Mountain Grove [a town eighteen miles from Mansfield] so no one here will get the address. When he was here I promised not to tell anyone he came or where he was. People ask me and no one seems to know. I will let someone else tell me before I admit I know. I don't know what his reason was and he may have told someone here by now. Thought maybe it was Dorothy Sue [his former girlfriend]. It is fine for him to send you the lovely gift and I am so glad he is making a start. Don't worry that I will write him anything but a nice letter.

Gee! I'm glad. Al is a brick [a slang term for a solid, trustworthy individual].

I hope John changes his mind back again. *Anybody* can be a lawyer.

I think he will do you credit someday. But of course he can't be expected to be settled in his mind at eighteen.

It has been more than a year that I have been trying to get Corinne's things moved out of my way. Still I ought not to be impatient, I suppose. And I should not have written boiling over a little. Sorry! [Corinne and Jack Murray occupied the farmhouse when Rose left the farm. The Wilders were eager to move back into their old home. Until they were resettled in the farmhouse, relationships were tense.] But surely you know I would not burn a good book, if it belonged to the old Nick himself. ["Old Nick" is a slang term for the devil.] It was just my temper boiling over a little. Sorry!

I am happy that the Christmas things came in so handy. What luck! Do you remember when you were in Crowley [Louisiana] and wanted a green dress? And how I made it for you for a surprise? [Rose spent the school year of 1903–1904 living with her aunt Eliza Jane Wilder when the dress was sent.] I seem to be fortunate that way. "Tis the sunset of life gives me mystical lore and coming events" told me you wanted those things [a quote from the Scottish writer Thomas Campbell].

The little dish I sent you for your birthday can be a pin tray or an ash tray. It is silver (?) and I found it in Linn Creek [Missouri] (Oh the town, You silly!) when we stayed there Christmas Eve on our way home from seeing you in Columbia a year ago. I got it just because I thought it was pretty.

The weather here is warm and foggy all the time. We have only had a couple of days of sunshine for three weeks now. Fog so thick it is dangerous to drive even with lights on for they don't penetrate it. There is no moisture and it is awfully dry here. Have you seen that the Mississippi River is lower than at any time since weather records have been kept in St. Louis, in 1861?

It is sweet of you to offer to pay for fixing the furnace but it is not necessary now. The furnace is working *perfectly*. I like the heat and there is nothing wrong except the expense. It is expensive to run. We will have the furnace overhauled and put in shape for winter, so it will keep through the summer.

I know the basement should be waterproofed and other things should be done on the place but we don't feel like putting any more money into it.

We spent our time fixing up the other place so we could leave it [a reference to the Rock House, occupied from 1928 to 1936]. All last winter and summer we worked and fretted and spent $ getting moved over and we are not settled yet.

Well, I'll be darned if we are going to spend *next* summer fixing up this place. I have gone on strike and called Manly out. We will spend our money for gasoline and our time burning it.

Now is the time to snort.

We can't go away and leave workmen to do things for they would do nothing right and would just put in their time doing nothing. It is almost impossible to get anything done. You have no idea what it is like. So as I said, we have gone on strike ourselves. I am glad 30,000 of the darned General Motors men are let out and I hope Roosevelt may enjoy the mess he has on his hands. [The famous 1937 sit-down strike in Flint, Michigan, was headline news. President Roosevelt rejected federal intervention. The aftermath of the strike was massive unionization; membership in the United Auto Workers soared to five hundred thousand.]

We had a very nice Christmas. Bruce [Prock] had a Christmas tree and we were there, also Mr. and Mrs. Prock [senior], Mrs. Bruce's mother, and Virgil Prock and wife who is the one you liked so well— who lived near Brown's Cave. John Williams [another neighbor] was there too. Mr. [Beau] Williams had a bad cold and did not come.

Mrs. Bruce tried to have things, as near as she could, like you did. She trimmed the tree with strings of popcorn and popcorn balls in green and red cellophane. For candles she stood small sticks of striped peppermint candy on end all over the tree. We, of course, gave the tree and the filled cheesecloth bags of Christmas candy to hang thickly all over it. Bruce, you know, has no electricity but the lamplight sparkled on the tree and made it very pretty.

Everyone had several presents and the kids had a grand time. Mrs. Bruce had the round table filled with dishes of fruit and nuts and homemade candy of several different kinds and gave us each a piece of pie, pumpkin, banana, or mince as we chose, with a cup of coffee. She is a good cook and makes delicious candy.

Mrs. Prock proposed and they all joined it, that the crowd send you their Christmas greetings with love and good wishes for the new year.

Christmas day we went to Mountain Grove for dinner at the Elliott Hotel. At last we have found a nice place to eat. Pity we couldn't have found it when you were here.

A lovely clean dining room with spotless white cloths on the tables, a low-spoken, soft-footed waitress, fairly nice china and *no coffee in the saucers*. The dinner was roast turkey, dressing and gravy, an extra gravy bowl, salad, celery, cranberries, green beans, mashed potatoes, candied sweet potatoes, brown bread, white bread and a Christmas plum pudding, with all the coffee we wanted. Price 40 cents.

There is a nice restful room to sit in, with couches and deep chairs, house plants, newspapers and a radio. We are going there some more.

I hope this letter isn't so long you get tired of it. Write me about your Christmas and the [Grosvenor Hotel staff, on lower Fifth Avenue]. Sounds like a novel of Lady So-and-so. [Rose has obviously deemed the hotel maids as so-and-sos; rude and annoying while she wrote *Free Land*.] Indeed I am glad you are so comfortable, and love you heaps.

Mama Bess

[ATTACHED SHEETS TO DECEMBER 29 LETTER]

Thought you might like to hear from Helen Stratte. I enjoyed the letters from your G.R.'s very much and shall write to them at once. ["Gentle Reader" is a term coined by Charlotte Brontë in *Jane Eyre* and later used by Nathaniel Hawthorne in *The Scarlet Letter*.]

I remember Pa's buckskin horse Charley, but cannot remember Mark Mason. Strange how the old timers would all like to go back to those old, hard times. They had something that seems to be lost. Perhaps it is our youth.

Mary Landon was an utterly strange name to me. It didn't bring an echo of Burr Oak. [Landon likely responded to mention of Burr Oak in Rose's short story "Silk Dress," published in the August 1937 issue of *Ladies Home Journal*.] But just as I began to go to sleep that night I saw, in my mind, the old school house. Two stories high it was. At the back a woodshed had been built against it over the windows on that side. The peak of the slant roof of the woodshed came up under the eaves of the school building and the joists where the ceiling of the shed should have been, reached from its far side to about two feet below the second story window of the school house and were fastened there against its wall.

We could raise the windows and step out and down onto an end of a joist timber. The wood was in one corner of the shed below and looked like a small pile. The rest of the way there was nothing below the joist but the ground, ten feet or so below us.

No one thought we would do such a thing, but at noon when both teachers were gone, we used to raise the windows, climb onto the joists and run across and back, seeing who would go out farthest and run back quickest.

I saw it, I said, as I was going to sleep and out in the middle of the joist stood a slim, black haired girl who flapped her arms against her sides like wings and *crowed* to beat any rooster. Mary Landon! Will I write to her! Manly came into the bedroom to see what I was laughing about.

I am so surprised that she said I was good looking. I always thought I was the homeliest girl ever and the only way I could endure myself was because I could outdo the boys at their games, and forget I wasn't pretty. Funny!

I have enjoyed the letters.

*At the end of 1937, Louise Raymond reported that* Plum Creek *is still flourishing and, "by the way, was listed in the last night's* New York Post *under the heading of 'Top-notchers of 1937.'"*

## A telegram to Rose

*In late 1937 Rose was consumed with the "Free Land" serial for the Saturday Evening Post. In her quarters in the Grosvenor Hotel in lower Manhattan, she often wrote twelve hours daily. As indicated by her mother's telegram, Rose relied on her parents' advice.*

JANUARY 4, 1938

Poland China black and white. Stop. White hog called Chester white. Mama Bess

## There is nothing new to write

JANUARY 6, 1938

Rose Dearest,

Just for your information—a Poland China hog is black with various white markings, as happens around the nose. May have white feet or not, or one foot white or two or three.

A Chester-white is all white, the original white hog. There are two or three other white breeds but all were derived from the Chester white. . . . Berkshire hogs are all black, a small breed. The Doric is a *red* hog. I suppose you had my wire in answer to yours.

We went to Springfield [the nearest large city; fifty miles from Mansfield] yesterday. Silas Seal drove and Mrs. Bruce went with me.

I went up for a haircut. Wonder if I told you that I am having my hair cuts in Springfield now, once a month or as near as possible. Jack Humble who used to work at Herr's beauty parlor is in a shop of his own now, and he cuts my hair. [Herr's was the city's leading department store, on the town square.] Ate lunch at the New England cafe. We went to Cabool for dinner, lunch to you, on Monday. There is a very good place to eat downtown there. [Cabool is twenty-eight miles east of Rocky Ridge Farm.]

We have been having nice weather lately, but *dry*. Letter from Grace today says they are having a nice winter. That means a dry season next summer. Said she hadn't heard from Carrie for months and neither have I. Not a word this Christmas.

Grace feels the same as we do about the farm bill and all the rest of the [New Deal] mess.

There is nothing new to write. We are both about as usual, and the goats are going dry. Then I suppose my stomach will have to be pampered again to keep it in good shape. [The Wilders believed that goat's milk was key to good digestion.]

I hope you have enjoyed all the Christmas letters I have been forwarding to you. I am glad Christmas is over and we are started on the way to spring. It won't be long now, just two months, and one of them short.

Here is a bit of news after all. A Long-King check for $35.00 was turned down a few days ago. "Insufficient funds." Guess they'll go under and it seems a pity.

This letter is dull and I'm quitting.

Much love,

Mama Bess

### *You are a wonderful Santa Claus*

JANUARY 12, 1938

Rose Dearest,

Such delicious candy and mints in the mail a few days ago.

You are a wonderful Santa Claus, before Christmas, at Christmas, and after Christmas. Thank you my dear! We enjoy them a lot.

A letter came from Mark Mason, the man who used to live in Dakota. He seemed very much pleased to have had a letter from you, and then one from me. [Rose often received letters from her mother's readers, asking her to forward them.]

I haven't heard from Mary Landon, the woman who went to school in Burr Oak.

A letter from Mabel O' Donnell of Row, Peterson Publishers, says they have gotten permission from Harpers to use two chapters from Farmer Boy and three from L. House in Big Woods.

Bruce [Prock] wanted me to send you the enclosed papers and tell you he was thinking of hiring money from them to start farming. Wanted me to ask you what you thought of the papers he must sign to get it. He and Manly got the papers from the government man at Hartville [county seat of Wright County]. No! I didn't say Bruce was thinking of getting the money. I said he told me to tell you that. The official told them that it is just an ordinary chattel mortgage. A great many of the farmers here are signing. They say they sign anything but a common chattel mortgage. No rain yet. We are well as usual. Manly & Bruce are at an antique sale.

Much love,
Mama Bess

## *I am the Laura in the books*

*Third-graders at Washington School (locale and date unidentified) studied pioneer living, focusing on the Little House books. They wrote: "All of us like Laura. We have been wondering, Are you the Laura in the books?"*

Dear Friends:

You guessed it right. I am the Laura in the books you have been reading and I am very glad that you like her and have enjoyed the stories.

The books are true, you know. All those things happened to me and my parents and sisters, just as I have written them. There is another book you should read. It is "Farmer Boy" and tells about Mr. Wilder when he was a boy in New York State so long ago that his mother spun on her spinning wheel and wove cloth for his clothes, so that it, too, was really pioneer times.

Laura met that farmer boy in Dakota Territory and married him when they grew up. I tell all about that in the stories that are still to be published. To enjoy these later books you really ought to read "Farmer Boy." All the books together make the complete story.

Thank you all for your nice letter. Wishing you the best of success in your school year, I remain,

Your friend,

Laura Ingalls Wilder

## We seem not able to agree

JANUARY 25, 1938

Rose Dearest,

To make the changes you want to make on Silver Lake, it will have to be practically rewritten.

We seem not able to agree on the start of the story.

Laura was 8 when she started school on Plum Creek. But there were two more years accounted for in that same book. She was 10 in Burr Oak. That would leave only two years unaccounted for between the books. She was 11 and 12 in Walnut Grove. [Laura is explaining to Rose the years she left unwritten, between Plum Creek and the family's departure from Walnut Grove in 1879.] Twelve when she went to Silver Lake and 13 in February in the surveyors' house. Fourteen the February of the Hard Winter. And 15 when she started teaching the Boucher school. [Laura Ingalls Wilder was actually sixteen when she began teaching, and seventeen when the school term concluded.] So she finished the term according to law, even though she jumped the tape at the start.

Laura covered all of importance in her reverie in the hotel parlor in Tracy. It is a perfectly natural way to see that time, for girls of that age have those dreamy spells, or did have them 60 years ago. [The original draft's opening chapter in *By the Shores of Silver Lake* used stream-of-consciousness and exposition to summarize the years between *Plum Creek* and *Silver Lake*.]

But if you want to make that change I don't know that it really matters. It will just be the trouble of making the change. But remember it is only two years *not* four.

Now about Aunt Docia. She was not a character in Big Woods. Laura just saw her dressing for the dance. She appears nowhere else, and has no personality. She danced in and out of the Big Woods. She drove in and out of Silver Lake. I have no idea what became of the other aunt, Aunt Ruby nor where she was at that time. [Docia and Ruby were younger sisters of Charles Ingalls.] Uncle Henry and Louisa were just mentioned in Big Woods. [Henry Quiner was Caroline Ingalls's brother; Louisa was Henry's daughter.] They were as you say, "only names." And their names appear again in Silver Lake. I have said that Laura and Mary did not go there [to visit Louisa in the railroad camp kitchen] "because Louisa was always busy." You know she must have been the cook for all the men in camp except perhaps half a dozen. Charley was given a character in Big Woods [where he annoyed the harvesters and was mercilessly stung by bees] and in Silver Lake I have only showed that his character was still the same. Instead of teasing and bothering Pa and Uncle Henry, he teased his small cousin. [Charley Quiner was excised from any role in the final version of *By the Shores of Silver Lake*.]

But I have attempted to show that Laura had a temper and it didn't grow any less as she grew larger. . . . It was a fact that her big boy cousins called her a wildcat because she bit and scratched and put up a good fight on occasion.

I did not intend to make it appear that Laura threatened to kill Charley with a common table knife. It could hardly have been done. She would only have struck his hands. . . . It was no question of sex, or protecting her virtue. Such a thing never entered my mind at that time. It was just the idea of being mishandled.

Remember this was 60 or 62 years ago. Boy and girl cousins didn't kiss then, or at least there, as they might now. I don't remember ever kissing one of my boy cousins much as I played with them, or *any* boy until I was old enough and went to a few play parties. I don't remember Ma ever telling us . . . but we understood that boys must keep their hands off us.

If you think best, take the knife out but leave the quarrel in. It shows them both unchanged only more so.

Remember Louisa and Charley were too busy to bother with me. And Ma wouldn't let Mary and me be at the boarding shanty any length of time.

I was with Lena [cousin; daughter of Docia] for a long spell every day when we took care of and milked the cows night & morning. Gene [Lena's brother] was always out with the men. That disposes of the cousins.

It was not a whole summer that we were so near them. It was only from the middle of September to the first of December before the camp was broken up and everybody gone. Just a little over two months and everybody busy, even Mary and I. . . .

I didn't write a day by day narrative of those days in camp [in her *Silver Lake* manuscript]. I only wrote of the interesting events that happened. . . . Otherwise the story would be too long.

The theme of Silver Lake is *homesteading*.

Pa bought the farm in Wisconsin from a Swede. In L.H. on Prairie Pa was a *squatter*. He had no title whatever. In Plum Creek he traded the team for the farm. What with the grasshoppers and sickness etc. he was only just where he was at the start after four years. Now here was a chance to sell the place on Plum Creek, take the money to give him a new start on a homestead which Uncle Sam would *give* him, a farm as good or better than the one on Plum Creek. And while he was finding the homestead he could draw pay from the R.R. Co. I am sure this was all plain in the story.

The idea of the homestead is never lost sight of. All the other things, the R.R. building, riots, winter in the surveyors house, living in town awhile, are obstacles to be overcome before the family could have a home again. On the homestead I am sure that shows all the way through the story. And I did tell that Mr. Nelson took them from the farm on Plum Creek to the depot in Walnut Grove [in the first draft of the *Silver Lake* manuscript]. The book is bound to be mostly about the R.R. and town, for securing the homestead *in spite of difficulties* is the story, and being at home at last on the homestead, at last is the climax and finish.

JANUARY 25, 1938, STILL P.M.
Rose Dearest,

There is a great speculation here as to what has become of Al. No one seems to know but they all want to find out. If you have occasion to write to *anyone* here, I would not, if I were you tell where he is. If he wants his address known here he can tell it himself.

I wrote him immediately after you wrote me where he was, just after you had your Christmas present from him. It was just a note saying Hurrah for you! etc. and in it I put a $1 bill telling him to buy his own Christmas necktie or whatever. And that I was mailing the letter in Springfield, which I did, so no one here saw the address. I am certainly pleased about Al and what he is doing.

Mrs. Carnell told the neighborhood club that John [Al's brother] was in Germany [Rose had sent both boys to explore Europe, suspecting another world war was imminent]. Don't know where she got the idea.

How did John come out on his exams; or hasn't he taken them yet?

Do you remember the cedar trees that were growing on the very edge of the right-of-way in front of the house just this side of the bridge? Two had been stolen for Christmas trees before this year. One was left, a beautiful tree, cut 4 inches through. Manly set those trees out you know.

Someone was out with a truck stealing Christmas trees. He was cutting that one down when Bruce saw him but before Bruce could get near enough to stop him, he had it cut so badly that it broke off the next day. We can't do a thing about it. It would be tried before a jury and likely they would say it was no damage and we'd have the costs to pay. Or if they gave us damages it wouldn't be enough to pay our lawyer. You know what people here think of cutting down a tree.

We saw the Highway dept. about it. They were going to prosecute and send a man to look the situation over. By measurement the tree was 2 ft 1 in. off the right-of-way so they could do nothing about it. Couldn't make a suit stick.

The tree is dead and won't sprout. I miss it, looking out of the front window. *Stealing Christmas trees* has got to be quite a business around here. We have so many little ones all over the place, but it is doubtful that we can save them.

We have had a rain at last. Two inches of rainfall in one day and several other rainy days besides.

The creek [behind the farmhouse] rose up and roared! It was a warm rain soaking into the ground. Sunday night it turned cold and all night and all day and night Monday the wind blew from the southwest like the norther we met in Texas [during the 1925 return trip from California]. I never before saw a wind like it here. It would freeze the marrow in one's bones.

That night the wind stopped and next morning it was only 4 above zero. It is still cold.

Thought you might like to see the clipping from Allen Oliver's Springfield Slants [from the *Springfield News and Leader*].

I spent Saturday afternoon with Aunt Daisy. She told me, she rents the apartment in her house for $15 a month and her other house at the back of the lot for $12. Her taxes on the property were $148.90. Out of what is left from her rent she must pay for insurance and up-keep. She said Mr. Freeman didn't leave her enough to live on and if she hadn't been wise enough to save what Mr. Bray, No. 1, left her, she didn't know what she would do.

Aunt Daisy sent you her love. Jessie [Fuson] said she saw in the Leader that someone from Springfield, she had forgotten the name, had gone to New York to visit Catharine Brody. [Brody, a novelist and later a Hollywood scriptwriter, made two extended visits to Rocky Ridge while working on a book. Laura disliked her, and eventually Rose also tired of her company.]

Aunt Daisy said too, that if there was a party next voting time that offered a chance to make a start out of this New Deal mess, she would vote their ticket, she didn't care what the party's name was.

Lots of love,
Mama Bess

## We can't spoil this story by making it childish

*It is unclear why Laura consistently referred to teaching at the age of fifteen. Official Kingsbury County records indicate that Laura was sixteen when she began her first teaching position at Bouchie School (called "Brewster School" in These Happy Golden Years).*

JANUARY 26, 1938
Rose, My Dear,

Just a word more about Silver Lake. You fear it is too adult. But adult stuff must begin to be mixed in, for Laura is growing up.

In three years she will be teaching school and we can't jump into grown up stuff all at once.

I thought I showed that Laura was rather spotted at the time, grown up enough to understand and appreciate grown up situations.

But at times quite childish, as when she quarreled with Mary over seasoning in the stuffing of the goose Pa didn't get. She followed the moon path and saw a fairy ring on the old buffalo wallow. There is this too, and I tried to convey the idea.

Mary's blindness added to Laura's age. Laura had to step up and take Mary's place as the eldest. She must help Ma for herself and Mary both, and had a responsibility for Mary besides. It is no wonder she was older than her years. . . . I tried to show this.

Can't we let the readers see the children were more grown up then?

We have got to show this for no 15 year old girl could or would teach school now. Laura did and we have got to tell that she did and make it plausible. If the critics say this book is too adult, how are we going to make them let Laura teach school at 15?

I don't see how we can spare what you call adult stuff, for that makes the story. It was there and Laura knew and understood it.

It was not all plain and simple. The riots were just plain rioting [the railroad men became restive at the end of the construction season]. It was a joke on Sullivan about the Sheriff. Neither Laura nor the grownups had any complicated thoughts about any of it.

If grown up readers see the beginnings of labor problems, where is the harm? I suppose it was. But what it grew into has no bearing on the story, nor would it prevent a child, then or now, from understanding the simple facts that occurred. Surely all these things, the riots, the mock sheriff, the railroad building and the town are told from a 12–13 year old point of view. Are they not?

I remember hearing Pa say he did "wish Docia and Hi would quit railroading and settle down somewhere." That they never would have anything until they did, for there was nothing "in this game of trying to out steal a railroad."

I believe children who have read the other books will demand this one. That they will understand and love it.

They all seem wildly interested and want to know how, where and when Laura met Almanzo and about their getting married. You should have seen the interest in their faces when I spoke of it at Detroit and lots of their letters want me to hurry up and write about it.

Surely Laura will have to be rather adult then. And I think it will be more reasonable and easier to begin mixing it in, in Silver Lake.

Why Francis [Prock; Bruce's son] would stand wide-eyed to hear about and understand the riots of the men, the joke on Sullivan if "Daddy and Mr. Wilder" did it; the way the railroad was built, etc. And Francis is only nine. He would be slower to understand the stealing, but in three years he could not be.

We can't spoil this story by making it childish. Not and keep Laura as the heroine. And we can't change heroines in the middle of the stream and use Carrie in the place of Laura . . . we must *not* spoil the story that way. It could easily be done.

Put these sheets with the letter I wrote you, so you will have it all together to refer to, if you want to read it over.

Much love,

Mama Bess

*I am going to insist*

JANUARY 28, 1938, FRIDAY A.M.

Rose Dearest,

Don't work on Silver Lake until you hear from me again. I am going over it carefully once more.

I like your idea of the beginning less and less the more I think of it. That was the way I tried to start it but all the objections I have mentioned cropped up as I wrote it. It made too much of Plum Creek. We don't want to go back there. It would make the book too long and nothing later can be cut out if the picture is to be true.

It made an unpleasant beginning, a tale of sickness and failure and

death. We don't want to tell of Jack's dying. Nor of Mary's sickness.
Nor of Pa's failure so that it was necessary for him to make a new
start because he hadn't gained anything by all his hard work. The
readers must know all that but they should not be made to think
about it. The story of Silver Lake is connected with Plum Creek close
enough in Laura's mind and her thoughts are given to the reader, but
it is second hand and the knowledge isn't even sad, as it would be your
way. It will be passed over lightly by the reader in the interest of the
new adventure which is already begun.

I am afraid I am going to insist that the story starts as I started it.
How about rhythm and balance in the sentences?

I was in hopes that I had profited enough by your teachings that
my copy could go to the publishers, with perhaps a little pointing up
of the highlights. If it could, then perhaps I could do the following
two books without being such a bother to you.

Let me go over it carefully again now and see if in your judgment
we can try it out on Harpers. I'll make it plainer that the story starts
in the fall of the year. I'll try to touch it up here and there myself, to
overcome some of your objections.

If I can do it, it will give you more time for your own work.

Manly's foot is all right again. He just has to be a little careful. I
am feeling fine.

Bruce's folks are well. Francis is growing up such a nice boy. He is
smart and quick and dependable. He can be trusted and is getting
good marks in school. He brings them up to show me. Paul [Prock,
another of Bruce's son's] is smart too, and mean as the dickens, but
the funniest kid. He says "I like Mama and Daddy and Francis and
Mrs. Wilder" plainly, but when he is excited his tongue tangles and
no one can understand.

It is a beautiful, sunny morning but cold.

Birdie Freeman (Mrs. Manie Freeman) is dead and was buried
Sunday. She was buried in Springfield.

Aunt Daisy is going to visit her brother again next month.
Very much love,
Mama Bess

P.S. Do you ever see Helen [Boylston]? I hear she is in New York.

## SILVER LAKE

*Laura drafted a defense for her method of opening the story of* By the
Shores of Silver Lake *for Rose's consideration. She added other background information with her four-page memo to Rose.*

Laura was impatient on the train. She was in such a
hurry that the train went slow.

I meant to show it that way but of course I didn't or you
would have gotten it.

Take a girl of 12, who is always active, set her on a red
plush chair in a stuffy hotel "parlor" and keep her still so as
not to wake the baby, or just being still because she was all
dressed up. Wouldn't the afternoon seem two months long?
Wouldn't she be bored? I meant she was tired of it, not physically tired. But again I failed to put it over or you are hyped
on the idea of malnutrition. Which I don't think.

Lena and Jean could not be Aunt Docia's children for
Docia was a girl in the Big Woods when Laura was 5. Lena
was older than Laura and . . . appears so in the story.

The house where they [Lena and Laura, in *By the Shores
of Silver Lake*] lived was a one story house squatted on the
bare prairie. There were no trees. Even at that time I felt a
distaste for it. But it was not a shanty. That area had been
settled long enough that claim shanties were not there.

The threshers were in a field at the back. For some reason they were threshing early, though it was the 9th of September. Threshing was usually done in the late fall when the ground was frozen and a cold wind blew. Remember how late Pa stayed away threshing in Plum Creek?

Jerry rode a white pony, not a horse.

Pa found the homestead when he went to hunt the wolves before Christmas. The family was pleased over it as Pa told of it. When he came back from filing on it the question "Did you get it?" meant that particular homestead—the N.E. ¼ of Section 3, Township 110, Range 56. As I remember it there was no great excitement. We were not excitable, usually Pa, sometimes and Laura, now and then.

I don't think Ma ever was. She would not be—was not excited at finding Uncle Henry at the R.R. camp. It seems to me we were rather inclined to be fatalistic . . . to just do things as they came. I know we all hated a fuss, as I still do.

I have just found an old notebook of Pa's where he says of those days:

"We used to keep a lamp burning in the window for fear that someone might try to cross the prairie from the Sioux River to the Jim River and that light brought some into shelter that must otherwise have perished on the prairie. The coyotes used to come to the door and pick up the crumbs that were scattered shook from the table cloth."

I had forgotten.

Change the beginning of the story [*By the Shores of Silver Lake*] if you want. Do anything you please with the damn stuff if you will fix it up.

*This is all in the old days, you must remember*

*Again Rose relied on her parents' familiarity with agriculture.*

FEBRUARY 15, 1938

Rose Dearest,

Likely you need not feel so badly over the threshing in your story. Threshing *could* have been done the last of July.

Remember, I am talking of spring wheat. Harvesting was done the very last of July or the first of August.

Wheat was left in the stack six to eight weeks to go through the sweat before threshing. After that when threshed the wheat could be kept in bins on the farm or in elevators for years, and stay sweet and good. If it were threshed before going through the sweat in the stack the grain would get musty and spoil so even the stock would not eat it. It could be saved by shoveling it over into other bins every few days. But sometimes when a man threshed too early he lost the grain entirely. Couldn't sell it if it was musty. So you see if harvest was in August, stacking in September, then left in the stack for 6 or 8 weeks, it would be the last of October before threshing would be on hand. Fall plowing was done before threshing because threshing could be done after the ground froze and plowing couldn't. The price was better for wheat that had gone through the sweat and was properly threshed, than for wheat that was threshed too early.

Still, if a man was in a hurry to get the money out of his wheat crop, he could thresh the first of August or perhaps the very last of July and sell the wheat at once. So perhaps your story is all right. This is all in the old days, you must remember. *Now* they use combines and cut the heads off the wheat, thresh it, and sack it in the field all with one machine, as you know. What they do about keeping it from getting . . .

[The letter's content takes an abrupt change as Laura resumes discussion of her own work in progress, *By the Shores of Silver Lake*. The following discussion refers to the "spring rush" of settlers who flocked into the future town of De Smet. The Ingalls family, living in the railroad surveyors' house, provided newcomers with food and shelter.]

The lamp was kept burning in the window in The Shores of Silver Lake. It was done only when the weather got cold and snowy. Mr. Boast saw the light, but they were not lost. I don't think we put the lamp in the window until Christmas for that was the first snow.

Mr. Alden and co. came to the house because they saw the light and I remember one load of awfully cold men who came to it. . . . I don't see how I forgot to put it in. We did not expect anyone to go through until spring and would not have thought of a lamp in the window until Boasts told us how they felt when they saw it.

I had Laura and Mary quarrel over the stuffing for the goose . . . to show the relaxing from the strain first of loneliness and then the hard work and excitement of so many strangers underfoot.

Usually, you know, Laura and Mary disagreed now and then. Now here they had been good for a long time. That was not natural, especially for Laura. Their tempers were a little frayed and I thought it very natural that they should snap when at last the let-down came.

I have the chapters for The Hard Winter blocked out a good deal as you suggest, even to Pa going hunting and not getting any game, which was true. I can make it interesting without the goose-stuffing incident. And don't you think it is best left where it is?

Aunt Docia and Charley's mother, Aunt Polly, were sisters. Pa and Uncle George, Uncle Peter, Uncle James and Uncle Hiram were brothers.

Uncle Henry and Uncle Tom were brothers and their sisters were Ma and Aunt Eliza and Aunt Martha. Pa and Uncle Peter married sisters, and their sister married a brother of their wives. Sounds like a Missouri family.

There are just two more books after Silver Lake. I will block them out soon and talk them over with you.

Your check was a big surprise [Rose had sent the annual $500 subsidy, which she had been providing since 1920]. I suppose it is meant for expenses of running the house on your "head of the household" exemptions. I can't think what else.

If something doesn't hinder, I'm afraid I'll come into income tax class this year. But I don't suppose that need hinder you keeping up your home here. Oh well! We'll think about that next winter.

Thanks a lot anyway for everything. I am sure you will be glad to know I made such a pig of myself with that enormous heart full of candy that I can't look a piece of it in the face anymore. I am *full*. But it's been fun.

Tomorrow I expect to go to Hartville club meeting. [This was the Athenian Club, of which Laura had been a founder in 1915]. They want me to give them the talk I made at Detroit and are making quite a fuss about it. Hope it will sell a couple of books.

A week ago Sunday we went to West Plains and visited with the Park Summerses. Manly said he couldn't remember when he had enjoyed himself so much. You remember he is interesting and she is a very nice person. They sent you their best regards and said lots of nice things about you. And they insist we shall go some Saturday and stay until Sunday p.m. with them. I think we will do so when the weather is settled again. It looks now as though we are in for a bad spell.

Manly and I have both had the flu again. Everyone is having it. I had a spell of asthma with mine and couldn't get breath enough to blow my nose.

It seems to be all over now and we will be all right again. We are just being lazy now with a good excuse. And it is pleasant to be lazy.

I guess Al has written to Dorothy Sue for Mrs. Hoover told that Al was working in a garage near St. Louis.

Mrs. O. B. Davis came out and spent the P.M. Monday. Had a nice visit.

Very much love,
Mama Bess

## ROSE'S EDITORIAL CRITICISM
## FOR SILVER LAKE

*By the Shores of Silver Lake was a difficult book to draft. In it, Laura's character reaches adolescence, and shifting the point of view was a challenge. After many exchanges, Rose and Laura reached an impasse. Rose finally took a hard-line editorial position, giving Laura an unvarnished assessment of the manuscript.*

The Grosvenor Hotel
New York City
FEBRUARY 3, 1938
Dear Mama Bess,

You are one of the few writers in the country who would turn down a collaboration with RWL, but go ahead. You certainly are handling the material much better all the time, and if you don't want this book touched, you're absolutely right not to have it touched. . . .

I don't say that Harper's won't take this manuscript as it stands. They'll take it on your reputation, and publish it; any publisher will. But you'll lose your audience for future books, and cut your income, unless you work it over, and work it over by concentrating on every word and sentence until you know precisely what its values are, why you use it. . . . There's a lot of fine stuff in it that doesn't need to be touched, and there is deadwood, and clumsy spots and a lack of sufficient sharpness of identification with Laura—your point of view wavers. . . . Stretches of dialogue slow the story. Dialogue is used to convey information, always an ineffective method. Dialogue should be used only to convey character and to keep the story moving. Paragraphing is poor. Every paragraph must have its own shape . . . its shape and cadence and color must be suited to the tempo of the mood. . . . Forget you are telling a story; you aren't, you are living Laura's experiences. Live every word and sentence and paragraph intensely enough, and you'll make them fit what you feel. . . . Go over this story living it, and you'll feel a complete despair at how meaningless all the words are in comparison with the experience. Every writer does. But the job is to get words that will be the experience. I'm glad you are taking on the job. It's your book, and if you want to send it to Harpers as is, that's all right with me. I'm only telling you what will happen if you do. You can do that, or you can work at the manuscript, till you bring it all up to the level of its best parts now. Unless you want to do that work on it, my advice would be to make it your last book and not do any more. This book as it is will go on your reputation, but it will not add to it, in my opinion.

## *You are a dear, sweet thing to us*

FEBRUARY 19, 1938

Rose Dearest,

You don't know how much good your letter did me and I can't tell you. You see I know the music but I can't think of the words.

I didn't suppose anyone else ever felt such a failure as I did. It surely was a sick stomach I had.

Anyway your letter picked me up and gave me courage. It is sweet of you to say the nice things you did about my writing and I will try to deserve them more. I wrote you in such a hurry to stop you worrying that I slurred over things.

I am beginning Hard Winter as you suggested, with the strangeness of the geese not stopping at the lake.

Laura and Almanzo are to meet when the blizzard closes the school. You remember when the school wouldn't follow Cap Garland and nearly got lost. I don't know how it will work out, but I'm going to have Laura go with Almanzo to town.

Your suggestions are all helpful and I'll send you the outline soon.

Here is what is bothering me and holding me up. I can't seem to find a plot or pattern as you call it.

There seems to be nothing to it, only the struggle to live, through the winter, until spring comes again. This, of course, they all did. But is it strong enough or can it be made strong enough, to supply the necessary thread running through the book?

I could make a book with the plot being Laura's struggles to be, and success in becoming a teacher, with the Hard Winter and all being obstacles overcome on the way. Laura taught the next winter you know.

I could tell of the hard winter, how school closed, Laura studied at home, going to school next summer from the farm. And how she was only well started in school the next winter when she had to quit to go teach. She would never be able to go to school and learn to be a teacher. She just was a teacher without. Get the idea? That would be a plot. It would not make the book too long. But it seems to weaken it. To be sort of anti-climatic after the Hard Winter and it couldn't have that name. I don't like it. But where is the plot in Hard Winter?

Rose, my dear, is there anything special about the place you would like to have us do with the $500 you sent? And can you spare it easily now? If not, I'll send it back and no one need know. You would have the check and the stub to show just the same.

We thank you a lot for sending us checks if you can spare them, but we, neither of us, want you to work so hard because you feel you must help us.

You are a dear, sweet thing to us all the time. You and your comfort and well being are more to us than anything else. So please take good care of yourself for us.

I had a lovely time at the club meeting in Hartville. It was a re-union with the old members. Three women from Mountain Grove stopped by for me.

After my talk two women said they were going to get my books for their children, so maybe I earned two bits.

It has rained steadily for more than a week, 3 in. in one day. The creek [behind Rocky Ridge farmhouse] is roaring. Water is all over the highways and roads are blocked at Ozark and Branson and Hol-lister. 12 ft. of water over the dam at Powersite. Up to the hotel on Rockaway Beach. Snowed a little last night and looks like more rain.

We are well as usual.

I thought you might be interested in the [readers'] letters. I am especially glad for the boys' letter. Shows these are not just girls' books. I had hoped they would not be.

Much love,

Mama Bess

*Enclosed with this letter was a note from Almanzo.*

Dear Rose,

I wrote you a 4 page letter telling how much I appreciated your nice Christmas gifts and all that and asked you what in the world I should do with that nice big check and all that sort of stuff and you never said boo. *Did you get it?*

Yours, A. J. Wilder

## *It hurt no one to tighten the belt a little*

*While* By the Shores of Silver Lake *was being prepared, Laura forged ahead on her sixth book, tentatively titled* The Hard Win-ter. *When this letter was written, Rose's "Free Land" weekly serial in the* Saturday Evening Post *was receiving great acclaim.*

MARCH 7, 1938

Rose Dearest,

No! The people in the hard winter were not "monsters." I haven't been able to get my leaning across to you. The teacher Florence Garland and her brother Cap were easterners and perhaps did not realize how serious a blizzard of that kind was. In one of those storms where it is a struggle to even breathe, one does not think much. If Cap thought at all I suppose he thought we would come to one of the long line of buildings along Main Street [in De Smet] which we did. It was no place to stop and argue. Get the cold and the confusion of it. I held tight to Carrie's hand. but I'm sure I didn't think about it. It was just instinctive I guess.

Cap and Miss Garland were nice, friendly, ordinary persons. I wish I could explain how I mean about the stoicism of the people.

You know a person cannot live at a high pitch of emotion, the feelings become dulled by a natural, unconscious effort at self-preservation.

You will read of it in *good* frontier stories. How the people of a community captured by Indians would hardly turn their heads as one or two at a time were taken away from the main party by their special captors—taken away perhaps to a fate worse than death in a blizzard.

Living with danger day after day people become accustomed to it. They take things as they come without much thought about it and no fuss, in a casual way.

When Old Man Brown [the Reverend Edward Brown, the first minister of the Congregational Church in De Smet] was lost for a bit in a blizzard and after wandering around a little, came home, we asked Ida [his adopted daughter; a schoolmate of Laura's] if she and her mother had worried much. "Oh no!" she said. "He had always got through and we thought he always would." They were easterners too and ignorant and a little stunned by nature's fierceness. As far as who were frontiersmen—likely it was the wildness of the country, the difficulties and dangers all around us that made us so apathetic. . . . Indians were like that you know and they lived under nearly the same conditions.

Manly did go after the wheat to feed the town so he might keep his own for seed. Risking his life for his seed wheat. He got the wheat before anyone went hungry.

We were shorter of food than any one . . . and Manly and Roy gave Pa breakfast and let him have wheat.

If anyone had been without food, they would have divided, but if the town had known the wheat was there, there would have been a rush for it. Even those who didn't need it badly would have taken as much as anyone.

It hurt no one to tighten the belt a little.

I can't agree with you about the Boasts. I think the fact of their not coming to town, much as they wanted to see us and we them, shows how afraid the people were to stir out. They would not move to town in the fall for they had several cows besides their horses and pigs and chickens. They hay was all stacked by the stable and it was 2½ miles from De Smet. They had no place in town. We had the place in town, our hay was only ½ mile out and we wanted to go to school.

The Boasts would of course come to our Christmas dinner in June, meet Manly and be the friends we visited on our drives in Prairie Girl.

The Christmas barrel came the first of June. Train got through in the middle of May but freight was so congested all along the line that it was not straightened out until June.

People were afraid to leave their homes that winter. Pa and the Wilders were about the only ones who would do so, except the mail carrier.

There are more objections to moving the Boasts to town to live with us. Leaving them on the farm all winter shows the fear of the storms. Having them at the Christmas dinner in June makes it a happy reunion. I think they belong in the place I have given them as friends. . . . We can't have them living with us because, if we do, Boast and his team would help haul hay and he would help twist it. He would help grind wheat, Mrs. Boast would leave the baby in a chair by the fire and help and the point of the situation would be blunted.

There would be need for Manly and Roy to haul a load of hay for Pa because it was so hard for him alone. . . .

I think that incident is too important to lose. It shows that there was kindness and helpfulness there, where there appears to be so much selfishness and aloofness. For Pa and the Wilders took their lives in their hands when they hauled a load of hay.

Roy and Manly hauled for the town, gaily, cheerfully, taking a chance. And then an extra load for kindness. As I said such things were done and accepted so casually.

Pa is alone. He must haul hay to feed Ellen and David and Sam [the cow and team of horses]. Sam won't work buried in snow half the time. He won't stand for Pa to dig him out. So Pa hauls with one horse on a sled. It takes most of his time. He freezes his nose and nearly freezes himself. He does the chores and starts the fire in the morning and helps grind wheat at night and twist hay. Ma and I twist hay and keep up the fire. We grind wheat and get the meals and with Carrie's help do the rest of the work and take care of Mary and Grace. You see it kept us all busy.

We can't have anyone live with us unless they are mean people who would not help as the Masters were, or the hardships will mostly vanish.

If we put the Masters in the story they must be as they were and that would spoil the story if we make them decent. It would spoil the story for me and lose Manly's kindness which I think is worth more than having a baby born. George Masters was a clerk on the R.R. work west of town. When he moved to town he wanted Maggie [his wife] to come west and board with us so she would be nearer him until the work stopped when they would go east. When Maggie came Ma saw she would soon have a baby, much too soon after the time she was married.

Maggie didn't want the baby to be born at her folks' and disgrace them. George's folks were mad because he married her and wouldn't have her at their house.

Maggie had always been a nice girl and Ma was sorry for her and let her stay. The baby was born before winter came. [Arthur Kingsbury Masters was the first child born in De Smet.] Work stopped and George came. We thought they were leaving but George put it off. The winter set in and caught them. There was nowhere else they could stay. Every house was full and Pa couldn't put them out in the street.

George paid Maggie's board while he was working. Afterward he paid nothing. He never went with Pa for a load of hay, he never twisted any. He just sat. He would have done differently or I'd have thrown him out, but Pa wouldn't. Sweet charity!

I have brought Edwards [a favorite character from *Little House on the Prairie*] into Silver Lake exactly in character. No one except such a man would have saved Pa's homestead in the only way it could have been saved. I am bringing him in again in both the other books. I have a use for him.

I guess I'd better bring Nettie Kennedy from Plum Creek and perhaps Nellie Oleson. There is also Mr. Alden who is directly responsible for Mary going to college, helping his "little country girls" again. I used Charley, Louisa and Uncle Henry to show how people made stops on the way to the far west. How families parted were again united and parted again, without any heroics as people say now—"Well, I'll be seein' ya." It was in that same careless matter of fact way. I suppose the underlying idea was that they would happen on each other again in their going hither and yon.

I think their appearing and disappearing as I have them do give a feeling of the march westward, of passing on of people and of their appearing unexpectedly. Also they make a contrast to the family left behind with clipped wings as Laura felt in that chapter.

This casualness in meeting and parting, this feeling that you call apathy and I call stoicism was there and a true picture must show it even to the children if we possibly can. I think neither of us has found the right word for it.

I am bringing Uncle Tom in again in Prairie Girl. I wrote him into Big Woods and I don't think he was cut out, but I have not looked to see. [Thomas Quiner is not mentioned in *Little House in the Big Woods*.]

We will have Pa play the fiddle when the Hard Winter is over.

We will have to skip from the June Christmas dinner to Laura beginning her school, I think. She can't teach school until she is 15, becoming 16 in February. The school was three months, Dec., Jan., & Feb. . . . . Laura and Manly could be engaged in the fall when Laura would be 17. . . . Let the book end with the engagement, which can be supposed to last a couple of years before the wedding, not to have a horrid child marriage.

I don't know how else to handle the last book, for the children will keep track of Laura's age. Unless we make the story cover two years and it is hardly worth it.

We can have Manly say at the end, "And while we wait, I'll build us a little house on the tree claim where it will be sheltered by the trees as they grow." I will block it out as soon as I can and let you see it. I am stupid just now and slow. Haven't got over the flu. Hope you are feeling more rested.

Love,
Mama Bess


*Thanks for the invitation to visit you*

*Flush with celebrity and cash from* Free Land, *Rose purchased a country home along King Street in Danbury, Connecticut. Ties to Rocky Ridge Farm were permanently cut.*

MARCH 15, 1938

Rose Dearest,

I think I will let Nellie Oleson take Jennie Masters' place in Prairie Girl and let her be the only girl from Plum Creek. Their characters were alike. [*Prairie Girl* was the tentative title for what was perceived as the last book in the seven-volume series. Later the saga stretched into two books instead of one: *Little Town on the Prairie* and *These Happy Golden Years*. Jennie Masters from Walnut Grove and Stella Gilbert were combined to create the persona of Nellie in De Smet.]

Nettie Kennedy can't come unless all the family came with her, so we'd best leave her out and let Laura make new friends. It would not be a true picture if there were too many from Walnut Grove. They didn't go west that way. De Smet was a mix of people from everywhere which added to the interest. Hope you like the outline [for *Prairie Girl*]. Aren't two families from Plum Creek enough? Mr. Alden is in Silver Lake and can appear again in Prairie Girl. Uncle Tom [Quiner] comes from the Big Woods. Mr. Edwards from Prairie and Silver Lake and the Boasts from Silver Lake, Manly and E. J. from Farmer Boy and all Laura's family from all the books, are in Prairie Girl.

Your letter was so nice and gossipy. I am pleased that you are going to keep that lovely old place simple and economical. [Rose had immediately started to renovate her home in Danbury, Connecticut, the process continuing for twenty years.] You shall have some strawberry plants, if they survived the winter, which they surely have. It is a shame about your income tax. Couldn't you work less and pay less and get by just as well? I mean—you say you can live in your Connecticut place for $500. Suppose then you write enough to earn $1000. That would cut out the tax not right of course, but there's the idea. As you say, "Damn" 'em. [Rose was paid $25,000 for "Free Land," which the *Saturday Evening Post* serialized in eight installments in March and April 1938. After repaying considerable indebtedness and buying her house, she was left with a significant income tax bill.]

How nice to see Dee again [unidentified]. I thought she was pretty, but am surprised she thought I was.

Thanks my dear. I am glad you think I am nice to look at, even at this late day in the afternoon. It must be my lovely character showing in my face that people see. And knowing me, I can't see that.

I suppose by now you have Farmer Boy and Prairie from Harpers, and Big Woods I sent you. What became of the copy of Prairie I sent you in Columbia? The autograph I wrote in it, you said, was the best bit of verse I have ever done. I remember I loved it myself but I can't remember a word of it and I have no copy. If you remember it, I wish you would write it to me. It bothers me that I can't think of it.

Thanks for the invitation to visit you in your Connecticut house. Who knows! Strange things have happened.

I love you very much,

Mama Bess

## Your G.R. was wrong

*Reader response to "Free Land" inundated the Saturday Evening Post offices. Many letter writers had lived through the homesteading era; they wrote to share their own stories. Others wrote to debate facts, considering the serial as fact, not fiction. Rose shared some of the letters with her parents.*

APRIL 15, 1938
Rose Dearest,

Your G.R. [Gentle Reader] was wrong as to the date of your story.

The events which you have written, building of the railroad west, Indian trouble on Turtle Creek, were in 1880.

David [David Beaton, the chief protagonist of *Free Land*, modeled after Almanzo Wilder] didn't have his wheat until after that. His buying of binder was in 1881 or 1882.

Manly took his homestead in 1879.

At least two years before that, while he was a boy in Minnesota, they had a team thresher there. He remembers surely because the owner hitched the engine to two lumber wagons and hauled his crew and others to a party in another town. Manly didn't go.

He says the harvester, on which two men stood and bound the grain, was as early as 1873.

And there were self binders using wire, for binding, before Manly went west in 1879.

It was found that the threshing broke the wire into bits which were in the straw and the grain and injured stock that ate of it. So, as soon as that was learned, twine was used instead of wire. It would not likely be more than a couple of years later. We don't know the exact date of the twine self-binder. But the fall we were married, 1885, Pa bought a twine binder at a sale. It was an old wreck so it must have been used for some years before that. Pa bought it for Manly and the two of them fixed it up so Manly used it to cut his grain for two or three years.

Manly remembers a treadmill thresher in New York in 1866. This is the way it stands:

Treadmill thresher in N.Y. 1866

Harvester where men stood to bind. 1873

Self-binder with wire before 1879

Twine binder certainly before 1882

Steam thresher in Minnesota in 1877 and were used in Dakota when we were married.

There were the old horse power machines, which were more generally used, because of the cost of fuel for a steam engine.

You see David's crops must have been in 1881 or 1882 and he could have bought a self-binder and a steam thresher.

The trouble with your G.R. is that he dated your story too early, and he did get some of his other dates wrong. Manly said the G.R. didn't get around much to know what was going on, and the place where he lived must have been awfully backward. Remember the R.R. was not completed to De Smet until the spring of 1880.

Turtle Creek and the Indian scare was that same summer so your story is dated 1880 and after. . . . [Rose included the tension between the settlers and the Native Americans in *Free Land*. An eastern man stole a mummified infant from a burial ground, intending to show it as a curiosity in the east. Times were tense until the corpse was returned.]

## *The very light in the yard is green*

MAY 4, 1938
Rose Dearest,

I am so sorry I did not tell you what my income was last year, until it was too late.

Time and time again I have read that a married couple paid no income tax until their income was $2,500.

And every year I have noticed that ours was not that much. I had no idea it made any difference whether you knew what it was until it reached that amount. Surely when our intentions were innocent, we will be allowed to make it right and not be punished, for my mistake.

I am well as usual. Manly is getting better of the trouble in his head. It was just the after effects of the flu.

Trees are in full leaf now and the very light in the yard is green. It is so restful on the eyes.

I have gone back to the glasses I wore six years ago. They fit my eyes better than any later ones. Must be my eyes are growing younger.

I am very busy so this must be a short letter.

Much love,
Mama Bess

## You are probably right about the beginning of Silver Lake

*After debating the beginning of Silver Lake, Laura and Rose reached a truce. Following Rose's admonition that Silver Lake would be the last book if Laura ignored her instructions, Laura compromised. In this letter, Laura gives an overview of her next two books. Later she realized that another volume was needed to complete the series.*

AUGUST 17, 1938

Rose Dearest,

I sent you the letter from Ida Louise telling how late it would do to send Silver Lake for publication this fall. If I remember correctly the deadline was August first. Anyway, at that time, I gave up thought of having it published this year . . . and there was no time to finish it, if you took any vacation getting moved and settled.

Mary was 15 years old, I was thirteen. Carrie was nine and Grace two . . . in the surveyors house on Silver Lake. The books made me six in the Big Woods. That would make me 7 in Prairie and 8 when we lived in the dugout on Plum Creek. Plum Creek is the story of three winters that would make me 10. Two years from the end of Plum Creek to the beginning of Silver Lake in the surveyors house. I would be 14 in the Hard Winter and 15 the next winter. That was the year I began teaching at Bouchie's in December, two months before I was 16 years old.

Sixteen was the legal age, but the superintendent of schools forgot to ask me how old I was, because they wanted me to teach that school. Mr. Boast had recommended me to his friends there. He got the school for me and my age was overlooked. Mr. Boast couldn't have done that if he had been Peter. I think it is important. It shows how few teachers there were. How glad the people were to find someone to teach their little schools! And the place the little schools filled in the new settlements. And also that in her haphazard schooling, mostly at home, Laura had learned enough that she passed examinations and got a certificate to teach when she was only 15. The age is important. She must not be more than 15–16 the next February. Where I caught up to the age given me in the books was the year out in Iowa and the two years Mary was sick and lost her sight in Walnut Grove. But we have dropped Iowa and Walnut Grove out of the story, leaving Laura on Plum Creek until she went to Silver Lake.

I hope this is clear.

You are probably right about the beginning of Silver Lake . . . but how to write that chapter and not have it too sad. On page 12 of Silver Lake, as I wrote it [in her penciled manuscript] you will find the financial situation. Not "poverty worse than ever" as you put it, but what I have said on page 12.

Surely, Ma charged all those strangers for staying overnight and for board, 25 cents a meal, 50 cents for a place to sleep . . . $4.50 a week for board and a place to sleep, not a room, just a bed on the floor. . . . Pa had nearly all the money he had earned on the railroad. Ma boarded Fred Fields and I didn't put that in the story, thought it was better to keep the family to itself. His board money would have paid for our groceries and there was no other expense. Without that our groceries would have cost very little. We had our milk and butter from Ellen and fresh fowl from Pa's hunting. Our winter supplies were in the surveyors' house and they cost us nothing but taking care of the property. Pa had his railroad money. I think Pa bought the lot [on the town site of De Smet] from the railroad. There was no depot, nor railroad agent there when he built, nor when the first buildings were put up. The town was staked out and I think the first comers simply squatted on the lots they wanted and bought them later. The lots sold for $50, an inside lot, $75 for a corner lot. A building worth $250 had to be built on a lot within six months to hold it.

Pa first built on a corner lot facing east with side street on the south side. That was where it snowed in on us in an April blizzard. He sold that place at a good profit on the lot because it was the most desirable location in town. Also he got pay for his work building the house and pay for the material, that would have bought material for building again, so he would have money left after buying the lot diagonally across the street with a west and north frontage. . . . This is where we lived in Hard Winter. It seemed to me not necessary to explain all this in the story. It would take too much space, and I thought, add nothing. The value of the building is that it is the town house where we lived in Hard Winter and while I taught the Bouchie School; where Manly brought me every Friday night and from where we went sleigh riding, with the town crowd, Saturday and Sunday afternoon, the length of the street and circle you remember. If we had lived in the country we wouldn't have been in that charmed circle.

About the characters I am sort of stumped. I put Louisa in Big Woods and you cut her out. I had forgotten that when I put her in Silver Lake. Let it be Uncle Henry, Aunt Polly and Charley in Silver Lake. Cut Louisa. On page 76 of Silver Lake I tell what became of them. So far as I ever knew until on our trip this summer. Carrie told me she had found Aunt Polly was buried in the old, old cemetery at Keystone, the Black Hills, you know.

Uncle George, Uncle James and their families stayed in the Big Woods so far as I ever knew. Laura Ingalls was Uncle James' daughter. I never heard any more of them. Grandpa & Grandma Ingalls lived their lives out in the Big Woods. Aunt Lottie stayed in Wisconsin, was married there, and I never saw her again. She was somewhere near Madison. Oh No! No! Uncle James was *not* John James Ingalls of Kansas. Uncle James was Pa's brother. J. J. Ingalls was a second cousin or even more of Pa's. And he was John J. Ingalls. [John James Ingalls was a Kansas politician; he served as a U.S. senator for eighteen years, starting in 1873.]

We bring all of our family, Pa, Ma, Mary, Laura, Carrie; also Uncle Henry, Aunt Polly, Charley and Aunt Docia from Big Woods into Silver Lake. It seems to me those are enough to tie it up. Then there is Mr. Edwards from Prairie, which hitches that book in. Also the Wilder boys. Mr. Edwards comes again in Hard Winter, and the Wilder boys from Farmer Boy. Unfortunately we have used real names in these books and must stick closer to the facts than otherwise we would need to.

Alice and Ella and their husbands come visiting in the last book, and Peter can come too, though he didn't come until after you were born.

Peter can't be Mr. Boast; Mr. Boast is a frontier character that Peter doesn't fit. Peter was near my age and Mr. Boast is old enough to own teams and a homestead and such. Besides, in going to the frontier, one meets strangers and makes friends and enemies. Friendships are made quickly. One doesn't move west with whole communities, nor with all their "uncles and their cousins and their aunts." None of the letters have asked about any of the characters that I have dropped except Black Susan, and I venture to say there will be no outcry over any except Jack.

We did not have the kitten until the summer after the Hard Winter. We were not civilized enough before that. That kitten was blue and white and I want it left that way. Leave Susan out, don't bring her in at all. It is a point . . . to show that there was only one cat in the community as late as after the Hard Winter and *none* before that. It emphasizes the newness and rawness. Leave Susan out!

I don't want the Huleatts either. I think they are not needed. As Laura grows up and moves on, she must leave people behind and make new friends.

I truly don't see why Uncle Henry and Charley must be used in the rest of the books or be substituted for by someone. . . . We have five principal characters who go all the way through, six, counting Almanzo. That is enough to carry the story.

We have Uncle Henry, Aunt Polly and Charley and Aunt Docia passing through, going on west. And a glimpse of the Wilder boys.

We have Mr. Edwards just passing in and out. In the next book . . . the Wilder boys become alive & a glimpse of Nellie Oleson. That is Hard Winter.

In the last book, Prairie Girl (?) we have the whole family, the Wilder boys, Nellie Oleson, Uncle Tom, with news [of the rest]. And Peter if you want.

. . . The new friends . . . will be Mary Power and Ida Brown, perhaps Stella Gilbert. Though I think I'll combine Jennie Masters and Stella in Nellie Oleson.

How does that look to you for a list of characters? They come and go, pass in and out of the story as they really do. And the story is carried on . . . through the Ingalls family. . . . I think to bring characters along as you suggest is unnecessary. I know it is unnatural and untrue of the times. . . .

When Alice and Ella and Uncle Tom come visiting, we can have news of all the people in L.H. in Big Woods and tie the first and last book closely together, ending the story. Please, can't we do it that way?

I do not remember more of "When I was one and twenty, Nell, and you were seventeen." Thought I had it but did not. Then I remembered it was in an old song book of Pa's. Carrie may have it or remember the song. I will write to her and Grace and try to find out. That would be the only chance. No one else in De Smet ever sang it and I don't remember that we ever did after the winter in the surveyors house.

I will send you a skeleton outline of the next two books in a few days. I made one for my own use. . . . The only way I can write is to wander along with the story, then rewrite and re-arrange and change it everywhere. I have 10 chapters of the first rough, very rough draft of Hard Winter. But you could not read them if I sent them to you. They are really nothing more than an arrangement of my notes. . . .

Must hurry to mail this.

Much love,

Mama Bess

## *That sort of ballyhoo would appeal*

*This letter was written while Rose was enduring the 1938 hurri-*
*cane, which damaged Danbury with high winds, flooding, and*
*downed trees. While Rose hosted marooned neighbors, Laura*
*drummed up interest in the Ludlow Amendment. If added to the*
*Constitution, the amendment stipulated that a national referen-*
*dum would be required before America declared war on any for-*
*eign power, excepting in the case of direct attack. Rose was an*
*advocate of the bill, during those isolationist times. She published*
*articles supporting the amendment, testified before the Senate Judi-*
*ciary Committee, and engaged Laura in a grassroots campaign.*
*The concept was not endorsed by President Roosevelt. Following*
*Germany's attack on Poland in 1939, public support waned.*

SEPTEMBER 26, 1938

Rose Dearest,

Your letter dated the 22nd came this morning. It was evidently
written before the storm was at its worst and we are anxious to hear
from you again. It seems bad enough the way you wrote and we are
hoping the *bad* storm passed you by and that your electricity being off
and wires down is only your part of that terrible storm. But you did
say "the clouds look threatening."

A note from George Bye says he mailed you Pioneer Girl. So you
can have it for reference. You will likely find the description of the
little house there and whatever else you need [a reference to information Rose requested for her editorial work on *By the Shores of Silver
Lake*]. We will study the book names awhile longer. I can't agree with
you about the short names. So many people have said "I love your titles. They are so descriptive." And letters have said, "I was attracted
by the title of L.H. on the Prairie" and another by "L.H. in B.W." To

be plain, I hate too short, two word titles. But I don't want to fight it out now. Instead, I'll tell you what I have done.

The whole Athenian Club of Hartville will write the congressmen to vote for the Ludlow Referendum Bill. There are 18 or 20 members, so quite a bunch of letters. Mrs. Davis is writing and will get others to. Mr. Davis brought out "To American Mothers" letter [Davis published the widely printed letter in the local newspaper]. Thought it would be good to send a copy to people in each state. That is, I send to 10 people, as far scattered as possible, and you do the same. Mr. Davis's idea is to leave them unsigned, just to call attention to the matter. He said that sort of ballyhoo would appeal to lots of people. I don't know, but it can do no harm. Perhaps the way Mr. Davis expresses it, the letter may appeal to the kind of people that nothing else would reach.

Mrs. Gere is going to write, and she is going to write also to her mother and sister in Colorado. Says she knows they will write their congressmen, for her mother is nearly crazy over it. She says she will tell her father to take it up and is sure he will. He is mayor of his town. They are Democrats gone Republican. Bruce and Mrs. Bruce want to sign, but I must write the letters for them. Makes me 24 letters to write. Don't you think I have done very well for the short time since you wrote? I'll be glad when I have all these letters written.

Mrs. Bruce had a nine pound girl. Has had a bad time but is doing all right now, except that Prock, senior, has rented his farm, and he and Mrs. Prock have moved in on Bruce. Bruce had a hired girl doing the work and she still stays. How Bruce can manage I don't know, nor how Mrs. Bruce stands it.

Mr. and Mrs. Gere took dinner with us yesterday, Sunday. This is the first time I have invited company to dinner since I can remember. We had fried chicken & gravy, mashed potatoes, sweet corn custard, hot biscuit and butter & honey, pineapple and olive salad, pumpkin pie with whipped cream, and coffee. Mrs. Gere is a wonderful cook.

We have been there twice, and I was scared to have them, but everything turned out good. They go, the fifth of October, for two weeks
in Colorado.

The goat kids are over in that pasture near the Geres, and Mrs.
Gere counts them every day and coaxes them with bits of bread and
parings.

I have had a run of company this week. Two from Hartville, one
from near Mountain Grove, Mr. and Mrs. Davis twice, the Geres,
and Neta Seal.

A letter from Child Life wanting stories.

Do you know anything about "Jack and Jill" magazine for boys
and girls, just started by Curtis Publishing Company? "A perfect
companion for the Saturday Evening Post, Ladies Home Journal,
and Country Gentleman." Might be a market.

Love to John and more especially to yourself. Let us hear from
you.

Mama Bess

*Our interests all centered at home*

OCTOBER 8, 1938

Rose Dearest,

Brookings was laid out, "staked out" adjoining the R.R. camp.
That was ten miles east of the river. Volga was later built on the
river. It is forty (40) miles from Brookings to De Smet. The river
there is the Big Sioux but it is so near the head that it is not a large
stream. Its source is north of Watertown, flows south through
Volga and Dell Rapids to Sioux Falls and still south to the Missouri
at Sioux City.

There were farms near the first camp, but none we saw on the
river. Within the 10 miles from camp to the river the prairie became
more rolling. We saw no bluffs along the river and I do not remember

any trees. It was just a prairie stream, bound to be low at that time of year.

I don't know that the land was rough enough to be called "breaks." It was just low rolling rises that we wound around among just before we came to the water.

I don't remember any cows at the first camp, I suppose Aunt Docia bought them from a nearby farmer, to take to Silver Lake.

I don't know really if we were first at Silver Lake, but I think we were. Not long enough that we would have minded being without milk. I don't know that it matters who was at Silver Lake first. I don't care either way.

I am sure that we slept on the floor of Pa's office-store and there was nothing left in it that night we stayed in the first camp, and we stayed only the one night. I think Silver Lake copy [manuscript] is right.

I don't remember ever seeing the black ponies at Silver Lake camp. I know Lena and I were together only at milking time. Uncle Hi might have put the ponies on the work somewhere or he might have traded them in on a work team. . . .

Strange how my memory fails me on all but the high lights. We were maybe queer not to have been more with the kinfolks, but we had very little to do with them. We were busy cooking for us all and Fred Fields and Big Jerry later on. There was Grace to take care of and Mary to read to and take for walks, washing, ironing, mending, sewing, water to bring from the well, wood to bring in, wild fowl to dress and only Ma and me to do it. Carrie was only nine years old and Mary was no help, of course.

Don't bring Aunt Docia, Uncle Henry and the cousins into the story more than necessary. I mean don't stress them, don't play them up. The story is of [our] family and the family life. Families lived more to themselves in those days, at least where we were. Our interests all centered at home.

Oh I don't suppose I am making you understand. I suppose Aunt

Docia and Uncle Henry meant as much to Pa and Ma as my sisters did to me, but at that time they meant nothing whatever to me. I feebly disliked Aunt Docia and Uncle Henry hardly made an impression. . . .

*While working with her mother's penciled manuscript of* By the Shores of Silver Lake, *Rose found it necessary to gain clarification about various relatives. Accustomed to creating fictional characters, she did not realize that her mother's uncle Thomas Quiner was known as a member of the Gordon Party, among the first to try settling in the Black Hills.*

Rose asked:

Would it be possible to substitute Uncle George for Uncle Tom? You remember Uncle George was "the wild man" in Big Woods. In changing the lead of SILVER LAKE to make it chronological and bring Aunt Docia in, she tells news of the folks in Wisconsin (and of Black Susan [the cat] which covers that point [children's letters had asked about the Ingalls family's cat]). She can say that Uncle George is now a river jack on the Mississippi; that sort of revives his memory. Then if he shows up later—Was it on his way east from the Black Hills—we revive "the wild man" memory that Laura has, and describe him as he is now, and he goes on back to logging on the Mississippi. So that his whole life is in the books, because in Big Woods he is the boy who ran away to the war as a drummer boy when he was very young.

Uncle Tom has not been in the books before.

Laura's response:

I hardly know what to think about this. There are records of that first party of white men in the Black Hills and there was no Ingalls among them. To make it historically correct, it should be Uncle Tom. But I don't suppose anyone will take the trouble to look it up and only a few are left who will know it is not correct. I can see how it will add to the story to let it be Uncle George. So if you think best, knowing the circumstances, you may make the change from Uncle Tom to Uncle George. Uncle Tom was in the Black Hills in 1874, the grasshopper year. He went in sometime during the summer and the soldiers took him out the next spring. He spent only the one winter there, then went back east. He had been west to Oregon . . . and was on his way east again when he stopped to see us [described in *These Happy Golden Years*] the next year after the Hard Winter. People were going back and forth, up and down, continually.

Uncle Tom had not seen Pa and Ma since he was in the Black Hills and so told them all about it. We knew, of course, that he had been there and come back, but not of his experiences. Uncle Tom was such a quiet, small man, no one would have thought him capable of the things he did. He ran logs on the Mississippi, handled log jams . . . and he couldn't swim a stroke. He was low-voiced and quiet spoken, one couldn't imagine it of him, but he had fought Indians and apparently thought nothing of that terrible trip into the Black Hills with ox teams and afoot, lost in the awful Badlands before they got there.

Remember the date and don't have the first white men in the Black Hills too late. That would be a bad mistake. It was in the spring of 1882—eight years later that Uncle Tom visited us in De Smet. If Aunt Docia told news of him at the beginning of Silver Lake, it must be of what he had done since he came back from the Black Hills.

## *Are you short of money*

*Rose remained tied to the Turner brothers, especially John. When John's tonsils were removed, Laura feared that the medical expenses may have cramped Rose's budget.*

JANUARY 10, 1939

Rose Dearest,

I am uneasy about you and reading over your last letter, December 12th, doesn't help.

Are you short of money, what with John's hospital bills and all. If you are, I have a couple of hundred loose, you can have it if it would help you.

Please don't laugh. I know that is only a tiny bit to you, but it might be of use. If you want it just let me know. I feel as though something is wrong, and if there is I want to help if possible.

We are about as usual.

The weather is very warm and a small rain yesterday. The longest spell of the warmest weather ever known in the Ozarks at this time of year.

Very much love, in haste,

Mama Bess

---

### LETTER FROM DAD

JANUARY 15, 1939

Dear Rose,

We did not hear from you for so long we were very much worried, you must not do that again. You're going to mind. Well, we were mighty glad to get a letter when we did. Glad John got along all right and I think he is right about leaving school if what I can get here and there about schools is true. I am sure the less he has to do with them the better he will be.

I think what a man needs most is good straight common sense and John has that.

Our richest men did not have college education, they just had good common sense.

We have been having the most wonderful weather here this fall, except we need more rain. You must not feel bad because we don't use the furnace, you see. (now listen, read this carefully and see how it looks.)

To use the furnace I had to get up in a cold room, dress, do the furnace and put more fuel in it than it takes to warm the six rooms we use for 24 hours. It took 2 hours to get the water to boil before there is any heat in the house. . . . Now with the heater in the corner of the dining room, when I go to bed I put in 2 small pieces of heating wood or 1 larger one & shut the draft, open the night draft, and in the morning the rooms are still warm because that wood keeps the 400 pound stove hot and it was throwing out heat all night. . . . Before I dress and step to the stove, I shut the night draft and open the front draft. Just a jiffy to let the smoke out of the stove, then open the stove door & a big bed of coals, nice popcorn fire. . . . I throw in a couple sticks of wood & by the time I can get my clothes on, it is plenty hot. A good many days just 3 or 4 sticks of wood is all we need.

You see, besides the extra cost, there is a lot of walking down to the furnace & back, to say nothing about shoveling 10 tons of coal & 18 loads of heating wood. I got me a little red wagon like the boys have to play with, took it to the tin shop and had it shortened a little longer than a heating stick of wood. At night I fill it up and draw it right in by the side of the heater, and there is the wood right by the stove all evening and all morning. After breakfast, then I pull it out.

If there is any wood left I cord it on the back porch. . . .

You remember when you bought your house in Danbury, you wrote us that just a little fire in the cook stove kept the whole house warm. That is just the way it is here now. . . .

Did I tell you what a wonderful trip we had last summer [to the West Coast, with Silas Seal doing the driving]? I guess I enjoyed it more than any of the rest of them. Sometimes I think I'd take a trip east next summer if I can get hold of the money & then I think I am getting old and had better stay by my nice bed and don't always get a good bed when you are on the road.

. . . You wrote me that I ought to spank Bessie and make her pay more of the expenses. Now there is where you got me wrong. I said I paid more of the expense, or something to that effect. Well it was this way. Mr. Seal was to pay his & his wife's expenses & I pay mine & Bessie's & I furnish the car & car expense. Well sometimes there would be a cheap place & Seals had to go cheap, so he would want to stop there. & I wanted a better place so we all got a good place. So to kind of make it right & all that sort of thing, I just paid the bill once in a while. Sometimes they would buy a few things and eat a lunch in the car & we would go get a dinner. Lots of times I said come on in and have dinner & I paid the bill. He was such a good driver & took such good care of the car it was worth a lot anyway. Bessie would have been afraid for me to drive those side trips up the mountains and that made the trip a lot better. I think we made the trip about the best time of the year all except the rose garden at Portland, Oregon. It would have been nicer in about 5 or 10 days but it was a wonder anyway.

Oh we had a wonderful trip anyway and I made it on that check you sent me and have enough left to start the next trip.

Now that is getting a lot for your money don't you think?
Mrs. Seal says Bessie can get more for her money than anyone she ever saw, but I think I did fairly well, don't you? Now
you can't say but what I write you a letter sometimes. Wilder
Thayer [Almanzo's nephew, son of Eliza Jane] sent us a half
bushel of oranges for Christmas and some little yellow things
about as large as plumbs. When you have time just say you
got my letter, then I will know you are all right.

From Dad

## She can think I have gone to Timbuktu

*On the reverse of a letter from Louise Raymond, Laura wrote
Rose. Miss Raymond's letter of January 23, 1939, said: "As you
have guessed, I am again asking you if you have any idea when we
can get the finished manuscript of SILVER LAKE. . . . It is entirely too long since I have had the pleasure of reading a new Wilder
book, and I am terribly impatient to see it!"*

JANUARY 26, 1939
Rose Dearest,

You must, I think, be in your apartment by this time, so we are
sending an express package to 550 East Sixteenth Street. Evidently
you have no mail box there yet or I would have heard word of it.

I have used up all my excuses, etc. and think I will just not answer
this letter. She can think I have gone to Timbuktu or am sick or mad
or just too lazy to write.

We have had two snows that were so deep, 10 inches once and
then 7 inches. We could not get up the hill with the car if we had gone
down, so we didn't go down for two weeks or more. I lose my breath

if I walk down the hill, so I don't do that, even for the mail and the house is getting awfully stale.

We are all right and comfortable, waiting for spring to come.

Much love,

Mama Bess

## What a wise woman I am to have a daughter like you

*The long dependency on Rose for the Wilders' financial support abated in 1939. With advances from Harper & Brothers for new books, and increasing royalties, Laura's income was adequate. She still practiced frugality, but seldom obsessed over money. Rose's own career as a highly paid fiction writer was on the wane. Free Land exhausted her. Her ideas for stories dried up, or were out of synch with editorial tastes. Rose transitioned; she committed to writing about current events and American individualism. The following letter, from Laura to Rose, is a mother's tribute to a daughter's generosity.*

JANUARY 27, 1939

Rose Dearest,

Yesterday I was thinking how unbelievable it is that we are so comfortably situated. What with the car license ($11) added to expenses, the $15 rent money [from the Rock House] wouldn't spread over the month. We used the dividend checks as they came and when they were gone, I took some out of the bank.

It was when I was drawing the check that I realized how lucky we are to have rents and dividends and money in the bank.

You see usually I don't believe it and when I do, it is with a shock of surprise.

When I realized it this time, I thought again who we had to thank for all our good luck. But for you we would not have the rent money. You are responsible for my having dividend checks. Without your help I would not have the royalties from my books in the bank to draw on.

I looked up to admire the new window curtain in the dining room and there was the dining table you gave us, with the chairs around it.

Over the new, blue glass curtains in the bedroom are the blue and rose drapes you gave me and beside the window is the dresser with the lovely mirrors and drawers full of jewelry you have given me.

I thought about you all day and when night came I lay on the Simmons bed you gave me and pulled over me the down quilt, a gift from you. I looked across the room at Manly in his Simmons bed covered with his down quilt, both gifts from you, as well as his chest of drawers I could see on his side of the window.

It is always that way. When I go to count up our comfortablenesses and the luck of the world we have, it all leads back to you.

And so, snuggled under my down quilt, I went to sleep thinking what a wise woman I am to have a daughter like you.

Oh Rose my dear, we do thank you so much for being so good to us.

Very much love,
Mama Bess

### I can't fit in with the crowd

*Laura's letter of January 27 included an additional page of local news.*

[JANUARY 27, 1939]

I have finished covering Manly's down quilt and it looks as good as new. A fine job if I do say so myself. The cover is American beauty rose satin. A good piece cost $5.

Now I am beginning on the curtains. Gosh! How I hate it! Always did dislike a tearing up job but I can't stand these old rags of curtains any longer, two pieced together to make one in some cases. They are what was given me as your curtains but I don't know where they were hung in the house, if they were [this remark is an allusion to what Laura considered Corinne Murray's careless ways when she vacated the farmhouse]. I should have put some up before now but couldn't drive myself to choose them and get them made.

The goods I have at last selected are not very expensive but I do think they will be pretty.

The over drapes are two-toned gold cotton & rayon damask. The design a lengthwise raised flowered stripe. The under curtains are a marquisette very fine, a Capri blue. Which is a very light blue? I am in hopes that they will look like a filmy, misty blue cloud against the windows. Seems like the colors will brighten the room.

Yesterday I put up a dotted marquisette of the same blue at the dining room windows. I like it very much. It is like the picture only not so deep over the window.

The Study Club meets with me the second Friday in February and I want the curtains up then.

I am going to serve a tea for refreshments.

And here is a way to make sandwiches for a Valentine tea. I am going to make them cut the slices of bread, equal number of brown and white, with a heart shaped cutter. Then out of the center of half the slices each, cut a smaller heart. Spread the whole heart and on it put a heart with the small heart cut out in the cut out place in a white sandwich. And in a brown sandwich put a little white heart.

I want some little tea cakes besides the sandwiches but don't know how I'll make them.

Since Mary Craig left, I have had to act as president but there is an election in March and I'll get rid of it.

I can't fit in with the crowd someway. Never could very well and now I am tired of them more than ever.

Guess I'll have to go with the old church crowd, Burney, Rogers, Hoovers (?)

Well, my dear I must get dinner now. Hope I hear from you soon.

Much love,

Mama Bess

## Hope you and John are well

FEBRUARY 3, 1939

Rose Dearest,

We sent you a shipment of books today.

The weather has been so bad that we couldn't get them off before. Snow and ice and cold fog.

Having no chains we don't drive when the hill is covered with snow and ice. Manly will not drive in the rain either so we are just now in hopes of being able to go again. Snow is gone and the sun is shining.

There were twelve (12) boxes sent you. When you get them better count. I am in an awful hurry so good bye.

Hope you and John are well and comfortably settled.

Much love,

Mama Bess

## God help the poor taxpayers!

*Laura's conservative bent escalated. Her reference to a birthday party for President Roosevelt was actually a fund-raiser to aid victims of infantile paralysis. Laura does not mention it, but Corinne*

*Murray was on the planning committee. The New Deal Works*
*Progress Administration had funded a sanitary sewerage project in*
*Mansfield, and a $5,000 vocational-agricultural building at the*
*high school.*

FEBRUARY 20, 1939

Rose Dearest,

The job of writing to you was all done up. And now comes the
goody Valentine which calls for another letter. Never mind! I like to
talk to you. And thank you for the Valentine box of candy. I may
wear store teeth, but my old sweet tooth has never been extracted.

There isn't much to write about, so I'll just gossip a little.

Have you celebrated F.D.R.'s birthday properly? Mansfield is all
torn up over it.

The tickets for Roosevelt's birthday party in the Masonic Hall
were 25 cents apiece and "they" couldn't sell them. There were less
than fifty people there. The refreshments were ordered from Springfield and cost nearly all the ticket money.

I really should have thought that there would have been the whole
town there.

Mansfield has got $65,000 from the WPA and is bonding the city
for $17,000, to be their share for building a sewerage system. The
town is already bonded for more than it is worth.

God help the poor taxpayers!

We have had a rain. For three days and nights it rained. Water ran
down the ditches and the creek roared. Yesterday it stopped and
turned cold. Last night there was a sprinkling of snow and today is
cold but the sun shines.

Have I told you we have lots of goat milk again? There are five little kids. We'll be getting fat now I suppose.

We will be going up to Springfield first of next week so I can collect $20 interest from the Union National Bank. I intend to buy a
mattress and blankets for my old oak bedstead on the sleeping porch

and enamel to refinish it, and the dresser and commode that go with it. Then my $20 will be spent. We are going to put some kind of wallboard on the sleeping porch and make it look nice again, as it did when you were here. Then I'll put a pretty linoleum on the floor. But we will not put in a bathroom upstairs, at least not now. It will take all my interest money to do the other things I want to do now. And we are living within our income, in spite of your advice. We feel easier that way. Besides, it would be a lot of trouble to put in a bathroom, and we are dodging all the trouble we can.

It is almost impossible to hire help here and when we do they are absolutely no good. Karl Tripp is almost impossible too.

But I had not thought the situation in New York could be as you write. [Rose had probably complained about New Deal programs hiring employees away from the private sector.] I wish Mrs. Roosevelt would have to scrub her own floors and do her own work.

Hope you are settled and comfortable. Much love,

Mama Bess

## *I am sorry you still have to work on my books*

MARCH 17, 1939

Rose Dearest,

We were so glad to have your letter of the 4th and I was going to answer it at once, but you know where good intentions are used to best advantage.

What a time you do have getting anything done! But at that we have almost as hard a time. How we are going to get the yard raked and such work done I don't see.

Bruce has more than he can do and can't get any help. Mr. Williams is not able to work much anymore and wants to hire a man to help with spring work but cannot find one. It is that way all around here. The P.W.A. [the New Deal's Public Works Administration,

which dealt with the construction of buildings for the common good]
is still going strong using all the men at that work should be helping
people to earn money to pay the P.W.A. workers, if you know what I
mean.

I am surprised that John [Turner] is in Columbia, but it likely is
the best for him. It surely is better for both boys to be on their own
and independent, rather than depend on you longer. By our old-
fashioned standards, they are men now and should look after themselves. I am pleased that they want to do it.

You have given them a good start in every way and it is time now
you looked after yourself instead of other people. I am really pleased
about the boys and hope you are not disappointed about John. They
are good boys and will make their own place.

It must seem strange to you, not to have anyone's expenses to pay,
except your own, and to have everybody, including us, off your hands.

I am sorry you still have to work on my books. I would like to have
you perfectly free for just your own affairs. But that trouble will soon
be over and you will get enough out of it to pay your rent for awhile
anyhow. I am glad you took a place so cheaply. It sounds like a nice
place and is much better than a more fashionable address and the
harder work to keep it up [Rose rented a "slum apartment" to use
during stays in New York City]. If you are comfortable, a little money
ahead or at least your bills paid so you don't have to worry over them,
it will add greatly to your happiness. Don't I know!

I haven't gone alone down that long, dark road I used to dream of,
for a long time. The last time I saw it stretching ahead of me, I said in
my dream "But I don't have to go through those dark woods, I don't
have to go that way." And I turned away from it. We are living inside
our income and I don't have to worry about the bills.

Speaking of economy—you see I am using up the scraps of paper.

Our fuel, wood, for this winter, both for heating and cooking, has
cost $10.00. We spent $20 getting the wood ready for use last fall and
we have used not quite half. We have enough left over for next winter.

Last winter, using the furnace, it cost something over $100 just for heating, and there were the electric bills for the cooking.

By fighting for it, making them [the power company] cut off the electricity for awhile, I got a contract so that the electric bill for last month was $7.42. There is a meter for Bruce, with Hyberger's consent, so he pays for what he uses and last month his part was $2.60, leaving our bill only $5.82. We use Frigidaire, lights, iron, and the stove for a quick bit of hot water.

I am glad you have come to agree with us about furnaces. I think you are wise to put stoves in the Danbury house. It seemed to us such a pity to tear up that lovely old house for pipes and radiators, to say nothing of the expense. Manly and I think you should get a hard coal heater. Hard coal is clean & the stove needs only one filling for all day. I suppose are much improved since you were creeping, eh?

I don't know just why the furnace did as it did here. Perhaps we didn't handle it right. But we went to bed at 8 o'clock, while you were up much later. That might have helped in the difference.

Since your letter, we have told Karl Tripp, and also Johnson at Mountain Grove, to sell it for us. Both have promised to try to place it.

Manly says to tell you, he does not want to go to the World's Fair [which opened near New York City in 1939]. That some way he doesn't care so much about going as he used to. We are glad we went west last summer when there were not such crowds everywhere as there would be this summer.

I am glad you know Laura Ingalls. It seemed all the time as though she must belong to our family, and it is nice that she looks like you, and that you like her. Adventuring seems to run in the family, and you and she must have a lot in common. Here's good luck to her. Hope she gets the backing she needs for her flight. [Laura Ingalls was a highly publicized female pilot of the 1930s, with many record-breaking flights to her credit.]

Dorothy Sue [Hoover] married a man in West Plains. Tom Carnell works at the Chevrolet garage. Joan Herndon has been going to teacher's college in Springfield. I saw her at Christmas time, home for vacation. She seemed very nice. [These were all high school students who were often guests at Rocky Ridge when the Turner boys lived there.]

Mr. Divan is about as usual. Mrs. Divan has nearly lost her mind. She never goes anywhere.

I am sending samples of the living room curtains.

There are no signs of another down comforter needing to be covered. They both are in perfect condition.

There is no use in trying to say anything about the news. We are probably thinking alike about things. Hitler's word is about as good as Roosevelt's, isn't it? I am worried though, for between dictators and Communism, what chance has a simple republic? If the dictators are stopped, the Communists will get 'em.

Oh Well!

Mrs. Gere is president of our study club now and I am loose again. We had our last meeting at Norwood [a town fifteen miles from Mansfield] with Alice Carnell Davis, Daisy Freeman's daughter. Her grandmother Alice Freeman raised her, you remember. Seemed someway strange to me to be in a club with Alice Freeman's grandchild.

Madelon Craig is going back to Guatemala in about three weeks. Bill Craig is already there, with a better job than he had before. I hate to see Madelon go. We all like her very much.

Manly and I are going to Hartville Wednesday. Mrs. Frink wanted me to meet her there. Mr. Frink is helpless, but more help to her than he ever has been before, as he draws an old age pension.

We have been to Springfield each week for two weeks now, and are going again the last of this week or first of next. I am trying, you see, to get a haircut and Jack Humble has been out of town. Manly and I are agreed no one else can do it. My hair is long enough to do up and I am tired of it. Am going to get a very short cut.

Very much love, I hope you are well and comfortable.

Mama Bess

*I am scared about what we are coming to
before long*

APRIL 2, 1939

Rose Dearest,

Silver Lake has waited until the deadline for fall publishing
has past. Ida Louise wrote me it was April 1st, as I wrote you some
time ago.

Do you suppose it would be possible to have it published this fall
anyway, if it is not much later? If not, then it will be three years between books. By then, I'm afraid I and my stories will be forgotten.

Your article on the Ludlow amendment in Liberty [magazine] is
great, so plain and fair and true.

But I simply gnashed my teeth when I read Mrs. Roosevelt's. It
evaded the truth—you proved that presidents cannot be trusted. She
said trust them. Also, she tried to scare people by completely ignoring
the fact that a vote would not be taken in case of attack.

My opinion is that Roosevelt has already made his secret agreement [with England] and Eleanor knows it. Your article touched
them in a tender spot by speaking of such a thing.

I am scared about what we are coming to before long.

Also I bragged too much in my last letter to you, though goodness
knows I only meant it in the way of thankfulness. Anyway it offended
some of "the Gods there be" [from William Ernest Henley's poem
"Invictus"] and I have no blue ring or bead.

Manly has had trouble with his head and ears and I went with
him to an ear specialist in Springfield last Monday. Since the treat-
ment the pains in his head have stopped and I think he hears a little
better. We are going up again last of the week. It is awfully dry again
and I guess we will have to put down a well and get a pump for the
other house. That will cost more than the year's rent. [Both the Rocky
Ridge farmhouse and the Rock House had relied on flowing springs

for their water source. Eventually the springs became unreliable and wells and pumps were installed.]

I strained my hand and a rheumatism has settled in it, so now I will have to hire the washing done and buy an electric cleaner to do the sweeping and someone, if possible to do housecleaning or let it go.

I can't even crochet much, so enjoy my handwork you have. I may quit doing any.

And I will have to cut expenses or increase income and how can I do either?

"But may I with fools and dunces everlastingly commingle, if ever."

I brag again about being on easy street. I am going to play poor as poverty and fool those jealous imps of misfortune.

Anyway I'm still thankful.

Things could be so much worse. I might have broken a leg instead of wrenching a hand. We are otherwise as well as usual and everything is all right.

Much love,

Mama Bess

## We have a little more time on Silver Lake

*Eager for a new Laura Ingalls Wilder title on the fall 1939 book list, Louise Raymond inquired about Silver Lake. "Don't fret about SILVER LAKE," she said. "I know you will get it done when you can . . . all the librarians and booksellers I met taxed me about there not being a new book by you. . . . If by May 15th you know one way or the other that you can or cannot get the book to us by, say, the end of June, won't you drop me a line and just tell me?*

APRIL 10, 1939

Rose Dearest,

You will see by this letter that we have a little more time on Silver

Lake. I am letting you know at once as I just got the letter this morning. I hope we can make it.

I have not been well for a week now. Everyone has had a queer sort of flu and I guess that was it. But I'm getting well now and there are no germs in this!

Dr. Fuson is in St. John's Hospital in Springfield, very low with pneumonia.

Mr. Frink was buried last week. Haven't heard from Mrs. F. since. [The Frinks were Hartville friends; Emma Frink and Laura Wilder were members of the Athenian study club.]

Much love,

Mama Bess

## We will be very careful

MAY 23, 1939

Rose Dearest,

I might have known you would fix things!

We are delighted that my business with Harpers can be done so speedily.

May I send you "The Hard Winter" now? I would rather you had it so if anything should happen on our trip you could finish it. Shall I send it to New York or will you be in Connecticut?

We plan to take our driving easily, stop early and lay over if we are tired. And not drive at all on Sunday when every drunken loon is drunk and on the road. If we find it too hard, we can come home any time. It is all right to have a driver but so many times we could have stopped comfortably for two but not for four. Anyone is always in a hurry and don't want to do the things we want to do.

We will be very careful, drive slowly and stop when we please.

You see if we are by ourselves we will be independent.

I must tell you how much I enjoyed reading your books about

central Asia and the Chinese and Tibet. "Beyond Khyber Pass" and the rest. Oh Rose! What a world! Thanks so much for letting me keep them to read. [The book was written by Lowell Thomas, a broadcaster and world adventurer. During the 1930s Rose did ghost-writing projects for Thomas.]

But now do you want us to send them back to you when we come back home? There will hardly be time to pack them up and send them, before we are gone. There are a lot of your books here yet. There is plenty of room for them to stay if you would rather they did.

I have handled over every book in the house this winter and spring and nowhere did I find Charlotte Temple [a British novel, published in 1791, one of the seduction genre, which was wildly popular at the time]. I am sure now that it is not here. I found some more, collections of Best Short Stories and there are all your gardening books.

About Silver Lake—it covers so much more than the homestead that I don't think the use of the word in the title would be good. "On the Banks of Plum Creek" went over so well that I think that sort of title is taking. But it isn't all about the shores, so I think By the Shores of Silver Lake would be better. It is no longer than the title of Plum Creek.

I think I wrote you about the teacher from Fort Wayne coming when I was just able to sit up after the flu. She said that what her children were wondering about most was whether Laura ever got to be a teacher. In Hard Winter I have kept that idea working.

Be careful with the copy of Hard Winter. I mean don't lose it, which of course you would not do anyway.

But it is the only copy. All I have besides are my notes. Because my hand was so lame, I did not make another copy.

I expect you will find lots of fault in it, we can argue it out later. If the manuscript is with you, it will be where you can work on it when you please and get it over with when you like.

It is good of you to tell me how to handle the business with Harpers.

Sometimes I have a suspicion that you are a nice kind of a person.

Much love,

Mama Bess

## *We are interested in all you do*

MAY 24, 1939

Rose Dearest,

House cleaning is mostly done and I will leave the house clean when we go.

You would not know the sleeping porch [the porch had been Rose's combination office and bedroom during her stays at Rocky Ridge]. The floor is covered with an all-over linoleum of "knotted pine" flooring. See Montgomery Ward [catalogue]! It looks like the real thing. The wall covering is my own idea. It was a problem what to do with the siding and boarded up window places for we did not want to spend much. It would cost a lot to take it off and use any of the wall boards in its place. Then I thought of real tapestry. And we covered the walls with an imitation of real tapestry, tacking it at the top and letting it fall smoothly to the floor. It hides the chimney which we built in the old place and makes two small closets, one at the side and one underneath. The tapestry hides them and looks as tho the wall were unbroken. Over the windows is a curtain like the sample. It hangs in an unbroken curtain the length of the south side and over the windows at each end. Between each two windows it is looped up and nowhere does it shade the windows, only enough to hide the rain spout at the top. The ceiling is painted ivory white and the casings a light cream.

Mrs. Gere and her mother raved over the room.

Bruce said it was "such a quiet, restful room."

The big, old, oak bedstead is in the west end [of the room] with a new inner spring mattress on it.

The old dresser and commode are refinished and stand by. Both desks are in their places and one of the big, Bruce-made walnut chairs, with new upholstery, stands by the windows between them. The spread on the bed is that Albanian silk one you gave me so long ago and afterward said I would never use. There are the pretty fur rugs on the floor, brown and white [the rugs were goatskins from Manly's herd].

The sleeping porch is not dark. So much light paint offsets the darkness of the tapestry and makes it just right. The flower pattern on the curtains is tulips, some larger than the sample shows.

The white bedstead in the north room has a new, good mattress. The cover is that silk crazy quilt I made so long ago, with a silk shawl as a cover for the pillows. The rose colored rugs from my bedroom are on each side of the bed and before the dresser. There is a lot of rose color in the quilt. The curtains are cretonne with rose colored roses on a light cream ground.

When you come you may take your choice of the rooms or use them both. Just to show you we are keeping the place up. Marion Dennis drove in with a register and he said, "You folks have the prettiest place in this whole country."

Am sending a sheet from Carrie's letter I thought might interest you.

How terrible about Catharine [Brody]. I wouldn't think she would want to come back to this part of the country after what she said about the people when she left. [Never fond of Catharine, Laura later snubbed her. As Catharine traveled cross-country by train, she stopped in Mansfield to visit; Laura refused to see her.]

What is Helen's address? You said, or wrote, before we moved over that she had written Corinne to send her, her doctor books that Corinne was supposed to pack and send them to her. She did not, or at least she did not send them all, for I found quite a lot of them.

If you will tell me her address, I will send them to her. I have already packed a box full, like those boxes we sent you.

Perhaps I have got it all said this time. I wanted you to know that we are keeping the places up and they are still the show places of the country.

I agree with you about Congress, but what can you expect? This is a representative government we have yet, and I ask you, does it not represent the majority of the people?

Our state legislature is as bad. We voted down an increase in their pay last election and they have fixed it so we will have to vote on it again next time.

We are interested in all you do, so write when you can and tell us all you want to.

Lots of love,

Mama Bess

## *Mr. Wilder and I are going wandering*

> By the Shores of Silver Lake *was finally completed. Laura and Manly planned their third trip back to South Dakota, this time driving alone. Before she left, Laura urged George Bye to secure good terms for her new book.*

MAY 29, 1939

Dear Mr. Bye,

A new book of mine is in the hands of the typist and will be delivered to your office as soon as it is typed.

Harpers is expecting it, and if they are pleased with it I hope you will get me a good contract. The last book has been so successful, I think Harpers should be willing to treat me well.

Mr. Wilder and I are going wandering this summer starting in about a week, so I am leaving in Rose Lane's hands the business of this new book.

Please refer anything concerning it at her Connecticut place, Route 4 Box 42, Danbury.

With kindest regards,

Sincerely,

Laura Ingalls Wilder

## *The place is so pretty*

JUNE 1, 1939

Rose Dearest,

Your tulip tree is blooming!! Manly said it was dead. Bruce thought it would die when trees in the timber were dying of drought.

And now it is full of bloom. Mrs. Bruce just brought me a blossom and leaves. Bruce sent word to tell you the tree is 25 ft. tall and 6 inches through the trunk at the bottom. I have never been to it and we can't see it from this place. I had no idea what it would be like, but it is as pretty as an orchid. It is a wonderful thing. We think it is about eight years since you set it out and this is the first time it has bloomed. [The tulip tree must have been planted across the road from the farmhouse, at the rented house where Bruce Prock and his family lived.]

The place is so pretty. I hate to go and leave it.

The little robins are running after the old birds all over the yard while the old birds pull up worms and poke down their throats. It is a funny sight for the young birds are larger than the old ones. It is a branch of A.D.C., Aid for Dependent Children, I guess. [Aid to Dependent Children was a New Deal program, enacted in 1935.]

What are those flowering shrubs? One in the corner by the west side of the garage and one down in the border west of the lilacs? They are a mass of white bloom. Lovely! We don't know them, neither does Bruce.

Bruce's baby is not doing well. Seems to be healthy enough but she weighs only 10½ pounds and she is eight months old. She doesn't sit up yet. They are doing everything for her that they or the doctors know. [The child died at a young age.]

Mrs. Bruce took her to a baby specialist in Springfield and he said just feeding and care, but she has had that all along. She went up with us yesterday. I got a haircut and Manly got a new summer suit. It is gray and I think very pretty. You remember the two suits you sent me last summer, the green and brown trimmed and the blue. I am taking the blue for my dress up in De Smet, if it should be cool, and the light figured summer dress, the blue, that you gave me from Columbia, to wear if it is hot.

It is cool here today, but yesterday it was frightfully hot in Springfield. It is always cool here in the shade of these big trees. . . .

## *It is selfish of me to leave you to proofread and everything*

JUNE 3, 1939

Rose Dearest,

We are expecting to start on our trip next Tuesday, June 6th and to be in De Smet the 10th. [De Smet's annual celebration was called Old Settlers Day, or "the Tenth of June."] Think we will stop there a few days. From there we will go to Keystone and likely stay there a few days, anyway until we feel like moving on.

A telegram would catch us at De Smet. If you write, address to Keystone, care of Mrs. D. N. Swanzey [Carrie Ingalls]. What a name, Swanzey!

I don't know how we will go from there, but will write you again as soon as I know where we will be next.

The key to the safety deposit box is in the upper right hand corner of my dresser, in the box where I keep my rings. The rings will be in safety deposit. Time deposit and Postal Savings certificates will be there too.

The little, old writing desk will be in the bank vault for safekeeping [a lap desk made by Manly, which was brought from De Smet to Mansfield in 1894]. Its key will be with the other key in the dresser drawer.

Notes for the last book are in the large envelop marked Pioneer Girl, in the tills of my old writing desk in the little study off the stairs.

You could write the last book from them and finish the series if you had to do so. I am sending you today by registered mail "The Hard Winter" mss. I think I wrote you that it is the only copy I have. My hand was so lame I did not copy it again. It is a rather dark picture, not so much sweetness and light as the other books, but the next one will be different so perhaps the contrast will not be bad. I wrote Harpers as you said. I also wrote George Bye that the book was coming and that I expected a good contract this time. That the contract was to be sent for consideration and that I would accept any contract you approved. Hope this is all right. Today I had a nice note from him in reply. He said Ida Louise was not well and was at her office only part of the time, but was still in charge of the department.

Can't think of anything more. It is selfish of me to leave you to proofread and everything, but I am doing as you say, going along and forgetting it.

You will hear from us along the way.

Very much love,

Mama Bess

P.S. Rose dear if anything should happen to us, I beg of you don't let Corinne and Jack, either one or both, back on the place. Do whatever else you please with it but not that.

## A Note from Carrie

*Laura included the following note from Carrie in her June 3 letter to Rose.*

Laura do you suppose Rose has any clothes she is giving to charity? If she has do you think she would send them to me? It would save me buying some things. Now if you had rather not—don't say anything about it—and above all don't send me any of yours. I can get along. I just thought if she was doing that I certainly would like to be the charity.

*Laura's note to Rose read:*

This note is from Carrie. I am taking her some of my things that I am tired of and I would rather use yours first if you have any to give away and pass them to her later.

## I am sorry to make you so much trouble

*The Old Settlers Day celebration in De Smet was a rainy affair, but Laura said no one minded; the long drought cycle was broken in South Dakota. While in De Smet Laura researched the Hard Winter of 1880–1881, the subject of her next book. She and Manly visited Grace and Nate Dow before driving across the state to the Black Hills. There they inspected progress on Mount Rushmore and visited Carrie in Keystone. They drove on through Colorado before returning home. By then, Rose was also on a car trip, to the West Coast, so Laura tended to the final details of* By the Shores of Silver Lake. *She addressed her concerns to Jasper Spock, a staff member in George Bye's office.*

JULY 1, 1939
George T. Bye & Co.
New York
Dear Mr. Spock,

I have no typed copy of "The Shores of Silver Lake."

A letter from Rose says, "Rialto Typing Service went haywire and sent two carbons to you in Mansfield, which should have gone to George Bye's office."

I have not received them and there must be a mistake about their having been sent to me. Evidently, they were not sent to Rose as she asks me to forward them to you.

Rose is traveling west and cannot attend to this, so will you please see if Rialto Typing can produce them. It seems to be the only chance.

I am sending you a check to cover Rialto's bill for typing the three copies which your office forwarded to me.

If you have paid the bill the check will reimburse you. If you have not paid it, please withhold payment until this matter of the two typed copies is settled.

I am sorry to make you so much trouble, but with Rose away there is nothing else I can do.

Sincerely yours,
Laura Ingalls Wilder

## *All of the books are <u>one story</u>*

By the Shores of Silver Lake *was published to resemble an adult novel in appearance. Laura clung to the square shape of the four earlier books, but eventually agreed to the new format. George Bye contacted experts in the children's book world, including Helen Hoke, an editor at Julian Messner publishers. Hoke proclaimed the change in format to be "a very brilliant move on the part of Harpers."*

JULY 10, 1939
Dear Mr. Bye,

It is a perfectly grand contract, with Harpers, that you have se-
cured for me. I am so pleased and thank you a lot. . . .

I have signed the contract and am returning it to your charge.

Harper's idea of making the format of "The Shores of Silver Lake"
attractive to adults as well as children seems to me to be good. But it
should be borne in mind that all of the books are *one story* and some
booksellers have intended selling them in sets when the story is completed. Because of this they should be made to look well together.

Again assuring you that I appreciate the good work you have done
for my book, I am

Very sincerely,
Laura Ingalls Wilder

*Do you think there would be any chance to serialize
the story?*

SEPTEMBER 12, 1939
Dear Mr. Bye,

The book to follow "By the Shores of Silver Lake" is now taking
shape on my desk.

It is a continuation of the story of Laura and her family at De
Smet, on the shore of Silver Lake, during what has always been
known as the Hard Winter.

Do you think there would be any chance to serialize the story? If
so, how long before book publication would you want to have the
manuscript?

Please let me know what you think about it.

With kindest regards,
Yours sincerely,
Laura Ingalls Wilder

*Sister Mary had quite a small library of those books*

OCTOBER 2, 1939

Dear Mr. Bye,

Certainly I give my permission for American Printing House for the Blind to publish Farmer Boy in talking-book form for use of the blind.

I shall be glad if it gives blind children any pleasure.

Sister Mary had quite a small library of those books. [Mary Ingalls owned raised print and Braille books, not "talking books" in the modern sense.]

Sincerely yours,

Laura Ingalls Wilder


*That chapter is fiction*

> *Because of children's letters asking about Mr. Edwards from* Little House on the Prairie, *Laura felt compelled to add him to a later book. In* By the Shores of Silver Lake, *Mr. Edwards reappears in the chapter "Pa's Bet." When Aubrey Sherwood inquired about the incident, Laura admitted that she had fictionalized the episode.*

NOVEMBER 18, 1939

Dear Mr. Sherwood,

Thank you for the copies of the "News" and for your write up of Silver Lake.

I am glad you enjoyed the book.

There are several typographical errors in the spelling, besides leaving out the "g" in Brookings. Mother's name is misspelled.

Mr. Wilder says lumber was hauled from Volga in the fall of '79, but in the spring, for the building of town, it was hauled from Brookings.

As to the place where homesteads were filed, that chapter is fiction. Such things did happen in those days and I placed it there to emphasize the rush for land. You understand how those things are done in writing.

Everyone spoke of going to Brookings to file, though it may well have been near there.

The book is not a history, but a true story founded on historical fact.

Have you an extra print of our picture used in your Old Settlers Day number? Rose was very much pleased with the write up you gave us and wants very much to have a print of the picture you used. If you can, please send me one for her.

Again thanking you for the copies of the "De Smet News" and the kind things you say, and your criticisms as well, of Silver Lake, I remain

Yours sincerely,
Laura Ingalls Wilder

## *It relieves my mind*

*The plan to change the appearance of the final four Little House books still concerned Laura. Helen Hoke again endorsed Harper's plan to give the latter books in the series a look appealing to older readers.*

FEBRUARY 14, 1940
Dear Mr. Bye,

Thank you for sending me Helen Hoke's letter. It relieves my mind about the change in format of Silver Lake. I appreciate her taking the trouble to write her views on the change.

We have had the coldest winter of record and it is still with us. We are well as usual. . . .

Sincerely,

Laura Ingalls Wilder

## *Rose tells me it should have gone through your office*

*The 1939 trip west was the Wilders' last extensive journey. Laura wrote an account of their visit to De Smet for the Christian Science Monitor. She called her nostalgic piece "The Land of Used to Be."*

FEBRUARY 26, 1940

Dear Mr. Bye,

I have sold to the Christian Science Monitor, for $15, a little article they ordered from me, and now Rose tells me it should have gone through your office. I am sorry I did not know this.

I have had so little experience of the way in which manuscripts should be handled that I make mistakes. Will you please have your office debit my account with the $1.50 commission on this article?

I have written A. C. Ellis, Superintendent of the American Printing House for the Blind, as you suggested, also referring them to Harpers.

I hope you have recovered from your latest storm which must have been more severe than ours which followed it. The sun is shining again today and that raises our spirits and our hopes of spring coming soon.

Yours sincerely,

Laura Ingalls Wilder

*I hope they will ask for more*

> Requests to reprint chapters from the Little House books in ele-
> mentary school reading textbooks created extra income for Laura
> and drew attention to the book series.

MARCH 4, 1940

Dear Mr. Bye,

Your letter came this morning. Certainly Row Peterson's offer is a
good one. Sell them the pages they want from Farmer Boy and I hope
they will ask for more in the future.

Yours sincerely,

Laura Ingalls Wilder

*You will . . . do whatever is best*

> Knowing of the substantial fees paid to Rose for her serial fiction,
> Laura hoped for the same for her own books.

MARCH 14, 1940

Dear Mr. Bye,

It will be grand if you can sell "The Hard Winter" as a serial and
I am pleased that you think there is a chance of doing so.

As to whether it is sold to Christian Science Monitor, or else-
where, I am, of course, leaving to your judgment. You will, I am sure
do whatever is best.

Thanks for sending me Miss Ince's letter.

Yours sincerely,

Laura Ingalls Wilder

## *Mr. Wilder and I celebrated our birthdays*

**MARCH 25, 1940**

Dear Miss Crawford,

As you thought my books are biographical. They are my earliest memories of Kansas and Indian Ter. in Little House on the Prairie.

My father's family lived there in 1870–71 exactly as I have written. As you see it was only for a short time.

The family records show that J. J. Ingalls of Kas. was a distant connection of my father. I think a second cousin. [John James Ingalls (1833–1900) was a Kansas politician elected to the United States senate in 1873.]

I was at first a little uneasy as to just how reliable my memory might be but I have had several letters agreeing with it [the accuracy of Little House on the Prairie] as yours does.

If there is anything more you would like to know about me I will gladly write again.

Mr. Wilder and I celebrated our birthdays this winter by giving a party to a crowd of friends. He was 83 and I 73.

Sincerely,

Laura Ingalls Wilder

## *I must tell you a story*

*This is the only surviving letter sent from Laura to Rose during the 1940s.*

**APRIL 3, 1940**

Rose Dearest,

Blow the bird up through the little plug at the back. Hold it so the air will not escape while you twist the plug a couple of turns to the right. You must hold it tightly so you can turn the plug. Stand the bird up on its feet and read what is printed on the back.

Does it remind you of anything?

I must tell you a story. When I entertained the Study Club, I asked them all to answer to roll call by telling the best short story they had heard recently. This is the one Jessie Fuson told:

Dr. Fuson had to do a small operation on a boy and Jessie gave the ether. Not being very used to it, she was anxious to have the boy come out from under and be sure he was all right. So as he began to come to, she talked to him.

"Have you any brothers?" she asked.

He said yes. She asked him how many and he said "three."

"Do you ever fight?" she wanted to know.

He said "yes."

"And who whips?" Jessie asked.

"Dad does," the boy answered.

Love,

Mama Bess

## It has been rather trying

The Long Winter *was completed in the spring of 1940. George Bye pursued serialization and negotiated a generous book contract. Considering the working title of "The Hard Winter" too grim, Ursula Nordstrom requested an alternate:* The Long Winter.

MAY 7, 1940

Dear Mr. Bye,

I am so glad you found The Hard Winter interesting.

It has been rather trying, living it all over again as I did in the writing of it and I am glad it is finished.

If you have not already, you soon will have the corrections, and the rest I leave in your hands.

Harpers is already enquiring about the book.

With best regards,

Yours sincerely,

Laura Ingalls Wilder

## I am trusting your judgment

*In this letter, Laura officially announced that her series would extend to eight books, not the originally planned seven.*

JUNE 21, 1940

Dear Mr. Bye,

Out of respect for your "gentleman's agreement" with Harpers, I am willing to sign the contract at "10 per cent for the first 3000 books and 15 per cent thereafter" on book sales.

But, like you, I do not approve of giving them 25 per cent of motion picture rights. If by good fortune, the story should be used in pictures, it will be at no expense to Harpers, but altogether through my hard work writing and your good salesmanship.

In consideration of our accepting the 10 per cent on book sales would Harper not be willing to take, say 15 per cent instead of 25 per cent of motion picture rights? If you are willing, let's make a try for this.

I am trusting your judgment and will sign the contract as it is, if it can be improved on this point, but am returning it unsigned this time just in hopes.

I had expected to finish the series with the seventh book, but, as I work on it, I am afraid it will stretch into still another, making eight.

In the last book, Laura will be eighteen and the story will be the courtship and wedding of Laura and Almanzo.

I suppose at that age it might be called adult, though I hope to retain the appeal to children. They are already writing me asking if A. J. Wilder is Almanzo, and when Laura marries him, if he is.

A story following the 8th book, telling of what next happens is taking shape slowly in my mind, but it is too soon to say if it will crystallize into a completely adult novel. I can only say perhaps it may do so.

Trusting to hear from you soon, I am

Sincerely yours,

Laura Ingalls Wilder

---

### "DEAR LAURA . . ."

*Laura not only wrote back to her readers, she also saved thousands of their letters, cards, drawings, and photos. Here is a sampling:*

Dear Laura,

Our teacher is reading your story of Little House in the Big Woods to us. We like it very much. We say "Read more!" when it is time for her to stop reading.

The way you lived when you were a little girl is very much like the way our great grandparents lived around here. So your story helps us to understand life around Plainfield many years ago.

We hope you had a happy birthday on February 7th. We are late with our birthday wishes because our school was closed for nine days because of icy roads. . . .

Vivian, one of our classmates, made this valentine for you.

We hope you are well.

Admirers of the Laura books

Third Grade

Plainfield, Illinois

Dear Mrs. Wilder,

I suppose that you will be perfectly fed up by the time this letter reaches you. For I suppose it has the same old stuff that all the others have.

I have read all of your books except Farmer Boy (that isn't fair to Almanzo is it?) and have enjoyed them all. I have finally gotten to read These Happy Golden Years and it has been of great interest to me, though I feel sorry for the book, since I have read it four times in the last two weeks. I think it is my favorite book. I disliked Nellie Oleson because she was so sure of herself and also think I would have been one of the boys that pestered Miss Wilder. It is really funny to read about Nellie so sure of herself that she would ride behind the Morgan horses, Prince and Lady, but only after you had ridden for a few dozen times did she get to ride twice. Ha! Ha!

Since you have written the books I have my heart set on South Dakota to homestead there and maybe raise some cattleoes, a kind of buffalo and cattle which can survive a Dakota winter. I certainly would like to know what became of Carrie and Grace. And is Almanzo still alive for if I go I would certainly want to have a fine pair of horses and I know that Almanzo could pick them.

I am only twelve and have a long way to go. . . . Again thank you for the wonderful books.

Your friend,
Jack
San Gabriel, California

Dear Laura,
Thank you.
Good books.

I like them.

I am seven years old.

Merrill

My dear Mrs. Wilder,

I am in the Third grade at school. We study Pioneer Life. Our teacher has read a number of your books to us. I like "Little House in the Big Woods" best. Our teacher also read that your gingerbread is famous.

Would you send me your recipe? If you will I shall allow the rest of the children to copy it. After our mothers have made gingerbread we shall put the recipe in our scrapbooks.

I was the one chosen by my teacher to make a picture of you in a pink dress with the buggy coming down the street. Thank you for the recipe if you care to send it.

Your true friend,

Madeline

Marion, Indiana

Dear Laura,

I enjoyed your books very much. I liked the time when Charley got stung by the yellow jackets.

I liked when Nellie Oleson went to the store and saw Laura. Laura, if I was you when Nellie Oleson bragged about her fur cape, I would have slapped her.

Thank you so much for writing the books.

With love,

Donald

Dear Mrs. Wilder,

This Christmas I received your new book "Little Town on the Prairie." I finished the day after Christmas, and have finished it a 2nd time. It is very good.

I have just finished telling my mother how the proposed paper shortage [during World War II] may cut out the publication of your books, and how we ought to get the rest of the books you have written. She looked as if the idea was good. . . .

One of the boys in my class, Cammie, has all your books, and he lent them to our school library, so I have read them.

The minute I received my present of your book, I sat down to start it. . . .

In reading I came across Nellie Oleson again. What became of her? And also Royal Wilder? Mary Power and Minnie . . . ?

Sincerely yours,

Rebecca

Newtown, Pennsylvania


Dear Mrs. Wilder,

I hope you are well.

I like best of all "Little House in the Big Woods," "These Happy Golden Years," "Farmer Boy," and "The Long Winter." I like them so well that I bought a series for myself. I earned the money picking beans on hot August days. When I get started I can't hardly stop. I have hardly ever read better books. I have been at Lake Pepin.

I wonder what became of Mary, Carrie, and Grace.

A Wis. Farm boy,

Paul

To my Valentine, Laura Ingalls Wilder

> *Although I've never seen your face*
> *I feel as though I had*
> *I've met you in your books, you know,*
> *And they have made me glad.*

Anne

## *I will try to answer all your questions*

JUNE 26, 1940

Dear Fifth Graders,

Such a lot of nice letters! And I wish so much I could answer each one, but there are twenty-eight of them and I really haven't time, besides there is the postage which does mount up when there are so many, many letters to write.

I will try to answer all your questions in this letter and send it to Miss Pearson, your teacher, for you all.

Sister Mary died a few years ago. . . . Carrie and Grace are still living in South Dakota, Grace a few miles from De Smet and Carrie near Mount Rushmore. Perhaps you know about the stone heads carved on the top of Mount Rushmore.

Oh yes! The trees we planted grew and are still there. I saw them last year when we drove there to see the place again.

I saw Nellie Oleson again and am telling about it in the book I am writing now.

No! I never went to college, but I taught school. I never went back to Plum Creek.

I have a daughter. Her name is Rose Wilder Lane. She writes stories and perhaps your mothers have read some of them, and her articles in different magazines.

Laura Ingalls, the one who flies an airplane, is a distant cousin, I believe. I never saw her, but she and Rose Wilder Lane are friends.

We never had another dog like Jack, but I and Mr. Wilder have a big bulldog now, who is very nice. But he is more Mr. Wilder's dog than mine.

The place where we found Grace among the violets is still there.

Grace and Carrie were both married. They have no children and Carrie is a widow now.

The balls of fire that came down the stovepipe on Plum Creek were electricity. A real Blizzard is an electric storm.

Grace had Ma's shepherdess, the last I knew about it.

Mr. Edwards came to our house once more. I have told all about it in the book I have just finished. It will be published this fall. Its name is "The Long Winter."

When you are reading my stories don't overlook "Farmer Boy" for there is where I tell about Mr. Wilder when he was a boy. He is Almanzo of that book. I am Laura of the others and the stories are all true, you know. . . .

I am working now on the next book, and hope to have it ready for you next year but don't know what I will call it.

I want to thank you, each one, for writing to me. It was kind of you to let me know you liked my stories.

Wishing you all success in your school and a pleasant summer, I remain

Your friend,

Laura Ingalls Wilder


P.S. I never heard of Big Jerry after the R.R. was built. I really did not want to be an Indian and go away with them, but I liked the ponies and the papoose.

*I appreciate the kindness of the children*

JUNE 26, 1940

Dear Miss Pearson,

I really couldn't answer each one of these nice letters, but I thought it might please the children to write one letter for all of them. I am glad you prepared them so they will not be too greatly disappointed.

I get so many letters from schools and classes and individuals that it is a problem to find time to answer all and to get the next book written.

Especially as I do all my own housework and care for Mr. Wilder and myself. He is 83 and I am 73 so we do not move as quickly as we used to move. I am sure you will understand and know that I appreciate the kindness of the children in writing to me. . . .

Yours sincerely,

Laura Ingalls Wilder

*We did not think it best to leave*

*Laura and Manly never lost their love for De Smet. Aubrey Sherwood printed this letter in the* De Smet News.

[JUNE 1940]

Dear Mr. Sherwood,

Mr. Wilder and I were so disappointed not to be with you all on Old Settlers Day this year. The way our affairs were, we did not think it best to leave the place.

Please give our best regards to any friends who may inquire and perhaps we may be among those present next year. I hope you and yours are in the best of health and spirits. We are about as usual.

Yours sincerely,

Laura Ingalls Wilder

## *Thank you for a better contract*

*Eileen Tighe, the editor of* Woman's Day, *was a friend of Rose's. Rose wrote extensively for the magazine. The Long Winter* was *considered for serialization in* Woman's Day.

JULY 5, 1940

Dear Mr. Bye,

I am pleased that you eliminated motion picture percentage from the Harper contract, also I note that second serial rights have been retained. Thank you for a better contract.

You have my permission to offer "The Long Winter" to Miss Tighe for serializing. I agree with you that it would not be well to interfere with the Christmas offering of the book.

I leave all this in your hands to do as you think best.

Sincerely yours,

Laura Ingalls Wilder

## *Children clamored for more stories*

SEPTEMBER 16, 1940

Dear Miss Crawford,

You will forgive the delay in answering your letter, I am sure, when you know how busy I have been.

No sooner do I get one story off my hands than I begin on the next. And I was just finishing the long-hand writing of the one to follow The Long Winter, when your letter came.

I was glad to hear from you again and to know you are so much interested in my work.

The first of my books, Little House in the Big Woods, was written to preserve the stories that Pa used to tell Sister Mary and me when I was a child. I felt they were too good to be lost and I wrote them for Rose, not for publication. She insisted that I have them turned over to a publisher.

I had no intention of writing any more, but children clamored for more stories; and Harpers insisted, so I have gone on, from one book to the next, until I have completed the long-hand copy of the seventh. There is still one more to do in the series and I promise myself that will be the last of my writing. But Harpers are asking for an adult book when the series is finished and one never knows.

I do my writing in a little room in a corner between my bedroom to the east and the living room at the north. It is a very small room with a window to the west and one to the south, looking out into the big trees around the house. The room is filled with my desk and a table, couch and small bookcase. It is usually a mess with papers and books and mss. scattered around.

I write whenever I can snatch the time from housework, telephone, callers, Mr. Wilder and Ben, the bulldog. I may have written you that I do all my own work, in the old-fashioned way mostly. And the house has ten rooms.

The way I work is a mixture of remembering, inspiration and just plain plugging.

While I am working at housework I study about whatever I am writing. Sometimes I can't sleep for trying to place the right word in the right place and again I will wake with a perfectly turned phrase in my mind, to be remembered and written down next day . . .

## *"The Long Winter" should be out by now*

OCTOBER 21, 1940

Dear Mr. Bye,

I have your letters of the 10th and 17th regarding use of excerpts from "Little House on the Prairie" by Mr. Harry C. Bricker.

It is all right with me to charge a fee of $25.00 for the use of three thousand words in his textbook, if you think that is right. I trust such matters to your judgment. . . . Of course you are not overlooking Harpers. I think they have the rights on such sales.

By the way—"The Long Winter" should be out by now. October 2nd was to have been the publication date.

We are having wonderful autumn weather, with just enough frost to color the leaves in the woods.

Yours sincerely,

Laura Ingalls Wilder

## *There is a lot about Almanzo in "The Long Winter"*

*Cammie was a young boy from Pennsylvania.*

JANUARY 8, 1941

My Dear Cammie,

Thank you for writing me such a nice letter. I am glad you like my books so much and hope you will enjoy "By the Shores of Silver Lake" and "The Long Winter" as well as the others. There is a lot about Almanzo in "The Long Winter."

Grace and Carrie are well and so is Almanzo. He is my husband, Mr. Wilder, you know.

Sincerely your friend,

Laura Ingalls Wilder

The Ingalls family in De Smet, circa 1894. Seated: Caroline (Ma), Charles (Pa), and Mary. Standing: Carrie, Laura, and Grace. *(Laura Ingalls Wilder Home Association, Mansfield [LIWHA])*

Laura Ingalls Wilder on the porch of the Wilder house in the town of Mansfield, early 1900s. *(Herbert Hoover Presidential Library)*

Almanzo Wilder, early 1880s. *(Herbert Hoover Presidential Library)*

Images not credited are courtesy of the author.

Laura and Almanzo at their newly completed farmhouse, circa 1915. (*Collection of Meroe Camp*)

Rose Wilder in Kansas City, 1906. (*Herbert Hoover Presidential Library*)

Laura in the ravine on Rocky Ridge Farm.

The house on Rocky
Ridge Farm, circa 1914.
*(Herbert Hoover Presidential
Library)*

The farmhouse
parlor, World
War I era. *(Herbert
Hoover Presidential
Library)*

The sleeping porch, later
the bedroom and writing
office of Rose Wilder
Lane, circa 1914. *(Herbert
Hoover Presidential Library)*

One of Laura's frequent letters to Almanzo, written while en route to California, 1925. *(Herbert Hoover Presidential Library)*

A postcard view of one of the California mountain roads that frightened Laura. *(Herbert Hoover Presidential Library)*

Almanzo and a Morgan horse on Rocky Ridge Farm, 1925. *(Herbert Hoover Presidential Library)*

Laura and Almanzo, 1933. *(The State Historical Society of Missouri)*

Almanzo, Neta Seal, and Laura in Yellowstone National Park, May 1938.

Almanzo and Laura in the *De Smet News* office, June 1939. *(Photo by Aubrey Sherwood)*

Al Turner in 1937.

John Turner studying
in Paris, 1937.

Rose Wilder Lane,
circa 1940.

Laura at seventy, September 1937. (*Burton Historical
Collection, Detroit Public Library*)

Rocky Ridge Farm, October 1944. (*Burton Historical
Collection, Detroit Public Library*)

Aubrey Sherwood at his *De Smet News* office, circa 1950. (*Laura Ingalls Wilder Memorial Society*)

*Right:* Laura's inscription in one of Nancy Sorenson's books.

Nancy and Alvilda Sorenson, South Dakota correspondents of Laura Ingalls Wilder.

Dear Nancy Lee

This is a true story of a little boy who grew to be a man and married Laura of the Little House stories.

They lived then on the prairies of Kingsbury County, South Dakota, that your Father and Mother know so well.

Laura Ingalls Wilder

Jack and Mary discuss the Little House books in the Wilder Room of the Pomona Public Library, 1950.

Garth Williams in his Aspen, Colorado, studio, 1950s. (*Dilys Williams Collection*)

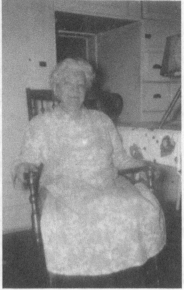

Laura in her rocking chair,
March 1953.

Laura's desk in her writing study at Rocky
Ridge Farm. (LIWHA)

At the Laura Ingalls Wilder Library in Mansfield, 1953. (LIWHA)

## Something very worthwhile

APRIL 14, 1941

My dear Mrs. Newman,

I thank you so much for your letter. You know, when one is seventy-four years old one begins to feel a little lonely, even when not alone and your words of appreciation warmed my heart. I am indeed glad if my stories of the long ago have helped you in any way, and it makes me happy that you too love Pa and Ma. There was something very worthwhile about those times and the people of their generation.

Sincerely, your friend,

Laura Ingalls Wilder

## I hope you had a happy Easter day

*The Newman family corresponded with Laura during the 1940s.*

APRIL 14, 1941

My Dear Patricia [Newman],

Such a pretty Easter card and so sweet of you to send it to me. I thank you a lot.

I hope you had a happy Easter day and many Easter eggs and cards.

Thanking you again for your thought of me, I am

Your friend,

Laura Ingalls Wilder

## *The Ozarks are beautiful at this time of year*

*A request for translation of a Little House book arrived at George
Bye's office from Sweden. Because of World War II, it was not
feasible to proceed with foreign editions until peacetime.*

**APRIL 15, 1941**
Dear Mr. Bye,

Whatever you think best to do about Swedish publication of "The
Long Winter" will be satisfactory to me. . . . I think, though, that
your office is entitled to something for your trouble in the transac-
tion.

There will be another book ready for publication this fall, but if it
will be in time to be serialized first I do not know.

I work so slowly and at times other things interfere with my writing so I seldom make any promises as to time.

I suppose if it seems more profitable we could sell it as a serial and
postpone the book publication a year. I will make it ready as soon as
possible and then we can decide about that.

Our spring has been very cold and dry, but at last we have had
rain. Fruit trees and flowering shrubs are in bloom and new leaves are
on the forest trees.

The Ozarks are beautiful at this time of year.

With kindest regards,

Sincerely yours,

Laura Ingalls Wilder

## *You and Rose are certainly in sympathy*

*Mayfair Togs, a national clothing manufacturer, proposed an ap-
parel line based on descriptions in the Little House books. The plan*

*included distribution coast-to-coast. Alongside the clothing, The Long Winter would be displayed for sale. George Bye reported the proposal, along with the news that "we visited Rose . . . and she told us of a little dirt road where there were some red trilliums growing wild. . . . I dug up a dozen of them, using a screwdriver!"*

MAY 15, 1941

Dear Mr. Bye,

Your letter just came and of course I am willing that the clothing manufacturer should use "The Long Winter" in a publicity stunt.

Seems crazy for them but fine for Long Winter. I am glad you gave them permission.

You and Rose are certainly in sympathy if you would dig up wild flowers, especially with the tools you had.

The hillside slope west of the house has been a mat of wild pansy blooms all spring. Rose says they do not grow there. These are not wild violets but regular pansies with two colors on each blossom and only a little smaller than the cultivated ones.

Sincerely yours,

Laura Ingalls Wilder

*I am sure Harpers are making a good thing on these books*

JULY 3, 1941

Dear Mr. Bye,

I am sending you today, by express, three copies of my ms. Little Town on the Prairie. I hope you will pardon the use of a second hand envelop, as I cannot get that size here.

Harpers is, of course, expecting this book, but I think they should give me a better contract than for The Long Winter or else a new contract for Farmer Boy, which I practically gave them.

I am sure Harpers are making a good thing on these books taken all together and naturally I want a fair share.

I am trusting you to do your best with the contract. . . .

By the way, whatever became of the deal with Mayfair Togs?

Yours sincerely,

Laura Ingalls Wilder

## *I hope you enjoyed reading Little Town*

Little Town on the Prairie *reached Harper & Brothers in July 1941. Ursula Nordstrom declared that it "seems to me to be absolutely perfect. Sincerely, it is beautiful. When Nellie Oleson came into the school I almost wept with pleasure and anticipation. Congratulations on a beautiful piece of work." A 15 percent royalty was negotiated "without much of a struggle," according to George Bye.*

JULY 15, 1941

Dear Mr. Bye,

Attached you will find the contract with Harpers, signed. I am pleased with it and the adjustment on Farmer Boy and appreciate very much the good job you have done.

I hope you enjoyed reading Little Town and that it was up to standard.

Rose writes me that the book market is bad, but I'm hoping not too bad.

Sincerely yours,

Laura Ingalls Wilder

## The days of Little Town were great days

*George Bye continued to praise* Little Town on the Prairie. *As Eleanor Roosevelt's literary agent, he was entertained at her social events. He once persuaded Rose to accompany him to the Roosevelt home in Hyde Park; she attended out of curiosity. In July 1941, Bye wrote to Laura that "I have covered a lot of ground in the last few days, going from a picnic given by Mrs. Roosevelt in Hyde Park last Saturday to another picnic given by a Connecticut park commissioner on Mohawk Mountain last night. . . . I found myself telling incidents from 'Little Town on the Prairie.'"*

AUGUST 1, 1941

Dear Mr. Bye,

I am pleased that you found my Little Town so interesting and flattered that you thought some of my anecdotes good enough to repeat. . . .

Ask Rose to tell you the one I told at Detroit Book Fair about the easterner who saw his first Dakota mirage and took a short walk to breakfast to the lake he saw from the hotel. Like all my stories, it is true.

Harpers have not been fair in making the adjustment on Farmer Boy. Like you, I think it is not so much the money for there is not much difference in that, but it is the recognition of the credit due the book. However, what is done is done, and we'll let it go at that.

The days of Little Town were great days and at times I have a strong feeling of nostalgia for them.

Sincerely yours,

Laura Ingalls Wilder

## *Greatly disappointed not to be at De Smet*

*In addition to the Wilders, Aubrey Sherwood befriended Harvey Dunn, a renowned magazine illustrator, teacher, and painter of the prairie. In 1938 Rose and Dunn met at the New York City Society of South Dakotans, where both gave speeches. Dunn was reared near De Smet. His uncle, Nate Dow, married Grace Ingalls. The artist made regular summer visits to the family homestead from his New Jersey studio. "Harvey Dunn has done a great thing in his paintings and it does seem as though they and my stories should be connected in some way. I should be proud to have our names connected because of our work," Laura remarked. Dunn admired her books, saying, "I would have been proud to illustrate the Little House books."*

AUGUST 20, 1941

Dear Mr. Sherwood,

Thank you so much for the photos, and the copies of the De Smet News. I am sending one on to Rose today.

Rose is at her place in Conn. Likely this is the reason she did not attend the S.D. Meeting in New York.

Mr. Wilder and I were greatly disappointed not to be at De Smet for the Old Settler's reunion this spring. We had fully intended to be with you on that date, but Mr. Wilder was not able to go. He has been in poor health all summer and is just now on his way to recovery. We hope for better fortune next year.

I have had one book published since Silver Lake. It is called "The Long Winter" and goes on with the story. Still true as to what it tells but not pretending to tell all the history.

Another will be published this fall. The title is "Little Town on the Prairie" going on with the story of De Smet.

The Long Winter was very well received and my publishers think

"Little Town" is even better. I think you would enjoy them for they seem to please grownups fully as much as children.

The De Smet News was very interesting though we do not find many names we remember.

Again thanking you for the pictures and the papers, we remain Yours sincerely,

Mr. and Mrs. A. J. Wilder

## I haven't decided on a title for the book yet

*By the end of 1941, the outline for* These Happy Golden Years *was complete. Laura previewed the book in her response to a reader.*

NOVEMBER 4, 1941

Dear Miss Bracket,

In the next book Laura really grows up.

She teaches her first school in the winter twelve miles from home, walking from her boarding place one half mile across the prairie to the schoolhouse which is an abandoned claim shanty.

Mary comes home for her vacation the next summer and Laura again sews for a dressmaker in town.

Refusing to teach the Brewster school again, she goes to school the winter following.

In the spring she teaches a country school near the claim.

She takes sleigh rides with Almanzo in the winter and buggy rides in the summer while he breaks horses and colts to drive.

She goes with Almanzo to singing school where they are taught singing in the old fashioned way. On the way home from singing school they become engaged.

The winter afterward Laura goes to school in the new graded school and the following spring she teaches school once more and for the last time.

Mary comes home again that summer.

Laura and Almanzo are married and Laura goes to live in another little house on a claim.

None of this sounds very exciting but it will give you something to work on and I hope it is what you want. I haven't decided on a title for the book yet.

Sincerely yours,
Laura Ingalls Wilder

*Have you seen the book in its published form?*

*The dust jacket for* Little Town on the Prairie, *with artwork by Mildred Boyle, caused a minor brouhaha. Laura's cheeks were enhanced by a brightly colored circular blush. Laura made one of her few complaints about illustration in the Little House books.*

NOVEMBER 19, 1941
Dear Mr. Bye,

Is Harper overlooking the payment of balance due on publication of "Little Town on the Prairie"?

They did before, you remember. If so please remind them. Not that I especially need the money, but I like to have it.

Have you seen the book in its published form? It is quite striking, especially Laura's cheeks, for which Miss Nordstrom apologized and promised correction in next printing.

We are having an unusually warm, wet season. Just now it seems to have set in for a Thanksgiving storm, but if it storms too badly, Mr. W. and I shall say we don't believe in celebrating the 20th anyway, and put off our excursion to the city in search of turkey until the 27th.

Wishing you a happy Thanksgiving, if it is still in the future in your state, I remain

Sincerely yours,

Laura Ingalls Wilder

## If Rose has any objection

*George Bye sent news that "the State of Ohio wanted to buy a special edition of Little House—running to three thousand five hundred copies—for public school use. . . . Harper's figure they can produce the book cheaply and sell it to The State of Ohio at 96 cents a copy. . . . The big point, according to Miss Nordstrom, is that this opens up a new field . . . and they will be able to go out after new states."*

DECEMBER 15, 1941

Dear Mr. Bye,

The news in your letter was certainly a surprise. It seems to me a very good proposition, but as usual I depend on your judgment. . . .

If Rose has any objection, you will no doubt hear from her. If she has I will expect you to consider it as you no doubt intended when you sent her a copy of your letter. Whatever you and she decide will have my approval.

Wishing you and yours a pleasant holiday season I am

Yours sincerely,

Laura Ingalls Wilder

## I was nearly swamped by my Christmas mail

*Signed copies of Little House books were cherished by Nancy Lee Sorenson. In Laura's reply to another letter from Alvilda Sorenson, she mentions the loss of her sister Grace Dow, who died in Manchester, South Dakota, on November 10, 1941.*

DECEMBER 29, 1941

Dear Mrs. Sorenson,

I hope your books reached you safely. Your letter should have been answered sooner, but hope you will excuse the delay for I was nearly swamped by my Christmas mail.

What a sorrow your little girl's deafness must have been to you and how proud you must be now that she has so far overcome the handicap. Please give her my love.

The death of my sister, Mrs. Dow, saddened the holidays for me. There are only sister Carrie and myself left of our family now. Because of Mr. Wilder's illness we were unable to make our usual trip to S. Dakota last summer, to see my sisters. Carrie lives in the Black Hills, near Mount Rushmore.

Wishing you and yours a Happy New Year, I am

Yours sincerely,

Laura Ingalls Wilder

## *You ask if Laura was a real person*

FEBRUARY 28, 1942

Stone School—4th Grade

Saginaw, Michigan

Dear Children,

I'm sorry to have been so long in answering your letter. Please excuse the delay, I have been very busy.

You ask if Laura was a real person. She was.

I was the Laura you have been reading about and all the books are true stories about me and my parents and sisters. All real people and things happened to them, just as I have told about in the books.

Mary never got her eyesight back, but she learned to do many things, besides getting her college education at the Iowa College for the Blind.

I am writing another book now that I hope to have ready for you next fall. Its name is not chosen yet, so I can't tell you what it will be called.

Your friend,

Laura Ingalls Wilder

## We used to drive that old road

JULY 29, 1942

Dear Mr. Sherwood,

Many thanks for the copy of The De Smet News and your kindness in vouching for the truth of my little books. I appreciate it.

Your description of the old prairie road to Lakes Henry and Thompson made both Mr. Wilder and myself very homesick for De Smet. We used to drive that old road on Sunday afternoon in our courting days.

We are well as usual and wish the best to you and yours,

Sincerely,

Laura Ingalls Wilder

## Begging your pardon for being a nuisance

*Aubrey Sherwood's advocacy for De Smet's history and famous folk was a frequent topic in his newspaper editorials and feature stories. Some wags, when picking up their weekly* De Smet News, *asked: "Wonder what Laura Wilder and Harvey Dunn are up to this week?" Aubrey never relented; in essence, he published a journalistic history of both creative former residents. The correct name Laura sought in this letter was Lake Kampeska.*

AUGUST 17, 1942

Dear Mr. Sherwood,

"One good turn deserves another," they say, and as you already have done the one I am asking for another, twisting the old words to my advantage.

There is, or was, a lake near Watertown—Lake Kampeskie—but I am not sure of the spelling and have no map showing the lake.

I will appreciate it very much if you will give me the correct spelling of the lake's name.

Also if you would send me another copy of your paper, the same date as the one you did send—vouching for the truth in my books and telling of the Old Prairie Road.

I sent it on to Rose neglecting to note the date and I would like to have a copy to keep.

Am enclosing 10 cents for the paper and begging your pardon for being a nuisance.

Yours sincerely,

Laura Ingalls Wilder

## The best I can do and all I can say

*The following three letters deal with the manuscript of* These Happy Golden Years. *The late submission precluded a pre-Christmas release date for the final volume of the series. In her letter of September 28, 1942, Laura makes an allusion to America's already heavy involvement in World War II. By spring 1943, when* Golden Years *appeared, publishers were dealing with rationed paper.*

SEPTEMBER 10, 1942

Dear Mr. Spock,

I am sorry I have made everyone so much trouble, but I could not get my new story ready any sooner.

Have written Miss Nordstrom that it should be ready for her in a few days and I hope it will be in time for this fall printing.

Neither Mrs. Lane nor I have an extra copy of mss. She will have it typed there for me and turn it over to your office as soon as possible.

That is the best I can do and all I can say.

Sincerely,

Laura Ingalls Wilder

## *Rose may be a little partial to my work*

SEPTEMBER 25, 1942

Dear Mr. Bye,

I am anxiously waiting for my carbon copy of my mss. which must by now be completely typed. Please send it to me at once as I need time to study it a bit before reading proof.

The haste and resulting confusion has left me somewhat vague as to a few details that need correcting and my hurry will not be over until the proof is read.

I do hope you will enjoy reading the book, but you must not expect too much of it, for Rose may be a little partial to my work.

Do please hurry to me the copy of the manuscript.

Sincerely yours,

Laura Ingalls Wilder

## *This children's story is now complete in eight volumes*

SEPTEMBER 28, 1942

Dear Mr. Bye,

Attached you will find the signed Harper contract. Considering the situation confronting us all, I think it is a very good contract. Thank you for your promptness in attending to the business.

I am eager to hear your judgment of the book when you have finished reading it. This children's story is now complete in eight volumes.

Sincerely yours,
Laura Ingalls Wilder

## I hope you get a copy for Christmas

*Years after Mary Phraner Warren asked Laura Ingalls Wilder about sourdough bread, she became the author of twenty-three books. She is among many who became inspired to authorship because of the Little House books.*

NOVEMBER 12, 1942
My Dear Mary,

I am glad that you and your sisters like my books. I have written the "one more book" you want to finish the series. It will be published this month and its title is "These Happy Golden Years." I hope you get a copy for Christmas and that you like it as well as the others.

Sour dough was really a substitute for sour milk and was used in cooking just as sour milk was.

We had no baking powder in those days and used soda with sour milk or sour dough. To start it, Mother mixed warm water and flour, a pinch of salt and a little sugar, making it about as thick as gravy. This was kept in a warm place until it soured. It was then used as sour milk to make the biscuit, but a little of it was left to help start the next batch souring. Enough more water and flour, sugar and salt were added to make enough for use again.

We used it only when we had no milk, which of course is better.

With love,
Sincerely yours,
Laura Ingalls Wilder

## *He is such a cute little rascal*

*Many of the children who wrote enclosed photos of themselves with their letters. Laura saved them all.*

JANUARY 10, 1943

My Dear Erma,

Thank you so much for your Christmas card and especially for the photo of yourself and your darling puppy. He is such a cute little rascal and I'm sure you love each other a great deal.

I would have written you sooner, but have had a lame hand and could not use it to write.

I wish for you a very happy New Year.

Sincerely your friend,

Laura Ingalls Wilder

## *Our rubber is good, our gas is short*

*Laura's wartime letters were peppered with references to the home front situation, including rationing.*

FEBRUARY 12, 1943

Dear Mrs. Masoner,

I was very much surprised and pleased to find the photo of you in your letter. Thank you a lot. It was a sweet thought. The picture is lovely and looks exactly like you. It seems as though you would look up and speak in a moment. I am proud to have my book photographed with you.

Glad you like my "By the Shores of Silver Lake" and am interested to know if you think my descriptive powers are as good in "The Long Winter." . . .

I find myself constructing sentences and situations in what might be another book, but I hope I will not be driven to write it, for there is really more than I should do without that.

There is so much to be done and "The bird of time has just a little while to flutter and the bird is on the wing."

I would like to see you again, but while our rubber [car tires] is good, our gas is short. Wishing you success in [the] "Writer's Digest" contest, I remain

Sincerely your friend,

Laura Ingalls Wilder

## *I appreciate the good words you have given*

FEBRUARY 23, 1943

Dear Mr. Sherwood,

This is a letter I had expected to write last fall and although it is somewhat late to answer yours of August 19, 1942, I still wish to thank you for telling me how to spell Lake Kampeska.

Under separate cover I am sending you my latest book, which I expected to be published last November. "These Happy Golden Years" is the last of the series of eight . . . and is the end of the story.

Like the others, this book is true to facts, with touches of fiction here and there to help the interest. Some names are fictitious for which you will see the reasons. I hope you will like Golden Years.

Have you seen Rose's latest book, "The Discovery of Freedom"? It was published in January by the John Day Company Inc., 40 East 49th Street, New York City. I think it is the best work she has ever done and it is fascinating reading.

Mr. Wilder and I are in the best of health and wish to be remem-

bered to any friends who may inquire. With kindest regards to yourself and family, I am

Yours sincerely,

Laura Ingalls Wilder

P.S. I appreciate the good words you have given my little books, and
any time I can return the favor let me know. L.I.W.


## *It seems that my mind is tired*

MARCH 1, 1943

Dear Miss Nordstrom,

. . . It seems that my mind is tired. It refuses to go to work again
on a new book, which is mostly floating around in disconnected anecdotes. But after I have recovered from making out income tax reports and
other first of the year business, I will see if I can make the new book jell.

Sincerely yours,

Laura Ingalls Wilder


## *I am getting some lovely fan letters*

APRIL 3, 1943

Dear Miss Nordstrom,

The book for Mrs. Wallace arrived yesterday and today I am sending it on its way, autographed. This is our first mail out.

Is "Happy Golden Years" getting good reviews? I am getting some
lovely fan letters . . . really fine ones. . . .

Rose writes me she thinks you did a fine job on the book which
pleases me, for Rose is nothing if not critical.

With kindest regards,

Laura Ingalls Wilder

## *The book is certainly being well received*

*These Happy Golden Years sold five thousand copies within six weeks of its publication in March 1943. Ursula Nordstrom begged the decision makers at Harper to reprint ten thousand copies immediately. She pled her case well, even citing "Rose Wilder Lane's attitude toward the House." But the large reprint was impossible; publishers were contending with wartime paper shortages.*

APRIL 16, 1943

Dear Miss Nordstrom,

I must write you a small note to say how pleased I am with the reviews of These Happy Golden Years, and to thank you for sending them.

The book is certainly being well received. Already letters are coming to me from children and teachers who have read it.

This is house-cleaning time so that I am very busy, but thankful I can still do my own work when help is so hard to get.

Sincerely,

Laura Ingalls Wilder

## *I will tell you in my rambling way*

*Ursula Nordstrom reported that Irene Smith of the Brooklyn Public Library was writing a profile of Laura's life and books for the Horn Book Magazine's upcoming September 1943 issue. Laura responded with information and anecdotes about her family and her current daily life.*

APRIL 26, 1943

Dear Miss Nordstrom,

It is great news that the Little House books will be given first place in the Horn Book. I will tell you in my rambling way what I think may be useful to Miss Smith and you can choose what you want from it.

Mary graduated from the Iowa College for the Blind in 1889. Her part in an entertainment given by her literary society was an essay entitled "Memory." You may recollect, in the books, I told of Mary's remarkable memory.

In the graduating exercises on June 10th, Mary read another essay, "Bide a Wee, and Dinna Weary," which showed the influence of Pa's old Scots songs. After her graduation Mary lived happily at home with her music, and her raised print and Braille books. She knitted and sewed and took part in the housework.

Pa and Ma and the girls lived for some years in the little house on the homestead, but later Pa built a house in the residential part of town and they moved there to be nearer church and neighbors.

Grace married and lived near the little town of Manchester, seven miles west of De Smet.

Carrie married later. Her home was and still is, at Keystone, in the Black Hills of South Dakota, near the foot of Mount Rushmore where the faces of four of our presidents are carved in the rock of the mountaintop. Carrie is a widow now, and she and I are the only ones of our family still living.

I never saw Nellie Oleson after she went east to N.Y. as told in "Golden Years." I heard some years later that she married and went with her husband to Washington state; that there the husband was arrested and sent to the penitentiary for embezzlement, and that Nellie died a few years later.

Cap Garland went his carefree, happy way for five years after Almanzo married. He was killed in an explosion of the boiler of a steam threshing machine.

Miss Wilder married and lived in Louisiana, where she is buried. Almanzo is the only one of his immediate family now living.

Almanzo and I came here in September of 1894 in a covered wagon and bought a rough forty acres of land, with five acres cleared of timber and a one room log house, where the only way for the light to enter with the door shut was through cracks between the logs where the chinking had fallen out. Another little house.

Through the years we added to our land until we owned 185 acres, cleared except for wood lots left to furnish wood to burn and fence posts.

We built the ten room Rocky Ridge farm house of materials from the farm itself, except for the pine siding on the outside. The oak frame of the house, oak paneling, solid oak beams and stairs in the living room are from our own timber, hand finished, and an enormous fireplace made of three large rocks dug from our own ground. The chimney is built of our own rocks.

There was also another house on the east end of the farm and another small house on the north.

We were very proud of our dairy and poultry farm, our Jersey cows and Leghorn hens.

We still call the place Rocky Ridge Farm but we are not really farming now. It has been increasingly difficult to get help and lately to do so at wages the farm could pay, so we have sold the other two houses and land to go with them. Now we have only 130 acres of land and the one house.

Mr. Wilder is 86 years old and I am 76. We can no longer do the work of a farm as you can see. Our land is now all in pasture and meadow, which we rent, and a larger timber lot. Mr. Wilder cares for our four milk goats and two calves in the morning, while I prepare our seven o'clock breakfast. Then he works in the garden or the shop where he loves to tinker, while I do up the housework and go down the hill to the mailbox for the mail. I take our big brown-and-white spotted bulldog with me and we go for a half mile walk before we come back.

After that the day is always full, for I do all my own work and to care for a ten room house is no small job. Besides the cooking and baking there is churning to do. I make all our own butter from cream off the goats milk. There is always sewing on hand and my mending is seldom finished. The town is near and I must go to church, aid society, socials, be entertained and entertain my friends now and then.

When Almanzo and the car go anywhere, I always go along, for I love to go for a drive as well as I ever did. We don't drive horses now. We drive a Chrysler.

And when the day is over and evening comes we read our papers and magazines or play a game of cribbage. If we want music, we turn on the radio. . . .

## *She is a better writer than I am*

MAY 10, 1943

My Dear Mrs. Phraner,

Your curiosity is justified but your guess is wrong. Rose Wilder Lane is my daughter. Our only child.

She wrote "Let the Hurricane Roar" before I had planned the Little House series. While her descriptions of storms and grasshoppers are true to facts, her story is fiction. She had of course learned of those things from us. Her use of family names and characters came naturally.

My series of stories, as you know, are literally true, names, dates, places, every anecdote and much of the conversation are historically and actually true.

When you read anything written by Rose Wilder Lane, just think of her as my little girl grown up.

Have you seen her latest book, "The Discovery of Freedom"? It was published in January.

I am glad you like my "Golden Years."

Sister Carrie writes me that after she read the book it seemed that she was back in those times again and all that had happened since was a dream.

I considered it a great tribute to the truth of the picture I had drawn.

I hope you will read some of Rose's books. She is a better writer than I am, though our style of writing is very similar.

Please give my love to Mary.

Sincerely yours,

Laura Ingalls Wilder

## *I am still surprised at the success the books have had*

These Happy Golden Years *won the* New York Herald Tribune's *Spring Book Festival Award for a book published for older children. "Hearty congratulations," wrote George Bye. "It was about time." Despite the accolade and a $200 prize, Laura was not eager to resume writing.*

MAY 10, 1943

Dear Mr. Bye,

It pleases me that you think "These Happy Golden Years" so attractive. I do think the book is a fine piece of work by artists and publisher.

Thank you for your wire of congratulations for its winning the award of the Herald Tribune and also your kind prediction of the success of the series. I am still surprised at the success the books have had so far.

It is not possible for me to do the short story you suggest as I have no contact with the working girls in industry today. I have no knowledge of their problems except through magazine stories and I think to write convincingly one must have a firsthand knowledge of their subject.

I believe Rose could write this story for you. She had the knowledge that I lack and is also familiar with the old fashioned, homely philosophy that is spread through the Little House series. Also she knows my character and disposition, and how I would react to situations.

Her name on the story would be worth more to your "exchequer" than mine. . . .

I don't know what to say about my writing more. I have thought that "Golden Years" was my last; that I would spend what is left of my life in living, not writing about it, but a story keeps stirring around in my mind and if it pesters me enough I may write it down and send it to you sometime in the future.

I appreciate the good work you have done for my books and thank you again for your kind appreciation of them.

Sincerely,

Laura Ingalls Wilder

*I am sending a collection of pictures for you to choose from*

> The Horn Book *article included an array of Laura's family photographs.*

MAY 22, 1943

Dear Miss Nordstrom,

You must think I am a long time in answering your request for pictures. I know it, but . . .

I sent Pa's fiddle to a neighboring town to get its picture taken and here it is at last. There is no one I could get to take a picture of the house so I am sending you some old ones. The furniture has been changed but the house inside and out is the same. The large picture of the house looks bare with the leaves off the trees so I am sending a small one taken last summer when the Scribblers Club of Topeka descended on me bringing a camera.

I am sending a collection of pictures for you to choose from. Not knowing what you might want I send those I thought may be interesting.

The [Ingalls] family group picture is so faded I feared I might lose it altogether so had a copy made some time ago. But the copy is so dark it does not look right and I am sending the original and copy both. . . .

You will note on the back of Mary's picture that it was taken in Vinton, Iowa, while she was going to college there. Mary's picture and Almanzo's were taken about the same time as mine that you used at the head of the circular. You can see how we all looked at the same time.

You still have that picture of me to use again if you wish. Please be very careful of these pictures and return them to me when you are through with them and the one of me, too, if it is still with you. There is no charge for the use of these pictures of course, but the expense of photographing the fiddle was three dollars. You might send me that amount if you wish, as you suggested.

I hope you will find what you want among these pictures and that you have not been bothered by their lateness.

With best wishes,
Laura Ingalls Wilder

*Please do give my love to Nancy Lee*

Alvilda Sorenson wrote to praise *These Happy Golden Years.* "Again, Mrs. Wilder," she wrote, "let us thank you genuinely for the lovely stories you and Almanzo brought into our home." Mrs.

*Sorenson also shared news of her hearing-impaired daughter, Nancy, who was successfully mainstreamed into her fifth-grade classroom.*

MAY 24, 1943

Dear Mrs. Sorenson,

It was nice to hear from you again and to learn that little Nancy Lee has done so wonderfully well in school. She must be a remarkable child.

I am so glad that you all enjoyed "These Happy Golden Years" and that it helped cheer the children in their illness. Please do give my love to Nancy Lee.

I am writing a note to Sylvia and Ann Rae today.

With kindest regards I am

Yours sincerely,

Laura Ingalls Wilder

*I am always surprised when one of my books is a success*

MAY 26, 1943

Dear Miss Nordstrom,

Your letter with the Herald Tribune check arrived. Thank you for everything. It is grand that "These Happy Golden Years" received the award.

I am always surprised when one of my books is a success and I'm glad that it is selling so well.

It pleases me that you dislike Nellie Oleson so much, which I suppose is un-Christian, too. She was a hateful girl.

By now you have the pictures. I do hope you can use some of them.

Sincerely yours,

Laura Ingalls Wilder

## *My sisters and I did have lots of good times*

*Letters from children in Detroit, Michigan, prompted this reply.*

JUNE 6, 1943
Longfellow School
Dear Children,

I thank you all for your nice letters and will try to answer your questions....

I am seventy six years old. Carrie is three years younger. She and I are the only ones of our family still living.

The bulldog, Jack, died long ago, but I have another bulldog. His name is Ben.

We have nine goats and two cows, but no cats.

My middle name is Elizabeth.

My sisters and I did have lots of good times when I was a little girl. It was fun sliding down the straw stack and going fishing. Whenever we felt like it, Mary and I would go down to the creek and catch a mess of fish for dinner, but I don't remember how many we caught.

It was many years ago when Pa built the Little House on the Prairie and I should think it would be gone now.

Sister Carrie has the china shepherdess.

I am sorry but I can't sell the books. They will have to be bought at a bookstore or from Harpers. I am glad you like my stories and think it kind of your teacher to read them to you. It is fine that you have such a nice teacher and that you like her so much. I am sure you enjoy her stories about Mexico and seeing the beautiful things she brought from there.

Your letters were so nicely written I shall keep them carefully. With love,

Sincerely your friend
Laura Ingalls Wilder

## We are safe from floods

JULY 6, 1943

Dear Miss Nordstrom,

Thinking you might be interested in the enclosed letter, I am sending it. What Mrs. May wants seems to be in line with material I have sent you.

Glad you like the pictures.

Rocky Ridge Farm was not in the flood area. The rushing waters swirled on every side of our mountain peak while rain poured down on us to run swiftly off the high land and raise the rivers still higher. We are on the very peak. Rain that falls on our Rocky Ridge runs from the north to join the waters of the Gasconade river, while the rain from the south goes on south to the White River.

We are safe from floods but our gardens were simply drowned and crops could not be planted until late. We are having hot, dry weather now.

I hope you are not suffering too much from the eastern heat wave.

Sincerely yours,

Laura Ingalls Wilder

## Canning berries and garden stuff

*Laura and Rose offered information for Irene Smith's article in the Horn Book Magazine.*

JULY 20, 1943

Dear Miss Nordstrom,

Sorry to have delayed so long in answering your letter. I have been very busy and canning berries and garden stuff. But the real reason for my slowness has been the difficulty of filling in detail that might be of use to you.

There are of course a number of books that might be written of our ups and downs, of sickness and loss, of gains and successes, for as with everyone our life has been full of such things, but for purpose of Miss Smith's article, they would go too far afield.

I am sorry I have no large envelop, but must crowd this into a smaller one. Hoping it will be in time for Miss Smith, I will mail it at once.

Yours sincerely,

Laura Ingalls Wilder

## *It is like getting a letter from home*

*In 1942 Harper & Brothers printed a four-page promotional brochure on the Little House books. Biographical information and photos of Laura at seventeen and seventy were included, to answer questions about her life and requests for photos. Aubrey Sherwood used material and book jackets from the brochure for articles in the De Smet News.*

NOVEMBER 22, 1943

Dear Mr. Sherwood,

Many thanks for the Nov. 11th copy of the "News" just received. Although most of the names mentioned are strange to us, still it is like getting a letter from home.

I thank you too for your nice feature on my books and family and am looking forward to seeing the next issue featuring my books as a series with reproductions of the covers.

Please send a copy of that number to Rose Wilder Lane, Route 4, Box 42, Danbury, Connecticut, and also one to Ralph O. Watters, editor, Mansfield Mirror, Mansfield, Missouri.

Mr. Wilder and I are as well as usual and wish you and yours a Merry Christmas and a Happy New Year.

Yours sincerely,

Laura Ingalls Wilder

# Laura Ingalls Wilder

LAURA INGALLS WILDER was born in the log cabin described in *Little House in the Big Woods*. That is to say, the Big Woods of Wisconsin near Lake Pepin in the Mississippi. Her earliest memories are of a venture into the Indian Territory of Kansas. She was about three then, and Pa was a pioneer hunter, trapper and Indian fighter. However, he soon took his family back to Wisconsin, and at that point the story of *Little House in the Big Woods* begins. From Wisconsin the Ingalls traveled west by covered wagon, through Minnesota and Iowa to Dakota Territory, where Pa finally settled. For a year Pa was a railroad man and the family spent one winter by the shores of Silver Lake, sixty miles from the nearest neighbor. Pa hunted and trapped and guarded property of the Chicago-Northwestern, then building, from outlaws in the Black Hills. In the spring Pa put up the first building on the new town-site, founded the Congregational Church, served as Justice of the Peace for a while, and so was one of the founders of what later became De Smet, South Dakota. The Ingalls' first winter there was the remembered "Hard Winter" of 1880-81, when the tiny settlement of scarcely one hundred persons was cut off from all outside help. There were no trains from October to May. When all the supplies were used up and there was no light, food or fuel, Almanzo Wilder and another boy risked their lives to drive forty miles across the prairie to get a little seed wheat from a farmer known to have some; women ground it in coffee-mills and the people lived on small rations of it made into mush.

Beginning in 1942, Harper and Brothers printed a four page brochure on Laura Ingalls Wilder and her books. Thousands were sent to readers by Harper and by Laura herself.

# CHAPTER 5

# THE LAST GOLDEN YEARS
## (1944–1949)

Laura and Manly at home on Rocky Ridge Farm, May 1947.

*As Laura neared eighty and Manly neared ninety, they were con-*
*tent with their peaceful retired life on Rocky Ridge. The farming*
*years were over. Laura's writing years were over. They had finally*
*reached a safe haven of financial security.*

*Laura was asked continually to write another book. But she*
*considered her story told. And her collaborator, Rose, was finished*
*with fiction. Rose was committed to write what Laura called*
*"American propaganda," referring to Rose's passion for a return to*

small government, absolute individual freedom, and a life free of interference by politicians in office. Those were underlying political subtexts that flowed as philosophical threads through the Little House books.

The closing years of Laura and Manly's companionable life together were sweet ones. As Laura wrote of their early married life, "It was a carefree, happy time, for two people thoroughly in sympathy can do pretty much as they like." It was always that way for Laura and Manly, and their years together ended as they had started.

## We have shared so many nearly alike experiences

JANUARY 28, 1944

Dear Miss Redmond,

Your letter is very amusing and interesting. There certainly should be a bond of sympathy and understanding between us, we have shared so many nearly alike experiences.

The Hambletonians were grand old horses, our favorites after the Morgans. They could travel so beautifully and swiftly. Mr. Wilder and I often bewail the fact that there are no such horses in these mechanized days.

I am sorry but I cannot tell you how to make those vanity cakes that Ma used to make.

It seems strange that I never learned to make them. I know they were mostly egg and were fried in deep fat as doughnuts are. They were to be eaten hot. Were crunchy, not sweetened and were so light, really a bubble that they seemed almost nothing in one's mouth. They were yellow in color when fried. I suppose the egg yolks helped in their coloring. They simply puffed up when fried until they were nothing but a bubble. *Vanity* cakes.

I have thought I would experiment and try to make some, but

never have. Mother was gone when I got around to wanting to know and my sisters did not know. Sorry!

Sincerely yours,
Laura Ingalls Wilder

## *All the children are begging for another book*

FEBRUARY 9, 1944

Dear Miss Nordstrom,

The Horn Book containing Miss Smith's article is a grand piece of writing and I am greatly pleased with her appreciation of the Little House books.

I would like some copies of the brochure on my books. I get so many requests for my photo, which I cannot afford to send, and one of the brochures would do even better.

It is out of the question for me to get any photos now. We had Pa's fiddle photographed just in time, for the studio is closed now, the photographer gone to the war.

All the children are begging for another book, and I must begin to think about it. . . .

## *They think of me as I am in the books*

*Schoolchildren from Saginaw, Michigan, developed a long correspondence with Laura Ingalls Wilder.*

MARCH 27, 1944

Dear Miss Dunning,

It is sweet of your boys and girls to call me "Laura." Of course they think of me as I am in the books when I would have been their playmate.

I thank you for your appreciation of my work and the kind things you say about it.

You must be a delightful teacher for those little third graders and I want to thank you also for the pictures they drew for me.

It was, I am sure, your idea and it must have taken a great deal of kindly patience to help them in their work.

With best regards I am

Yours sincerely,

Laura Ingalls Wilder

## We would leave the violin with some museum

*In 1931 Laura and Manly brought Pa's fiddle, the most treasured family heirloom, from South Dakota to Rocky Ridge. No one knew how Charles Ingalls acquired it on the frontier; it was likely an inexpensive German copy of the work of the Italian violin maker Nicolò Amati of Cremona. When Ursula Nordstrom proposed a department store window display of the Little House books in New York, she asked Laura for family artifacts to exhibit. "She sent us Pa's fiddle!" Miss Nordstrom exclaimed. A label on the violin suggested it was an authentic Amati. Harper could not be responsible for an Amati, and returned it promptly. In 1944 Laura offered the fiddle to the South Dakota State Historical Society.*

APRIL II, 1944

Dear Mr. Fox,

I am sure you will pardon my delay in replying to your letter when you learn that I have been quite ill and unable to attend to it.

Today I am mailing you autographed books as you requested and I take pleasure in presenting to South Dakota Historical Society the three volumes needed to complete the set of my "Little House Books."

I have the old violin, "Pa's fiddle" that he played through all my books. It is a "Nicolaus Amati Cremonensis" and still has a beautiful voice.

Would your historical society like to have this violin to keep on exhibition with my books? If so what arrangements could be made and what assurance could you give me that the instrument will be preserved safely and with the care necessary?

Neither my daughter Rose Wilder Lane, nor my sister Mrs. Caroline Swanzey of Keystone, South Dakota, has anyone to whom to bequeath the violin and none of us can play it. No one else has any interest in it as we are the only ones of the family living.

We have thought we would leave the violin with some museum or the like. It only remains to decide where.

If you are interested please let me hear from you.

Yours sincerely,

Laura Ingalls Wilder

*My favorite . . . is the very first one*

MAY 6, 1944

Dear Miss Fosness and Pupils,

I am very glad you like my Little House books so much, and I thank you for your nice letters.

It must be great fun to go to such a small school. Really, your letters made me rather homesick for the little schools I used to go to when I was your age and for the two nice ones I taught. The first one I taught was pretty bad, but there are not many like that.

I think my favorite among the books is the very first one, "Little House in the Big Woods." I always loved the stories Pa used to tell us.

Again thanking you for the kind things you say of my stories and for recommending them to others for reading, I remain

Yours sincerely,

Laura Ingalls Wilder

## *Today I am sending you . . . my father's violin*

*Lawrence Fox commented, "I have read of your career with much interest and I rejoice at the success you have attained. I don't see how you found time for everything."*

MAY 15, 1944
Mr. Lawrence. Fox
Pierre, S. Dakota
Dear Sir,

I hope you have quite recovered from your indisposition by now. Spring here is very backward also, rainy and cold.

Today I am sending you, by express, collect, my father's violin.

My sister, my daughter and I have . . . the stipulation that it be played at least four times a year. Kept in a case on display the rest of the time.

Perhaps your Society has meetings where its music would be suitable or you may have, in your city, violinists who would find it interesting to play this violin. As no doubt you know, if it is played its tone will constantly improve . . . but if it is not played it will deteriorate. If it is kept in voice there is no reason why it shouldn't be playing the old music in South Dakota a hundred years from now. It has not been played for over a year and I am anxious it should be as soon as possible.

As you see, the bow is not in shape. It needed re-stringing, but the attempt was a failure and the mother-of-pearl holder was broken. Another bow would need to be used in playing the violin.

I am enclosing copy for a card, I should like to have printed and placed on display with the violin.

As you see the violin is the property of your Historical Society. I am trusting it to your care with the feeling that it has found its proper home and I trust it will create interest and give pleasure for many years to come.

Yours sincerely,
Laura Ingalls Wilder

## *They are poor little rich children*

*Dorothy Nace Tharpe read the Little House books to her students in Cleveland, Ohio, in the 1940s. "We've been reading them all year," she wrote. "I just had to pick up the book to have complete expectant silence waiting for me.... I hope that when I have a family of my own, I may be able to read all the books as part of the household tradition." As a professor's wife, Dorothy Tharpe introduced the books to her own children. The family traveled to the books' sites. Dorothy researched and wrote on the subject, and gave many presentations about Little House lore.*

MAY 19, 1944
Dear Miss Nace,

It pleases me very much that you have enjoyed my books and perhaps they have had a good influence on the children in your school.

The children today have so much that they have lost the power to truly enjoy anything. They are poor little rich children.

I fear my letter is late for your school term, but perhaps you can let the children know that I answered their letter.

Yours sincerely,
Laura Ingalls Wilder

## *Much different from the schools I knew*

MAY 19, 1944

Pearl Creek School

Dear Fourth Graders,

Your letter is very interesting. It must be fun to ride in the busses to school and it certainly is much different from the schools I knew when I was young.

We have only one child, our daughter Rose Wilder Lane. You may know of her for she writes stories. She lives in Connecticut.

We moved from De Smet nine years after the time of "These Happy Golden Years" so you see we have lived here a long time.

Wishing you all a happy vacation,

Yours sincerely,

Laura Ingalls Wilder

## *Such terrible things are happening in the world*

*A few days after D-Day, the 1944 Allied invasion of France on the Normandy beaches, Laura wrote to George Bye and alluded to the war.*

JUNE 10, 1944

Dear Mr. Bye,

Please use your own judgment in selling The Long Winter to Columbia Broadcasting System . . . whatever you do will be perfectly all right with me.

I shall be pleased to have the book used in a broadcast. . . .

The Ozarks are beautiful now and in our quiet home it seems impossible that such terrible things are happening in the world.

Please do excuse the writing in this. It looks like a fan letter from one of my nine year old readers. My ink is poor but not pale.

Sincerely yours,

Laura Ingalls Wilder

## *Hope I have not bored you with my reply*

*In June 1944, Mrs. George Jones of Rocky Hill, New Jersey, wrote: "I read the Little House books to my small son who is 7 years of age. He enjoyed them and now wants me to start all over again.... Haven't you ever read a wonderful story and then said to yourself, 'I would like to know the author?' That is the way I feel."*

JUNE 27, 1944

Dear Mrs. Jones,

It was a pleasure to have your letter, but I have been so busy with the last of house-cleaning and company that I have been slow in answering. I do all my own work and a ten room house takes some doing....

You are right in thinking I am the Laura of the books, which are altogether my memories.

These Happy Golden Years is the last book I expect to write, though there are many stories in the years that followed. But I will answer some of your questions.

We have one child, our daughter Rose, born in the little house. You may know of her—Rose Wilder Lane. She is a writer of short stories, books and magazine articles. Her home is in Connecticut. She has no children, so I am not a grandmother. Carrie and Grace married, but had no children.... Carrie and I are the only ones of our family now living. Mary never recovered her sight and did not marry.

De Smet is a large, very modern town now, but we left there fifty years ago and have lived here ever since.

I have worn my hair short for a good many years, tailored cut in the back and long enough in the front to curl and fluff around my face. No permanents, just a homemade curl.

I never smoked nor drank nor do I wear skirts so short as the fashion is. Do not paint my finger nails nor use rouge, just keep my complexion good and powder lightly. My hair is perfectly white. By no stretch of the imagination could I ever be called ultra-modern. My wedding band was a medium wide, plain gold band.

Almanzo and I live by ourselves on our farm, but we do not farm now. The farm at one time was 200 acres and we kept a herd of cows, mostly Jerseys. Also we kept a flock of leghorn hens, which were my especial care. And always we had fine horses.

Now we have only three milk goats—Saanens. We have sold the land until we only have 75 acres with the old farm house.

The land is all meadow, pasture and timber, for Almanzo is 87 years old and I am 77, not able to do so much work now, glad and thankful we are still able to care for ourselves and each other. We have no horses now. Drive a Chrysler car instead.

I thank you for your kind letter and hope I have not bored you with my reply.

Yours sincerely,

Laura Ingalls Wilder

## I am glad you like my stories

*Gloria from Greenwich, Connecticut, wrote praising the Little House books. She prized her answer from Laura, and later sent her a picture she drew. Laura responded: "It is a fine drawing and you are a fine artist. I thought you might like to see what I really looked like when I was seventeen. The printed pictures were taken from photos." (Laura sent the Harper & Brothers promotional brochure.)*

AUGUST 8, 1944

My dear Gloria,

I am glad you like my stories. . . .

All my schoolmates were scattered long ago. I know of none of them still living.

Almanzo is very well. We still live by ourselves in our home here.

Our house burned many years ago and the rag doll Charlotte burned with it.

With best regards,

Laura Ingalls Wilder

## *You must be very proud of your son*

*Carrie Ingalls Swanzey made her final visit to Rocky Ridge Farm in October 1944. Laura and Manly took Carrie sightseeing and they talked over old times. Laura's pleasure over the family reunion is indicated in this letter, as well as her admiration for the McCallum family's sacrifices for the work of the war.*

OCTOBER 23, 1944

Dear Mrs. McCallum,

Your letter should have been answered before now, but sister Carrie has been visiting me and there seemed no time for letter writing. Carrie and I are the only ones of our family still living and our talks brought the old days back very realistically. She has returned now to her home in the Black Hills of South Dakota and I miss her so much.

I am glad you and your daughter and friends enjoyed my books. I have certainly enjoyed your letter telling me of it.

Yes! I am still quite a busy woman though not as usefully as yourself. You must be very proud of your son and anxious of course. Also glad you are doing your part in the world's work.

I thank you for your kind letter and good wishes, and with all good wishes for you and yours, I am

Yours sincerely,

Laura Ingalls Wilder

## *It was a good and pleasant life with work and play*

*In February 1945 Congressman Clarence E. Kilburn from Malone, New York, wrote: "It seems Mrs. Kilburn and I have been living with you and Almanzo because we have gotten every one of your books from the Congressional Library. . . . This spring when we get home, we are going to try to locate Almanzo's old farm. I have been over on the floor of the House and had a visit with Dewey Short, your Member of Congress. He knows your daughter Mrs. Lane, and I didn't realize until talking with him that she wrote Let the Hurricane Roar. . . . I have read it twice a year ago." Laura and the congressman corresponded, and on March 9, 1945, she sent him a copy of Rose's Give Me Liberty. She also spoke passionately of her concern for America.*

We are looking forward to our Congress to save us from the situation which is developing and I respectfully beg you to use every effort to preserve the way of life which has proven such a good way all through the long years since "Little House in the Big Woods."

It was a good and pleasant life with work and play, careful planning and saving. What we accomplished was without help of any kind from anyone. There was no alphabetical relief of any description and if there had been we would not have accepted it. Now here we are at 78 and 88 years old, with our farm idle for lack of help, still doing our own work and paying taxes for the support of dependent children, so their parents need not work at anything else; for old age pensions take care of those same parents when children are grown, thus relieving the children of any responsibility, and all of them from incentive to help themselves.

Rose stopped writing fiction in 1937 and has done nothing but American propaganda since. She says she doesn't think this is the time for any American to do anything else.

> *Congressman Kilburn responded that "I agree with you about Congress, and imagine we feel the same." He also inquired about the Wilders' lives after the book series: "If you get a chance I would greatly appreciate hearing from you again giving me a little more on what happened to you since 'These Happy Golden Years.'"*
>
> *Laura replied:*

Both Mr. Wilder and myself were much interested in your letter. . . . The Wilder farm, north and west of Burke, on the old map, belonged to Almanzo's uncle, William Wilder. The farm described in Farmer Boy, belonging to Almanzo's father, was south and west of Burke, about ½ mile south of the main road from Malone to Burke and nearly midway between the two towns. Our daughter Rose Wilder Lane, found the farm a few years ago. . . .

Almanzo came with his father's family to eastern Minnesota and from there he went to Dakota Ter. where he again enters the story in By the Shores of Silver Lake. And from there on through the series. . . .

In those days, you know, young men went west to "grow up with the country." I am the little Laura, grown up now. It may interest you to know that the names, dates and circumstances of all the books are actually true—all true—written from my own and Almanzo's memories.

It is a long story, filled with sunshine and shadow, that we have lived since These Happy Golden Years.

In the first few years of our marriage we experienced the complete destruction of our crops by hail storms; the loss of our little house by fire; the loss of Almanzo's health from a stroke of paralysis and then the drouth years of 1892–1893–1894.

In the fall of 1894 we, with our seven year old daughter, Rose, left Dakota, by way of a covered wagon holding all our worldly goods, drawn by our team of horses. We arrived in Mansfield, Missouri, with enough money to make part payment on a rough, rocky forty acres of land and a little left to buy our food for a time. The only building on the land was a one-room log cabin with a rock fireplace, one door but no window. When the door was closed light came in between the logs of the walls where the mud chinking had fallen out. We lived there a year.

Almanzo had recovered from the stroke but was not strong. He changed work with neighbors to build a log barn for his horses and a henhouse for a few hens.

In the spring we planted a garden and together we cleared land of timber. I could never use an ax but I could handle one end of a cross-cut saw and pile brush ready to burn. Almanzo made rails and stove wood out of the trees we cut down. With the rails he fenced the land we cleared; the stove wood he sold in town for 75 cents a wagon load with the top on. I hoed the garden and tended my hens. We sold eggs and potatoes from our new ground planting besides the wood and when we were able to buy a cow and a little pig, we thought we were rich.

After that it was much easier. We worked and saved from year to year, adding to our land until we owned 200 acres, well improved; a fine herd of cows; good hogs and the best laying flock of hens in the country.

These years were not all filled with work. Rose walked three-quarters of a mile to school the second year and after and her school-mates visited her on Saturdays. She and I played along the little creek near the house. We tamed wild birds and squirrels; picked wild flowers and berries. Almanzo and I often went horseback riding over the hills and through the woods. And always we had our papers and books from the school library for reading in the evenings and on Sunday afternoons.

P.S. I cannot resist telling you that when we were building up our 200-acre farm we also built a 10-room farm house, using mostly material from the farm. We used hand-finished oak lumber from our own trees to panel rooms and build the open stairs, and hand-finished oak beams in the ceiling. At the time there was no planing mill to finish the lumber.

Please pardon me for this extremely long letter. But as we say of one who gets what he richly deserves, "You asked for it."

## *"The Long Winter" was on the radio*

MAY 4, 1945

Dear Mrs. Masson,

I thank you for your kind appreciation of my books. If they have helped children a little I am very glad indeed.

"The Long Winter" was on the radio, Blue Network last January but I missed hearing it, so do not know how it was presented.

My New York agent, George Bye, will get it in the movies if there is a chance, I am sure. All such details are in his hands. . . .

## *Things have been rather __up in the air__ ever since*

> On April 12, 1945, Ursula Nordstrom wrote a chatty letter, inviting Laura to New York City to meet booksellers and librarians. Later that day, President Franklin D. Roosevelt died suddenly at

*Warm Springs, Georgia. While Americans huddled around ra-*
*dios, absorbing the unexpected news, strong cyclones hit Oklahoma,*
*moved east through Missouri, and then entered Illinois. Seven died*
*in Missouri; at Rocky Ridge Farm, Laura and Almanzo barely*
*escaped calamity.*

MAY 7, 1945
Dear Miss Nordstrom,

It was a pleasure to have a letter from you and I would have an-swered sooner, but on the night of April 12 (date of your letter) we went through a cyclone, and things have been rather *up in the air* ever since.

We were very fortunate in that our house stood, with the loss of only some of the shingles and one of the big windows in the living room. It is one of the wonders of the cyclone that the house was not blown away.

Our big trees in the yard on every side of it were pulled out by the roots, broken and twisted in every shape. Big oaks were thrown across our driveway from both sides and for two weeks we could not drive out, had no telephone connection nor electricity. It was quite a return to former times being isolated with our coal oil lamps for lights. Neighbors' buildings were blown away . . . highway and country roads were blocked with fallen trees; fences all through the neighborhood were blown flat or torn down. But no one near us was injured, though they were a few miles away.

You see Almanzo and I have had still another adventure and es-caped.

I would love to visit New York and am happy that a welcome still awaits me, but it will have to be at some unknown time in the future.

I am sorry too that I cannot see my way clear to writing another book soon. My mind is filled with what might be written, but I lack the time and energy.

You would be astonished at the number of letters still coming,

from five or six a day, to letters from schools enclosing 12 to 20, three
such last week, each asking questions. I answer most of them for I
cannot bear to disappoint children.

    With kindest regards,
Laura Ingalls Wilder


## *I lost my sense of time in writing these books*

*A class from Los Virgenes School in Calabasas, California, wrote
letters to Laura, which she answered "all in one," as she said. The
children's teacher received a separate reply.*

MAY 7, 1945
Dear Mrs. Kelley,

    A fountain pen sometimes plays tricks. Please excuse it. [A blob of
ink stained the letter.]

    I am sorry I have no photograph I can send you. Perhaps Harpers
would send you one for the school if you asked them. The printed
ones on the pamphlet enclosed are the best I can do, as our photographer has gone to war.

    I am so glad that you and the children enjoy my books and your
little school must be delightful; the letters are so nice. I have answered
the children's letters the best I could and hope their curiosity will be
satisfied in a measure.

    I lost my sense of time in writing these books from memory and it
was hard to bring myself altogether back to the present time, so I can
understand the children's point of view.

    Yours sincerely,
Laura Ingalls Wilder

## We are having an awful spring

MAY 21, 1945

Dear Carrie,

This is just a note to tell you I have sent De Smet Cemetery Association $5.00 in your name and mine for care of Ingalls family lot. So you need not bother to think of it.

We are having an awful spring. First planting of potatoes and garden seed rotted in the ground it was so cold and wet. Since then the ground has not been dry enough to plow. Corn can't be planted, hay spoils before it dries and it looks as though we will be needing more food than will be raised this year.

Well! the big oak trees in front and west of the house are all cleared away. A cyclone did it. It uprooted them, just tore them up by the roots. It tore out a big walnut tree by the barn and split the elm by the iris bed. The great, old oak close in front of the house was broken in pieces and trunk split the whole length. Some shingles were torn off the house and the big south window in the front room was blown out, but we were lucky the house didn't go. A good many houses did, and people were hurt. It was two weeks before we could get the big trees out of our driveway so we could get out. Telephone and electric wires were down two weeks.

Am looking for that letter you were writing at once.

Lots of love,

Laura

## I would be glad to have you call on me

Clara J. Webber, a children's librarian at the Alliance, Ohio, Public Library, noted the intense interest readers showed in the Little

*House books. She began a long correspondence with Laura Ingalls*
*Wilder, asking her many questions that the children posed.*

JUNE 15, 1945
Dear Children,

Thank you for your nice letters. I am glad you like my stories of long ago when I was a little girl.

It was rough riding in covered wagons in those days. It was quite different from riding on soft cushions over springs of a car as we do now, and we did have hard times but we didn't let them beat us. We had good times and were happy even if we sometimes had bad luck.

I fed chickens and milked cows too for many years after I was married and 300 chicks are a good many to raise, but they are lots of fun to watch grow.

Almanzo and I still like animals. We have a big brown and white bulldog now, three milk goats and a Rocky Mountain burro. They are all spoiled pets.

When our only child Rose was a baby we had a great St. Bernard dog who used to take care of her.

Almanzo is eighty-eight years old . . . and I am seventy-eight.

I am glad you liked to hear Pa's fiddle in the stories. You may like to know that . . . I gave the fiddle to the South Dakota Historical Society. . . .

If any of you come past here I would be glad to have you call on me, but perhaps you would be disappointed to see Laura so grown up for it has been many years since she was the girl in the stories.

With love to you all, I am

Yours sincerely,

Laura Ingalls Wilder

*Please give my love to the children*

Miss Crawford of Winfield, Kansas, was one of Laura's periodic correspondents.

DECEMBER 29, 1945
Dear Miss Crawford,

A little late to send Christmas wishes, but in time to wish you a
very happy New Year.

I am glad to hear from you again and also that my books are still
popular.

Please give my love to the children of Winfield and Cowley county.
Tell them I am wishing them all a very happy New Year.

Yours sincerely,
Laura Ingalls Wilder

*The boundless sweep of the prairie*

> Teacher Ida Carson read the *Little House* books to her classes in
> South Dakota and Iowa.

MARCH 25, 1946
Dear Mrs. Carson,

I am glad to have your letter. It is interesting to hear from someone who knows the Dakota prairies so well and who feels their fascination as I do.

We have been away from them, living here, for more than fifty
years, but we still are homesick for Dakota at times. On our several
visits back to De Smet we came away still unsatisfied: the country
and the town are so changed from the old, free days, that we seem not

able to find there what we were looking for. Perhaps it is our lost youth we were seeking in the place where it used to be.

But there is something about the boundless sweep of the prairie that makes it unforgettable. . . .

[Rose's] two books "Let the Hurricane Roar" and "Free Land" are Dakota stories. Her latest books, "Give Me Liberty" and "The Discovery of Freedom" are well worth reading, especially for educated persons. . . .

Almanzo and I are living by ourselves on the farm where we have lived for fifty years. We do not farm now, being too old for hard work and not able to get help. We have sold a part of the land and what we have is in pasture that we rent. Almanzo is 89 years old and I am 79.

I enclose a brochure, thinking it may interest you. With kindest regards, I am

Yours sincerely,

Laura Ingalls Wilder

## *I'm sure they are great kids*

APRIL 23, 1946

Dear Mrs. Carson,

Thank you for the picture of your school. The children look so interesting. I'm sure they are great kids.

Pa and Ma, Mary and Grace are buried in the De Smet cemetery. They never went farther west.

Cap Garland was a very real person and did and said the things I have told of him. I never knew of any connection with Hamlin Garland.

I hope you read Farmer Boy sometime. I am sure you would enjoy it. Royal died many years ago at his home in eastern Minnesota.

I wish you a pleasant visit in S.D. I would be glad to spend some time there this summer, but I suspicion that our traveling days are over.

Yours sincerely,

Laura Ingalls Wilder

## The Wilders always called me Bessie

*Perley Day Wilder was born in 1869, twelve years Almanzo's junior. Most of his youth was spent on the Wilder farm in Spring Valley, Minnesota. During his early twenties Perley traveled south on the Mississippi on a skiff called* Edith. *He kept a log of the trip. His daughter Dorothy and her husband, Carl, were visitors on Rocky Ridge.*

JUNE 9, 1946

Dear Dorothy and Carl,

The picture [enclosed] is rather faded as you see, but can be photographed and give you a more lasting one. Perley is on the right. My cousin Peter Ingalls is in the middle and cousin Joe Carpenter to the left. You are to keep the picture. The picture of Almanzo was taken from a badly faded photo.

Because there was already a Laura in the family, the Wilders always called me Bessie. . . .

The New Dealers are in control of most publishing houses in New York and because they think Rose's "Discovery of Freedom" teaches ideas contrary to their plans, they are working against its publication and distribution [this was Rose's hypothesis]. Even the publishers of the book are trying to stop it, so I doubt if you can get it from them. The address where you can get it is on the printed sheet. I have marked it in red. I am sure you would find the book interesting.

There have been two days of sunshine here. My cough is much better.

We both send love and hope you arrived home safely. We are delighted that you came and shall look forward to seeing you again.

Uncle Almanzo and Aunt Bessie

## *Impossible for me to dictate another book*

JUNE 24, 1946
Dear Mrs. Carson,

I hope you will pardon my delay in answering your letter. I have been so very busy there was no time for letter writing.

It is impossible for me to dictate another book for the reason that there is no one I could dictate it to.

All my books were written in longhand and sent to New York to be typewritten. There is no one here who does such work and I cannot go away to find a stenographer.

Five years after I was married Cap Garland was killed in an explosion of a threshing machine engine. He was an interesting person to know and one of our best friends. . . .

I am the only one of the C. P. Ingalls family left and Rose is the only grandchild. There are Wilder and Ingalls kin scattered all over the country, but the Almanzo Wilder branch will die out with us. . . .

## *There is material there for an interesting story*

The "atom bomb test" that Laura refers to in this letter was the first of twenty-three nuclear weapons tests conducted by the United States at Bikini Atoll in the Marshall Islands.

JULY 1, 1946

Dear Dorothy,

The "Log of the Edith" arrived safely and I do thank you for it and for binding it so nicely. We enjoyed reading it very much. Manly especially enjoyed reading "The Log" and says to thank you for him.

There is material there for an interesting story, but it would need a great deal of padding to make it salable. A lot of research work would need to be done to make the fiction added true in detail to the time and the different places mentioned.

There should be a reason for the trip and an idea followed as a thread through it all to the end accomplished.

I can see it all as it should be and if I were a few years younger would like to rewrite it myself. Of course as you so kindly say it is not expected of me now. Nor do I know of anyone who would undertake it at the present time. Rose is so tied up and so overworked or I would suggest it to her.

Perhaps some time later someone will like to have the chance to use the material. If Carl feels like trying, tell him there must always be a first time.

Here's hoping the atom bomb test tonight will do no harm more than expected.

Love,

Aunt Bessie

## Going back anywhere is apt to disillusion

*Carrie Ingalls Swanzey died in Rapid City after a short illness on June 2, 1946. She was buried with her family in De Smet.*

OCTOBER 1, 1946

Dear Mrs. Carson,

Your letter should have been answered before now but I hope you will pardon the delay. My mail got ahead of me and piled up on my desk. Being almost eighty years old slows one down.

We did not go to S. Dakota this summer.

Carrie died suddenly so there was not time for us to get there while she lived and conditions of travel were such that we could not attempt the journey. We did not know Carrie was ill until we got a message that she was dead. After that we received delayed telegrams and miss-sent letters.

I have no snapshot of Almanzo nor myself. I'm sorry. Perhaps you will like my printed photos. Or have I sent you them before?

Thank you for your photo. You look like a person it would be pleasant to know.

We left S. Dakota because Almanzo could no longer endure the winters there.

We are in very good health considering our age. He will be ninety in February, though I think I wrote you that before. I have so many letters to write that I am apt to repeat myself.

Our weather is quite cool now at night, warm and sunny daytimes.

I too long sometimes for the prairies but S. Dakota has changed so much it is a disappointment when we go back. I think going back anywhere is apt to disillusion anyone.

With kindest regards, I am

Yours sincerely,

Laura Ingalls Wilder

*There is a space of years unaccounted for*

OCTOBER 28, 1946

Dear Ida Carson,

Thanks for your very interesting letter.

Believe me I love to have your letters, but it *is* becoming difficult for me to keep up with my correspondence.

I know there is a space of years unaccounted for in the Wilder family history between Farmer Boy and the Little Town on the Prairie. One book anyway, perhaps two, which will remain unwritten. I'll try to condense them for you.

Almanzo's father had a friend who moved from N.Y. to eastern Minnesota. He liked it there and Mr. Wilder went out to visit him and look the place over.

Mr. Wilder liked the country so well that he bought a farm near Spring Valley, which is thirty miles south of Rochester, which is the nearest large town. The Wilder family moved to the new farm, all of the family except Royal and Almanzo who stayed behind and ran the old place for a year.

At the end of the year their father and mother were so well satisfied with the new home that they sold the New York farm and Royal and Almanzo drove a team with covered wagon from there to Spring Valley.

One book.

But you know in those days once people started going west they usually kept on going, making stops along the way.

Royal and Almanzo went from Spring Valley to Marshall and later from there to De Smet where they took homesteads and appear once more as characters in the Little House Books.

And all this would make another book. I hope I answered your questions in this synopsis.

You see there was really no reason for the Wilders' move except to follow Horace Greely's advice and go west.

If as you suggest we make this the end of our correspondence, please remember that I have enjoyed it and am glad to have known you.

Sincerely your friend,

Laura Ingalls Wilder

# FIRST TOURISM AT THE LITTLE HOUSES

*Following World War II, American families piled into new cars for summer road trips. Little House readers stopped at Rocky Ridge to meet Laura and Manly, who were always welcoming. Others arrived in De Smet and sought out Aubrey Sherwood for information. He interrupted his editorial duties to show travelers around town and country. "Often I had letters from Mrs. Wilder on my desk, and showed them to the wide-eyed children," he recalled. When the travelers arrived home, they wrote Laura about their visits.*

*Esther Clifton described her family's 1946 trek to South Dakota:*

I was born in Bruce, South Dakota, near De Smet. My husband is a professor of Bacteriology at Stanford University and we have two sons, Charles is 8 and John, 6. . . . A friend suggested that we read your Little House books, but Charles couldn't wait for our reading periods and simply ate them up. When June came I went to the library and got the last four books, intending to have them for summer reading, as we planned to spend the summer in the Middle West. Both boys were absolutely fascinated. . . .

Late in June we went to South Dakota. We spent one night in a camp in Keystone. It seemed strange to me upon leaving that Carrie had lived in Keystone. The next day we stopped in De Smet . . . we all felt we simply could not pass De Smet without trying to find out something about your family. As we drove down the main street the boys kept guessing at buildings—which one had been Pa's store? I got out—not being at all certain. As I walked down the street I came upon three ladies "visiting." . . . I told them what I wanted and could hardly believe my ears, for one of the ladies was Mrs. Sterr, who knew. . . . She told us about Carrie's recent passing, and that you were still living in Missouri. Then she took us to her garage and showed us the old pictures [framed portraits of Pa and Ma] and dishes, trunks etc. [Mrs. Sterr had taken these items from the Ingalls home at Carrie's request.] She let each of the boys take a little button from Ma's sewing box and their joy knew no bounds. We saw an old teapot and we were just sure it had been Pa's.

Another lady, a Mrs. Bowes, drove with us over to the house where your family had lived [the Ingalls home on Third Street]. She was a dear little lady. We came away from De Smet feeling as though we had actually visited all of you.

I can't begin to tell you how much I have enjoyed your books, too. Just today the librarian sent me a copy of "The Horn Book" magazine and the whole family has enjoyed reading about you. . . . I hope I have not bored you, Mrs. Wilder. We all say thanks a million times for giving us so many happy hours.

## The real things haven't changed

The Carson Pirie Scott department store of Chicago sponsored an eightieth birthday party for Laura at the Merchandise Mart in February 1947. Hordes of children attended; first they witnessed a live radio broadcast of the store's Hobby Horse Bookstore Presents; Hugh Downs was the announcer. A letter from Laura was read on the air and refreshments were served. The guests signed a huge oversize birthday card, which was sent to Laura. It is now displayed at the Laura Ingalls Wilder Historic Home and Museum. Laura was overwhelmed by the honor. By a majority of 1,734 votes in a poll of Chicago children, she was proclaimed the city's favorite children's author.

[NO DATE]

Dear Children of Chicago:

I am sorry I cannot make a personal appearance on your program and thank you for wishing me to do so. Instead, I greet you by letter.

I was born in the Little House in the Big Woods of Wisconsin just eighty years ago the 7th of February, and I'm calling this my birthday party. Living through all the Little House books, as told in those stories, I came fifty years ago with Almanzo and our little daughter Rose, to live on our farm in the Ozarks. Rose, now Rose Wilder Lane, grew up and went away. Her home is in Connecticut.

Almanzo and I still live on the farm but are not farming now. We care for our pet bulldog, our comical Rocky Mountain burro and our milk goats. We no longer keep horses but still go driving together in our car. Schoolmates and friends of the Little Town on the Prairie are scattered. Perhaps you would like to hear about them. Ida married her Elmer and went to California where her children and grandchildren are now. Mary Power married the young banker and did not live many years. Nellie Oleson married; later separated from her husband. . . . Cap Garland was killed in an explosion of a threshing machine engine soon after Almanzo and I were married.

[Laura continues by explaining the fates of her parents and sisters, and mentions that Pa's fiddle is now on exhibit in South Dakota.]

The Little House books are stories of long ago. The way we live and your schools are much different now, so many changes have made living and learning easier. But the real things haven't changed. It is still best to be honest and truthful; to make the most of what we have; to be happy with simple pleasures and to be cheerful and have courage when things go wrong.

With love to you all and best wishes for your happiness, I am

Sincerely, your friend

Laura Ingalls Wilder

## *The cards are wonderful*

*Children from Saginaw, Michigan, sent eightieth-birthday greetings.*

FEBRUARY 15, 1947

Dear Miss Dunning,

I have been quite seriously ill and am only now able to be up. This explains the delay in acknowledging the birthday cards sent me from your third grade pupils. The cards are wonderful and I thank them all so much because they made them for me. They are all so quaint and pretty. I don't see how they could do it.

Dr's orders are that I shall take it more easy, slowing up on my activities.

There are 225 cards and letters on my desk waiting to be answered and it seems a hopeless task. . . . I shall have to stop writing so much.

Again thanking you and the children I am with love your friend,

Laura Ingalls Wilder

## *I have thoughts of Burr Oak as a lovely place*

*Although the Ingalls family lived in Burr Oak, Iowa, in 1876 and 1877, Laura never mentioned the era in her books. In May 1947, L. Dale Ahern, editor of the* Decorah Public Opinion, *wrote Rose, asking her to confirm that her mother spent time in Burr Oak. Rose replied that Laura "had very clear memories of the place and the people" and would elaborate on them. Laura complied and her letter was printed in the newspaper on June 18, 1947.*

Dear Sir:

My family did live in Burr Oak for nearly two years, but I fear my memories of that time will not be very interesting as they are more of the place than the people.

At first we lived in the old Masters Hotel. My parents were partners in the business with the new owners, Mr. and Mrs. Steadman. Their two boys, Jimmy and Reuben, were about the age of my sister Mary and myself and of course we played and quarreled together.

The hotel still stood when Rose saw it a few years ago [1932] as it was then even to the bullet hole in the door between the dining room and kitchen. It was made when the young man of the house, being drunk, shot at his wife who slammed the door between them as she escaped. This had happened some years before, but the bullet hole in the door was thrilling to us children.

Pa used to play his fiddle in the hotel office, and one of the boarders, a Mr. Bisbee, taught me to sing the notes of the musical scale. We stayed there most of the winter, then moved to rooms over Kimball's grocery.

One night Ma woke Mary and me, telling us to dress quickly. The second building from us, a saloon, was burning and we must be ready to leave quickly if the fire should spread toward us.

Ma and Mary and I stood at the window where we watched the flames and the men in the street carrying buckets of water from the town pump to pour on the fire. Pa was one of them.

The men stood in line. One would fill his bucket and run with it to the fire, while the next man instantly took his place. On returning he took his place at the end of the line, which was constantly moving.

But they all stood still for some moments, with the same man at the pump. At every stroke of the pump handle he would throw up his head and shout "Fire." Then someone pushed him away and took his place. The bucket which he was frantically pumping water [into] had no bottom in it.

The fire was put out after a while and we all went back to bed.

Mary and I were going to school. It seemed to us a big school, but as I remember there were only two rooms. One began in the downstairs room and when advanced enough was promoted upstairs.

Downstairs we learned to sing the multiplication tables to the tune of Yankee Doodle. Next term we went upstairs to the principal whose name was Reid and who came from Decorah. He was an elocutionist and I have always been grateful to him for the training I was given in reading. I still have the old Independent Fifth Reader from which he taught us to give life to "Old Tubal Cain," "The Polish Boy" and "Paul Revere."

We had friends among our school mates. I remember their faces and occasionally the names escape me.

In the spring [1877] we moved to a little brick house at the edge of town. It was a happy summer. I loved to go after the cows in the pasture by the creek where the rushes and the blue flags grew and the grass was so fresh and smelled so sweet. I could see the old stone quarry, but was forbidden to go to it as it was filled with water.

Often on Sunday afternoons my friend, Alice Ward, and I would walk out on the other side of town, past the Sims' rose-covered cottage to the graveyard. We would wander in the shade of the great trees, reading the inscriptions on the tomb stones. The grass was green and short and flowers were everywhere. It was a beautiful, peaceful place.

I spent a great deal of time that summer caring for baby sister Grace, with the big blue eyes and soft fine hair.

That fall we left Burr Oak and drove in our covered wagon back to Walnut Grove, Minnesota, and the banks of Plum Creek.

As you see, these are just dim childish memories, but I have thoughts of Burr Oak as a lovely place.

Yours sincerely,

Laura Ingalls Wilder

## *I'll answer your questions*

MAY 22, 1947

Dear Mrs. Carson,

This will be too late for this school term, but I'll answer your questions anyway.

Pa's fiddle is in the museum of the [South Dakota] State Historical Society at Pierre. . . .

Ma's china shepherdess was at home when I left there. I do not know what became of it afterward.

Cap Garland never married. He was single when killed.

I never saw Grandma Ingalls after the dance.

This last year I received a letter from the other Laura's granddaughter. Her grandmother was dead sometime ago.

Since the books were published I heard from cousin Lena who drove and rode the black ponies.

Mother's maiden name was Quiner.

Almanzo is not very strong but he is very well for ninety. Rose is 60. I know what it is to be tired for I am eighty.

Yours sincerely,

Laura Ingalls Wilder


## *I have never gotten over my timidity with perfect strangers*

JULY 31, 1947

Dear Mr. Sherwood,

Thank you so much for copies of "The De Smet News" sent me recently. You are very kind to me and my "Little House Books" and I appreciate it.

It is surprising how many people are interested in my account of early times. I have letters from all over this country and Canada. One came from Holland this week.

I am glad if I have made them all interested in De Smet for we have always been proud of the town.

A great many people traveling through stop to see me and I am glad not all come this way for I have never gotten over my timidity with perfect strangers.

Under separate cover I am sending you a photo of Pa which you may like to have in your collection of early De Smet souvenirs. If you already have one, perhaps the school library would be the place for it.

Mr. Wilder and I are very well for persons ninety and eighty years old. Still caring for ourselves and our home.

Rose is well and very busy at her little place in Connecticut.

Best regards to yourself and family and any enquiring friends, if any.

Yours sincerely,
Laura Ingalls Wilder

*I am writing to offer you enlarged photographs of Pa and Ma*

*The Ingalls home in De Smet was sold by Carrie in 1944. After the deaths of Caroline and Mary Ingalls in 1924 and 1928, the house was rented, with a room reserved for Ingalls property. Following Carrie's death in June 1946, a De Smet friend took charge of the Ingalls belongings. She recognized the oversize portraits of Charles and Caroline Ingalls, and shipped them to Laura. Laura decided her parents' portraits would complement the exhibit of Pa's fiddle at the South Dakota State Historical Society.*

AUGUST 2, 1947
Secretary, State Historical Society
Pierre, South Dakota
Dear Sir,

You will remember having some correspondence with my sister, the late Mrs. Caroline Swanzey, regarding Ingalls family exhibits in your museum.

There are "Pa's fiddle," a set of my Little House books, and perhaps some other items which she intended sending you.

I am writing to offer you enlarged photographs of Pa and Ma, Mr. and Mrs. C. P. Ingalls, to place with the exhibit. The photos will be unframed for greater safety in mailing, but if you will have them framed under glass, I will gladly pay for it if you will send me the bill.

If you will accept these pictures for your collection let me know and I will send them.

Yours sincerely,
Laura Ingalls Wilder

*You can see photos of Pa and Ma*

OCTOBER 24, 1947
Dear Mrs. Carson,

I was glad to hear from you and hope you will forgive me for being so long in replying. It keeps me busy just doing the work and letter writing is neglected.

You must have had a wonderful vacation in California. I have visited the state three times and would like to go again.

Almanzo and I are well as usual and busy as always.

On your next visit to S. Dakota, if you should go to Pierre, you can see photos of Pa and Ma in the museum with Pa's fiddle.

With kindest regards,
Your friend,
Laura Ingalls Wilder

## *I feel sure his illustrations of my stories will be beautiful*

*In 1946 Harper & Brothers decided to issue a uniform-size edition of the Little House books, with new illustrations. It was a complex plan, as postwar difficulties still plagued publishers. Ursula Nordstrom envisioned the new edition as a grand marketing technique to reach upcoming baby-boomer readers. She engaged Garth Williams as the artist; his illustrations had graced the 1945 bestseller by E. B. White, Stuart Little. Williams met with Rose Wilder Lane for advice. She urged him to visit her parents, and he did.*

NOVEMBER 3, 1947

Dear Miss Nordstrom,

I thought you would like to know that Mr. Garth Williams, wife and little daughter arrived here safely and visited us on Thursday of this week. They are very charming people and I think I helped a little in his work. He made drawings of old family pictures I have of the same dates as my stories and seemed very pleased to have found them. I feel sure his illustrations of my stories will be beautiful.

One thing I should have told him is that "Jack" the bulldog was not as pictured in the published books. I think that strain was developed later. Jack's legs were straight and stood tall on them. His face was not wrinkled all out of shape but was smooth with powerful jaws. He was tall enough that I rode on his back without touching the ground.

Mr. Williams will know that kind of English bulldog and if he is told he will make no mistake if he should picture Jack.

With kindest regards,

Laura Ingalls Wilder

## *I love those old missions in California*

NOVEMBER 24, 1947

Dear Miss Nordstrom,

I am a little late in doing so, but still I do thank you for the book, "The Good Night at San Gabriel." It is a sweet story.

I love those old missions in California and long to go back and see them again.

In my book "By the Shores of Silver Lake," there is a mistake in spelling the name of a town east of De Smet. I must have spelled it wrong and then let it get by me in reading proof. In the last paragraph on Page 157 "I'll get to *Brookins*" should be spelled Brookings.

Again on Page 212—4th paragraph it should be spelled *Brookings*.

Also on Page 205—2nd paragraph, the g is left out of the word.

I think those three pages are the only places the name of the town is mentioned. I have thought it did not matter, but I did not realize the books would be used in schools and as historical reference.

I would like to have the spelling corrected anyway in the new edition, for the name of the town is Brookings.

Again thanking you and wishing you a happy holiday season, I am

Yours sincerely,

Laura Ingalls Wilder

## *The complicated system of life that has been thrust upon us*

*Once again Laura's dissatisfaction with American government and modern life is referenced in this note.*

DECEMBER 5, 1947

Dear Mrs. Newman,

Thank you for thinking of us so kindly. We are well as usual, still taking care of our home and ourselves, by ourselves.

You ask what I think of life today. I will say this. I think it was easier and we were happier fighting all the difficulties and dangers of our pioneer life, than anyone is fighting the complicated system of life that has been thrust upon us now. Space is too small to say what I think of it but I am hoping that conditions will change if we all do our best to bring it about.

Love to you and Patty,

Your friend,

Laura Ingalls Wilder

*I cannot agree with what is said about the Ozarks*

*Children's Book Week in the Syracuse Public Library system was celebrated with exhibits concerning the Little House books.*

JANUARY 3, 1948

Dear Miss Nordstrom,

Even though a little late I still want to say thank you for your Christmas greeting and the book "Inside the U.S.A." It is very interesting, though I cannot agree with what is said about the Ozarks, or I should say, about the people of the Ozarks.

Yesterday I wrote the answer to the last of my 210 Christmas cards and letters.

I wrote Miss Wise [Doris Wise, the head of the Syracuse library's young reader department] as you wished and later a letter in answer to those the children wrote me. Featuring Little House books in Syracuse libraries was certainly grand publicity and I hope I expressed my appreciation rightly to Miss Wise. I am glad to have the picture of the display of the books.

By the reports N.Y. is having very bad weather. I hope you are not too much discommoded by it. Our weather was fine until New Year's day; then snow came and ice, making highways unsafe. But now it is again warm and sunny, with snow rapidly disappearing.

I trust you had a Merry Christmas and wish you a Year of Happy Days. With kindest regards,

Yours sincerely,

Laura Ingalls Wilder

## Sometimes I feel lonely

*The renown of the Little House books prompted old childhood friends and relatives to reconnect with Laura. Lettice Carpenter Axtell, a first cousin from Wisconsin, was one of the letter writers. Her mother was Martha Quiner Carpenter, Laura's aunt.*

JANUARY 20, 1948

Dear Cousin,

Your letter was a pleasant surprise. It had been so long since I have heard from you, and as you say "years and age have crept up on us."

I am sorry about you having rheumatism. My hands are not as nimble as they used to be, but still I am very well for 81 years old in February. Manly is rather feeble, being crippled in his feet. He is ninety one. We are living by ourselves in our old farm house and I am doing all the work for ourselves and the house. We have good neighbors just across the road and Manly drives the car so we go to town quite often.

[The letter continues with a summary of her family members and Rose's career as an author.]

Sometimes I feel lonely when I stop being busy enough to think.

It does keep me hurrying to do the work and write as much as I must to keep with the people who write to me after reading my books. The books are selling well. I had more than 200 Christmas cards and letters to answer. . . .

Give Alice my love and tell her I will be looking for her letter. It is nice that you can be with her. I was glad to have your letter and hope to hear from you again.

Lots of love,

Laura Ingalls Wilder

## Perhaps better in the telling than I deserve

*Elizabeth Rider Montgomery was an educator and author. She is best known for creating the first* Look and See *reading primer in 1940, with the characters Dick, Jane, Sally, and their dog, Spot. Her 1949 book,* The Story Behind Modern Books, *included a chapter on Laura Ingalls Wilder.*

JANUARY 24, 1948

Dear Mrs. Montgomery,

I am pleased with the chapter about me and my books. It is all true though perhaps better in the telling than I deserve.

There is one wrong impression that I have corrected in the copy. The stories Pa told us were only in the Little House in the Big Woods and were so indicated. All the rest is from my own memories.

If you will take out the paragraph I have surrounded, page 3, and insert it where I have marked X on page 5, perhaps beginning it with the line I have written at the bottom of page 5, I think the impression I have pointed out will be corrected. All the rest is absolutely correct.

Thank you for the list of the books you are writing about. My Little House in the Big Woods is keeping very good company indeed and I am proud of it.

It was kind of you to tell me where my books stand in popularity.

I had never thought I was in any way remarkable for having my mss. accepted. It may be as sister Carrie once said to me, "You are always so busy doing, you never stop to see what you have done."

I wish you success in the book you are writing and if I can be of any help, let me know.

Yours sincerely,

Laura Ingalls Wilder

## It is flattering

*Dr. Irvin Kerlan worked in Washington, D.C., on the staff of the Food and Drug Administration. He started collecting children's books as a hobby, especially signed copies, and original art and manuscripts. Laura's inscription in his copy of* By the Shores of Silver Lake *reads: "Dear Dr. Kerlan, Some day when I have passed away / (The flowers will bloom just the same.) / Someday my face will be forgot / My only memory be a name." Dr. Kerlan's collection expanded; he offered it to his alma mater, the University of Minnesota. The Kerlan Collection is one of the world's greatest repositories of rare children's books and memorabilia.*

FEBRUARY 2, 1948

Dr. Irvin Kerlan

Washington

Dear Sir,

I will be pleased to autograph copies of my books if you will send them to me by mail with return postage.

It is flattering that you should wish to add my series of "Little House" books to your library and I thank you for the compliment.

Hope you will be able to secure the eight books.

With kindest regards,

Laura Ingalls Wilder

## *I do not wish my letter to seem abrupt*

*Robert and Ella Boast, friends of the Ingalls family in De Smet since 1879, died in 1921 and 1918, respectively.*

MARCH 18, 1948

Dear Mrs. Carson,

I have so many, many letters to answer that sometimes I am far behind with them. Now that Spring is here and house-cleaning on hand I shall have to stop writing altogether I fear.

It is not possible for me to get help for housework so I must do my work whether I can or not. So far I have been able to keep it up after a fashion for which I am thankful.

We are both very well though it has been a long, hard winter and we are glad Spring is here. We have tomato seeds planted in the house and six little kids at the barn.

The Boasts have both been dead for many years.

Rose is well, but the winter there has been very hard.

I do not wish my letter to seem abrupt. I have written so many letters, my hand cramps.

With kindest regards,

Your friend,

Laura Ingalls Wilder

## *Sir Walter Scott and Tennyson's poems were great favorites of mine*

*In response to a survey of childhood reading experiences of children's authors sent by the Denver Public Library, Laura wrote of her early meager memories of books.*

APRIL 29, 1948

Dear Miss Watson,

It seems I must have done without all the good books when I was a girl. The two checked on the list are all of the list I knew. [A book list was submitted to authors, asking them to check books familiar from their childhoods; Laura noted only *Uncle Tom's Cabin* and *Lorna Doone*.]

The poems of Sir Walter Scott and Tennyson's poems were great favorites of mine.

My father gave me a little book of verses called "The Floweret" in 1872. It was published by Lee and Shepard in Boston. I still have the little book, but of course it is long since forgotten by others.

My sisters and I read our stories in the old Youth's Companion which was no book but a children's paper.

Sorry to be of so little help to you.

With kindest regards,

Laura Ingalls Wilder

*I must tell you how much I enjoyed it*

APRIL 30, 1948

Dear Betsy,

I have so many, many letters to answer that I have made a rule to write only once to each person. But your letter is so interesting that I must tell you how much I enjoyed it.

It is wonderful to live where you can watch the wild animals and birds. I would love to see them. Thank you for writing me about them.

Yours sincerely,

Laura Ingalls Wilder

## *You certainly had courage to live on your claim*

MAY 3, 1948

Dear Mrs. Schaefer,

Your letter is most interesting and inclines me to think, as we so often have said, that the world is small.

I did not know the Billy Allens, but that is understood when one remembers how many strangers flocked into that new country. Mr. Wilder probably knew him, but it is so long ago that he does not remember.

I wonder if Mr. Allen and Rita Allen know that Carrie died two years ago this June. Grace, my younger sister, died four years before that, and Mary several years before her.

I am the only one of the family left and I was 81 last February. Mr. Wilder is 91.

You certainly had courage to live on your claim so far from any one as you did. No one who has not pioneered as we have can understand the fascination and the terror of it.

Royal Wilder married in eastern Minnesota and lived there until his death years ago. He left one daughter. Eliza, the sister, married and lived in Louisiana. She also died years ago, leaving one child, a son, Wilder Thayer, who lives in Louisiana.

We lived on the claim for four years, then spent one year in Minnesota and one year in Florida. Went back to De Smet and lived in town, coming from there here in 1894.

Please give my regards to Mr. Allen and Rita.

Yours sincerely,

Laura Ingalls Wilder

## *I remember how lovely the bluffs along the lake were*

*Reba Wakefield was a children's librarian in Saint Paul, Minnesota. "For many years," she wrote Laura, "I have given your books to boys and girls to read . . . they love them so much that they are always out of circulation." Her family also had lived in the Pepin, Wisconsin, area, so "with the feeling that Lake Pepin is a bond of kinship between us, I couldn't resist writing you."*

JUNE 7, 1948

Dear Miss Wakefield,

Thank you for your most interesting letter and the old fashioned name card.

The card is quaint now and pretty and your recollection of your mother's stories of her childhood are so near my own it seems to make us almost kin folk as we say here.

Indeed I do remember Pa and Ma often speaking of Stockholm and I knew it was not far away.

Also I remember how lovely the bluffs along the lake were then and my memory was refreshed when my husband and I re-visited that country about 58 years ago.

I would love to see it again, but likely never will for my traveling days seem to be over.

Again I thank you for telling me of Lake Pepin as it is now.

Yours sincerely,

Laura Ingalls Wilder

## *Things of real value do not change*

The United States' State Department compiled a list of American books for translation into Japanese as part of a reeducation program in the occupied country. The Long Winter *was one of the first titles published. Laura was asked to write a message to Japanese children as a result.*

Rocky Ridge Farm
Mansfield, Missouri U.S.A.
JULY 8, 1948
Dear Japanese Children.

Though you are far away and speak a different language, still the things worthwhile in life are the same for us all and the same as when I was a child so long ago.

Things of real value do not change with the passing of years nor in going from one country to another.

These I am sure you have.

It is always best to be honest and truthful; to make the most of what we have; to be happy with simple pleasures, to be cheerful in adversity and have courage in danger.

With love to you all and best wishes for your happiness, I am
Sincerely your friend,
Laura Ingalls Wilder

## *My schoolmates are still very distinct in my mind*

The Kennedys are mentioned in On the Banks of Plum Creek.

AUGUST 16, 1948

Dear Mrs. Spears,

Your letter was a pleasant surprise. It is so interesting to hear from one of the Kennedy family. I am sure it must be the one I remember.

There were Daniel and Christy. Then if I remember right, Cassie, Sandy, Nettie and a smaller girl whose name I do not remember. If I am right, this smaller child was a baby when last I saw the Kennedy family which was about three years after meeting the others at school.

It is so long ago that my memory may not be accurate, but those who were my schoolmates are still very distinct in my mind.

Plum Creek was two miles north of Walnut Grove or as it was sometimes called, Walnut Station.

A friend [Garth Williams] who is to illustrate a new edition of my books visited Walnut Grove and Plum Creek recently so I know they are still there.

Thinking you may be interested I am sending you a list of my books.

Yours sincerely,

Laura Ingalls Wilder

*I think I have had letters from every state*

An educator asked to examine a sampling of Laura's fan mail from children.

OCTOBER 1, 1948

Dear Frances Mason,

I hope the enclosed letters will be what you want to see. They are from scattered points as you notice.

The children send me their pictures, Christmas cards and presents, Valentines, birthday cards and gifts.

I think I have had letters from every state and have always answered them all until recently. Rheumatism in my hands now makes it difficult and at times painful for me to write, so I am not answering all and wish the children might understand how I cannot continue writing so many letters.

With kindest regards,

Yours sincerely,

Laura Ingalls Wilder

*Your father certainly was a grand man*

*This letter to Mrs. H. R. Richardson of Minneapolis indicates Laura's respect for courage and individuality.*

OCTOBER 6, 1948

Dear Mrs. Richardson,

It is indeed a pleasure to hear from you and know that you once saw Ma and Mary and that your father attended the college for the blind with Mary.

Those were great days when your people came to Arlington. Mr. Wilder and I are at times homesick for them. We were saying only the other day that we wanted so much to go back again to De Smet. When you next visit Arlington I do hope you visit De Smet. But I hope you will not be disappointed.

The city drained Silver Lake and the Big Slough to get more plow land. As though the hundreds of acres of dry land was not enough!

Your father certainly was a grand man to do so well without help. In those days people who were worthwhile did not beg for help as many do now.

I am the only one of my family living now. . . .

I thank you so much for your letter, it means a lot to me; and for the kind things you say about my books.

With kindest regards
Your friend,
Laura Ingalls Wilder

## *I do envy your seeing the Wessington Hills*

OCTOBER 23, 1948
Dear Ida Carson,

Glad to have your letter with news of your trip to S. Dakota.

Almanzo and I were speaking of De Smet the other day and of how we were still homesick for Dakota.

We are very well for our age and enjoying our nice weather. Oh! Of course we tire easily and have twinges of rheumatism, but that is to be expected. Rheumatism in my hands makes it hard for me to write. But we are still living by ourselves and doing all our own work.

I do envy your seeing the Wessington Hills and Huron and Mitchell, but am glad that you did.

We are having a dry fall here, but a few showers faded the colors of the forest leaves.

I am wishing you another successful school term.

With love, your friend,
Laura Ingalls Wilder

## *Mansfield is on the exact top of the Ozark Hills*

*Laura was vague in reporting the family history; Charles Ingalls died in 1902; Caroline in 1924; Royal Wilder in 1925.*

DECEMBER 13, 1948

Dear Mrs. Marshfield,

Thanks for your season's good wishes.

Answering your questions—Royal Wilder died several years ago. Almanzo is the only one of the family living. Pa died thirty years ago and Ma soon after. I am the only one of the family living.

Mansfield is at the exact top of the Ozark Hills. Water to the north drains away in that direction into the Gasconade River, while on the South the water runs south into the White River.

The Ozarks, you know, are not mountains as are the Rocky and Coast ranges. They are as we always speak of them, the Ozark Hills.

I wish for you and yours a Merry Christmas and a very Happy New Year.

With kindest regards,

Laura Ingalls Wilder


*I had some surprising good news yesterday*


DECEMBER 14, 1948

Dear Ida Carson,

Your telling me of your South Dakota trip made me homesick for those prairies. How I would love to see them again, but I fear I never will. Just now I should be thankful we are sheltered in the Ozark hills from South Dakota winter winds.

We have had a wonderful fall and so far this month, no snow or cold weather. Just now it is raining steadily but still warm.

Mr. Wilder has not been well and we have been staying close to home so I have not seen the stores in their Christmas dressing.

Rose was well a few days ago when writing her latest letter. She is very busy and tied up with affairs at her home in Connecticut.

I had some surprising good news yesterday. The Detroit Public

Library is opening a new branch library and it will be named the
Laura Ingalls Wilder Branch Library.

You have certainly served your time teaching school. Such a record deserves public recognition of some kind.

I wish you a Merry Christmas, a Happy New Year and again a
successful year in your chosen profession.

Yours sincerely,

Laura Ingalls Wilder

## *I am overwhelmed*

*The post–World War II baby boom and the expanding suburbs
created a need for additional libraries in Detroit, Michigan. Ralph
Ulveling was the director of the Detroit Public Library system.
Bedtime reading for his children included the Little House books.
He had great respect for Laura Ingalls Wilder; his own ancestors
in Adrian, Minnesota, had endured the Hard Winter of 1880–
1881. Ulveling and his staff agreed that a new branch library should
bear Laura Ingalls Wilder's name.*

DECEMBER 15, 1948

Mr. Ralph Ulveling

Detroit Public Library

Dear Sir,

Your letter is indeed a pleasant message and a great surprise as
well. To say that I am deeply gratified is not enough. I am overwhelmed that such an honor should be given me. I am certainly least
among those so honored.

I would be glad to be present at the opening of the library, but it is
not possible.

Mr. Wilder, Almanzo, the Farmer Boy, is ninety-two years old
and not well, so I cannot leave home.

I thank you for the invitation, also for your kind letter and the two copies, one of which I am sending to my daughter, Rose Wilder Lane, and the other to Harper and Brothers as you suggested. I am sure they will all be greatly pleased.

I thank you and the others of the Staff for the great honor bestowed upon me and wish you all a Merry Christmas and a very Happy New Year.

Yours sincerely,

Laura Ingalls Wilder

## *I am doing no writing and very little reading these days*

*Margaret Kinison from Illinois wrote about children who lived in New Salem, the early home of Abraham Lincoln.*

MARCH 15, 1949

Dear Miss Kinison,

Thank you for the nice things you say about my "Little House Books."

Your stories "Children of New Salem" must be very interesting and I wish you a great success with them. Being so busy with other things I am doing no writing and very little reading these days.

With kindest regards,

Yours sincerely,

Laura Ingalls Wilder

## *I can send you the mss.*

*The use of Laura's name on the library marked the first time Detroit had designated a building for a living person and for a woman. Other*

*Detroit library namesakes included Benjamin Franklin, Thomas Jef-*
*ferson, and Thomas Edison. Ralph Ulveling wrote: "This enduring*
*honor is in recognition of the fine social history of pioneer days which*
*you have presented in your series of books so beautifully and clearly."*
*He invited the Wilders to the dedication, asked for items to display at*
*the event, and requested a formal response from Laura to be read.*

MAY 3, 1949
Dear Mr. Ulveling,

Much as I would like to be present at the opening of the Laura
Ingalls Wilder Branch Library it will not be possible.

Mr. Wilder's general health is better but he is ninety-two years old
and not strong. It is not safe for him to be alone and we two are by
ourselves in the old farm house. There is no help to be hired and I
cannot leave home. Please understand that it is not from any lack of
appreciation that I do not come.

I am sorry to disappoint you also about the photograph. There is
no photographer in our town and I do not feel equal to a trip to the
city to have one taken. The picture I am sending was taken when I
was writing "By the Shores of Silver Lake" about twelve years ago. I
have no pictures of any scenes in my books. It was long ago and taking
of pictures was not common as now.

I haven't the mss. of "Little House in the Big Woods" but I can
send you the mss. of "The Long Winter" or "These Happy Golden
Years" one or both. The original drafts are written with pencil in
school tablet. If you want them I will send those and also the revised
typewritten mss.

If you would care for them I will send you to keep also the reader
and history I studied in "Little Town on the Prairie." Let me know
what of all above I shall send.

I hesitate to write anything to be displayed at the opening or read
on a program. Frankly I don't know what to say. The enclosed is my

attempt to accede to your request. If it pleases you, use it in any way you wish. If not, ignore it.

I will be glad to autograph books for the libraries.

With kindest regards from Mr. Wilder and myself I am

Yours sincerely,

Laura Ingalls Wilder

### *I am proud and grateful*

*Laura's message was read at the dedication of the Laura Ingalls Wilder Branch Library on May 12, 1949.*

Dear Friends,

Although I am not present, I join with you in being glad that you now have a Branch Library in your community.

I am proud and grateful that it has been named for me and that my "Little House Books" will be among those you may read.

Unless you had lived as I did, where books were scarce and so prized greatly, you cannot realize how wonderful it really is to have a whole library so convenient for your use.

With congratulations and all good wishes, I am

Yours sincerely,

Laura Ingalls Wilder

### *At times it has seemed incredible*

JUNE 2, 1949

Dear Mr. Ulveling,

Many things conspired to delay my writing to you, but I assure you your kindness in sending me so complete an account of the

Laura Ingalls Wilder Branch Library is none the less appreciated.

The Branch being named for me is such a wonderful thing that at times it has seemed incredible. Your letter has made it more real.

Thank you for the delightful broadside, the clippings, the pictures and the check.

The books to be autographed have arrived and will be started on their way to you as soon as I can go to town.

You may be interested to know that I have just received a letter from a twelve years old Japanese girl in Japan, a reader of my books, who quoted Tennyson's "Sweet and Low, Wind of the Western Sea."

Mr. Wilder is feeling better, but is quite feeble.

With kindest regards from us both I am

Yours sincerely,

Laura Ingalls Wilder

## *This arrangement should have been made long ago*

*Rose edited the National Economic Council's Review of Books and lived modestly in her Danbury house during the 1940s. Continual improvements on her home indicated more income than she officially earned. Perhaps her parents shared proceeds from the sales of houses and land on Rocky Ridge. To give Rose a dependable income, Laura directed George Bye to send her daughter a percentage from the Little House books' royalties.*

JULY 16, 1949

Dear Mr. Bye,

I think the enclosed assignment will give you the authority needed for paying Rose 10% of my royalties. If anything more is necessary please let me know. This arrangement should have been made long ago.

I wonder if you were as surprised as I by the naming of the Detroit Branch Library for me. You and I as well as the Little House Books seem to be getting quite a bit of publicity. . . .

*Laura's nebulous description of Rose's role in the writing of the Little House books indicates that both mother and daughter desired their collaboration to remain secret.*

JULY 16, 1949
Mr. George T. Bye
New York City, N.Y.
Dear Sir,

I owe Rose, for helping me, at first, in selling my books and for the publicity she gave them.

In payment for this debt I hereby assign to Rose Wilder Lane (10%) ten per cent of the royalties on my "Little House Books."

Please pay her this amount from those royalties received by you from Harper and Brothers.

Laura Ingalls Wilder

## *He is nearly helpless*

*The summer of 1949 was a difficult one. After suffering a heart attack Manly was extremely weak; Laura left home only briefly, to tend to errands in Mansfield. That summer, in Malone, New York, Frances Smith and her daughter Dorothy found the location of the old Wilder farm. The Smiths, who were related to Manly, wrote about their discovery.*

OCTOBER 1, 1949
Dear Miss Smith,

Your interesting letter would have been answered sooner, except for the serious illness of Almanzo.

He suffered a heart attack the last of July and is only slowly recovering.

Due to shortage of nurses I have had to take all care of him and still do as he is nearly helpless.

Almanzo remembers his uncle, Andrew Day, and his wife who was his father's sister. As you know James Wilder was Almanzo's father.

With kindest regards from us both,
Sincerely,
Laura Ingalls Wilder

## *Almanzo died of a heart attack*

NOVEMBER 8, 1949
Dear Dorothy,

This is to bring you the sad news that your Uncle Almanzo died of a heart attack October 23d. He was buried in the Mansfield cemetery on Oct. 28.

Rose came but could only stay a week.

We had sold the farm retaining possession of the house and grounds and I am staying on here for a time at least. My future plans are uncertain.

With love,
Your Aunt Bessie

## *It is very lonely without my husband*

*Laura appreciated the friendship between Ernest and Minnie Green and her family in De Smet. In 1902 the Greens rented rooms from Caroline Ingalls. After the couple moved to their own home they continued their rapport with the Ingalls family, assisting them faithfully. Laura met Minnie Green on her 1931 visit to De Smet. Her letter refers to Judge Green's death, earlier in 1949.*

NOVEMBER 18, 1949

Dear Mrs. Green,

I thank you for your kind letter and your sympathy. It is very lonely without my husband as you so well understand, but there is nothing left but to go on from here alone.

I have often thought of you and of the many kindnesses of you and Mr. Green to my mother and sisters and although I never saw you but the once I have counted you both as friends.

As we do not take the De Smet paper I did not know of Mr. Green's death. You have my heartfelt sympathy knowing what you have suffered.

It pleases me that you like my little books.

Those dear old days seem so far away now and sometimes I am homesick for them. But "The moving finger writes and having writ moves on."

With kindest regards,

Yours sincerely,

Laura Ingalls Wilder

*I am so tired*

*Laura informed her semiregular correspondent in Glidden, Iowa, the teacher Ida Carson, of her husband's death.*

NOVEMBER 19, 1949

Dear Friend,

This is only a note for my heart is too sore to write more. Almanzo died October 23d and I am very lonely.

My plans are uncertain and I am so tired for I nursed Almanzo through a 3 months sickness.

Sincerely,

Laura Ingalls Wilder

CHAPTER 6

# THE AUTHOR OF CLASSICS
## (1950–1956)

Laura at the dedication of the Wilder Library in Mansfield, September 28, 1951. The *Springfield News-Leader* wrote: "She was a striking, charming little woman. . . . She wore a beautiful, very dark red velvet dress, at the shoulder of which a friend had pinned a large orchid. It was difficult to believe she was 84. . . . "

*Laura was shattered by her husband's death. As a friend expressed it, "For Mrs. Wilder, all was well with the world until Almanzo died."*

*Laura stoically rejected well-meaning attempts to find a companion to tend her. She loved Rocky Ridge Farm too much to leave. Gradually, the self-reliant pioneer girl created a life without Manly. She resumed her attendance at the Methodist church in Mansfield. She continued her Wednesday tradition of shopping and visiting in town at midweek. In good weather, she took a long morning walk before tending to housework. Reading and needlework filled her time.*

*Friends and neighbors were solicitous. They telephoned and dropped in to visit. Neta and Silas Seal spent Sunday afternoons with her. The Jones family, who lived next door, was faithful. The two young brothers, Sheldon and Roscoe Jones, were Laura's surrogate grandchildren. They brought the mail, assisted with outdoor chores, and spent time simply visiting. The boys were deep into reading the Little House books, but better yet was listening to "Mrs. Wilder" herself telling stories. To the boys she was a grandmotherly figure, smiling and affectionate. She paid them liberally for chores they performed, and shared boxes of candy she received from readers.*

*Rose made extended visits to Rocky Ridge during the 1950s. She was good company, but had grown increasingly cantankerous about politics and government. Sometimes her rants were wearing. She found Mansfield as provincial as ever, and its lingering clannishness annoyed her. "We only came in 1894, and are still 'furriners,'" Rose fumed.*

*Without the responsibility of Manly, Laura could participate in her fame as an author. She entertained the local fourth-grade class at Rocky Ridge, and visited the school to tell stories. A Laura Ingalls Wilder Day was held in nearby Hartville, and Laura attended. She also went to Springfield to speak to a college class, appeared at a library event, and signed books at a well-attended autograph party.*

*Families, educators, and librarians from all over America stopped at Rocky Ridge, hoping to meet Laura. If she wasn't feeling well, the Jones boys fended off the callers. Usually Laura received her unknown friends, answered questions, posed for pictures, signed books, and proudly showed the visitors through her unique home.*

*And always, the letters continued to arrive, and Laura diligently replied to them.*

## *I long so much for the old places and the old times*

Evelyn Wenzel wrote an article on the Little House books for
Elementary English *magazine*.

JANUARY 10, 1950
Dear Miss Wenzel,

Thank you so much for the picture of Pa's fiddle and for your interesting letter. I am glad you saw the museum and the town of De
Smet.

At times I long so much for the old places and the old times. Especially is this so when I am so lonely for Almanzo.

Ah Well! "The moving finger writes, And having writ moves on."

Again I thank you for the picture of Pa's dear old fiddle.

Yours sincerely,

Laura Ingalls Wilder

## *I do not mind living alone*

FEBRUARY 1, 1950
Dear Mrs. Carson,

I thank you for your kind letter and for your friendly interest
in me.

Almanzo is buried in the Wilder lot in the Mansfield Cemetery.
Our daughter Rose Wilder Lane came from Connecticut. She is the
only near relative living. There are only scattered nieces and nephews
and distant cousins besides. Rose stayed a while and then had to return to her home. . . . She will come again in the Spring.

The farm was already sold but I have life tenure of the house and
grounds and am staying here. There are neighbors just across the
road and just a short distance to the side. Groceries are delivered to

the door; mail every morning to the box by the road; my fuel oil tank for my heater is kept filled with no trouble to me and electricity and telephone ready to my touch. The house is warm and comfortable.

Two boys from the neighbors on the East come every day to see if there is anything they can do for me and a taxi from town is on call to take me wherever I wish to go. Friends from town, only ¼ mile away, come often to see me.

I think I am as well situated as I could be in town with none of the town annoyances. Never having been timid, I do not mind living alone except for missing Almanzo. I am very lonely for him, but that would be so wherever I am.

We have had a wonderful winter so far. The last few days have been cloudy and gloomy and there is some ice which does not bother me as I do not have to go outdoors. The boys bring my mail from the mail box; wood and water are inside the house. Wood is for the cook stove when I rather use that than the electric cook stove.

With kindest regards,
Your friend,
Laura Ingalls Wilder

## Pa did not keep a diary

MARCH 30, 1950
Dear Mrs. Carson,

My mail is so heavy it takes me a long time to answer a letter, for I am always behind with my writing.

March weather here has been very unsettled, warm one day and cold the next. People have been suffering with colds and flu because of it. But I have kept well, not even a cold all winter. It looks now as if the worst was over and Spring is here.

Pa did not keep a diary. It would be very interesting if there were one.

Mary Power and Ida Brown died years ago. Mary left no children but Ida's children and grandchildren live in California.

My daughter is a widow with no children.

Almanzo's sister Alice married. Her home was in Florida and her children and grandchildren live there now.

It seems strange to me that of all the people I wrote about I am so far the only one left.

Yours sincerely,

Laura Ingalls Wilder


## *It is hard for me to even write a letter*

*The fifth-grade classroom and their teacher in East Jordan, Michigan, received replies from Laura while her grief over the loss of her husband was especially acute.*

APRIL 14, 1950

Dear Miss Liskum,

Thank you for all the kind things you say about my little books. But you must be tired of reading them so many times.

You have my permission to use my letter to the children in any way you please.

Since Mr. Wilder's death it is hard for me to even write a letter so I hope you will excuse my answer to the children being so short.

With kindest regards,

Yours sincerely,

Laura Ingalls Wilder

## *It is fun to have pets*

APRIL 14, 1950

Dear Children,

I am so glad you like my stories and hope the last ones of the series will please you too.

It is fun to have pets like cats and dogs and they will be such good friends if you train them that way. Just now I have only a cat.

I am sure you will be sorry to know that Almanzo died last October. . . . Your letters would have pleased him and I thank you for writing for him as well as me.

Love to you all,

Your friend,

Laura Ingalls Wilder

## *You ask how I spend my time*

*Clara Webber accepted the children's librarian position at the Pomona Public Library in California in 1948. She held back tears as she was shown the dreary children's room. She vowed, "As soon as I get this place looking like something, it will be named for Laura Ingalls Wilder." Early in 1950, plans were afoot to dedicate the library room. A huge wall map was created to trace the journeys of the Ingalls family; the dedication was set for May 25, 1950.*

APRIL 19, 1950

Dear Miss Webber,

It is not possible for me to locate on the map exactly the place of Little House in the Big Woods. The map does not show Lake Pepin which is in an enlargement of the Mississippi River some miles north of Winona, Minn., which is of course on the other side of the river.

I have marked with a blue cross the approximate place The Little House was, about seven miles into Wisconsin from the lake in the river. I do not know the route we followed going to The Little House on the Prairie, being much too young to remember.

On the Banks of Plum Creek I cannot locate exactly as the towns of Tracy and Walnut Grove are not shown on the map. I know it was west of New Ulm and so have put a cross there.

In going to Little House on the Prairie I know we crossed a corner of N. Missouri and through Independence, Kas. to 3 miles over the line into what was Indian Territory [the Osage ceded lands, technically not open to white settlement].

De Smet, South Dakota is the scene of the rest of the story. I have marked it with a blue cross. Blue is the only colored pencil I have.

Malone, New York, scene of Farmer Boy and Almanzo's birthplace in the country nearby is extreme N. New York. I have marked it with a blue cross, but have no idea the route the family followed going West to Minnesota.

I fear my map markings will not be much help. I am sorry.

Mansfield is marked in blue.

I will not be able to make a tape recording. There is no one here to do such work.

My daughter, Rose Wilder Lane, lives at her home near Danbury, Connecticut. She intends to make me a visit this summer. It is hard she lives so far away but her work is there and mine is here.

You ask how I spend my time—

There were only forty-nine letters in my mail yesterday morning. Most of them must be answered. I do all my own work and it is now house cleaning time for this ten room house. I call a taxi once a week for shopping and visiting and to church Sunday.

I am living alone and it is very lonely without Almanzo, but it would be lonely anywhere and I would rather stay in my own, old home.

[Clara Webber had asked for Laura's famous gingerbread recipe to serve at the library dedication, and Laura included it in this letter.]

1 cup sugar, 1/2 cup shortening creamed. Add 1 cup molasses. Mix.

1 teaspoon baking soda in cup. Fill with boiling water letting foam run over until there is one cup of water.

Add three cups flour sifted with 1 teaspoon each of ginger, cinnamon, allspice, scant spoon cloves and a pinch of salt. When well mixed add 2 well beaten eggs. Mix well and bake in a moderate oven 30 minutes. Raisins and candied fruit may be added if wished. Good luck!

Yours sincerely,

Laura Ingalls Wilder

## *The news of Pepin is very welcome*

APRIL 20, 1950

Dear Mrs. Anderson,

Hearing from you is like getting a letter from my youth. I was 17 when I received the last letter postmarked "Pepin."

I feel certain that the Laura Ingalls your father knew was a relative of mine. A cousin of my own age with the same name lived there when my family did. The families did not keep in touch but there are Ingalls in northern Wisconsin I know, and Laura was a family name.

I do not know the name of the man to whom Pa sold his farm near Pepin. I remember only that he was a Swede. As you know, it was a Swedish settlement. I have no memory of the name "Schruth." I am sorry but I was five years old when we came away and so much, so very much, has happened since. Please give your father my best regards.

The news of Pepin is very welcome. I'd love to see the place again. But never will I'm sure. 83 is too old to travel.

Think of me as your friend,

Laura Ingalls Wilder

## *It is kind of you to keep me informed*

*As a gift to the Pomona Public Library, Laura sent her penciled manuscript of* Little Town on the Prairie.

MAY 20, 1950

Dear Miss Webber,

Your letter came this morning and I have no mail out until Monday, the 22nd. I hope this will reach you in time for your use.

It is not possible for me to talk for a radio record. Please convey my regrets to Mr. Caldwell.

The enclosed letter is for you to read at the dedication if it meets with your approval. I'm afraid it is not good but since Mr. Wilder's death my thoughts do not flow freely. I am still rather stunned from the shock.

It is kind of you to keep me informed regarding the dedication and I will be glad to have the newspaper. I would love to be with you at that time for I am sure it will be a grand occasion. I wish you the greatest success and am sorry I cannot do more to help with it.

Yours sincerely,

Laura Ingalls Wilder

P.S. The books to be autographed have not yet come from Harpers.

## *I was far from a library in those days*

MAY 1950

Dear Friends,

It makes me very proud that you have named this room in your library for me. I do appreciate the honor you have given me.

You make good use of your library I am sure. How I would have loved it when I was young, but I was far from a library in those days.

As you read my books of long ago I hope you will remember that the things that will give you happiness are the same now as they were then.

Courage and kindness, loyalty, truth and helpfulness are always the same and always needed.

With kindest regards and all good wishes,

Sincerely your friend,

Laura Ingalls Wilder


## *I am indeed proud to have my name connected with it*

*Clara Webber hoped to visit Laura Ingalls Wilder when she traveled east for the American Library Association convention in Cleveland during July 1950. As Laura indicated in her letter, Rose planned to visit Rocky Ridge. The mother and daughter did not, however, make a vacation trip.*


MAY 31, 1950

Dear Miss Webber,

Thank you so much for the clippings and the photo of the library. It is a beautiful building and I am indeed proud to have my name connected with it.

It seems to me you must have had an enjoyable time at the dedication. Already I have had a letter from a little girl who enjoyed the gingerbread so you must have been successful with the recipe.

I am so glad Pa's old tunes were played. That surely gave the touch to bring to memory the past.

I would love to meet you, but my daughter Rose is coming in July.

She writes that she is going to take me away for a month's vacation. She did not say where. I suppose that it is to be a surprise. So I will not be home in July. I am sorry.

I thank you for your letter so kindly telling me of the things that happened. You are a sweet person.

Sincerely your friend,

Laura Ingalls Wilder

## Black Susan, the cat

JUNE 3, 1950

Third Grade

Franklin School

Dear Children,

Thank you for all your nice letters. I enjoyed them very much.

I am glad you like my stories.

The color of the Christmas horses was bay. Black Susan, the cat, stayed in the little house with the people who came when we went away.

Wishing you all a happy vacation,

With love, your friend,

Laura Ingalls Wilder

## Memories of our childhood are so much alike

JUNE 3, 1950

Dear Miss Panzram,

Your letter is very interesting. The memories of our childhood are so much alike and so different from now, they should make us friends.

What a thrill we had on some sunny spring day when we first took off our shoes and stockings and ran outdoors barefoot for a short time.

I am indeed glad if my books are a help in your school work.

Yours sincerely,

Laura Ingalls Wilder

## If I am at home I would be glad to see you

*Irene Fosness visited Laura on Rocky Ridge in August 1950.*

JULY 14, 1950

Dear Mrs. Fosness,

I cannot promise to be at home the last of August as my daughter, Rose Wilder Lane, is coming soon and insists that we take a trip somewhere together. As I do not know what her idea is, where it may lead us, nor for how long, my plans are rather uncertain as you can see.

If I am at home I would be glad to see you, so if you pass this way, please stop and see if I am here.

Thank you for the kind things you say of my little books. I am glad you like them.

With kindest regards,

Laura Ingalls Wilder

## Inquiries from people who want to give them for Christmas

*When Laura wrote this letter, Garth Williams was in Rome, working on the new Little House illustrations. "We have finally decided on an absolutely beautiful technique," wrote Ursula Nordstrom, "with a carbon pencil, and they will be reproduced in halftone . . . they will be perfect I know."*

NOVEMBER 25, 1950

Dear Miss Nordstrom,

Can you tell me when the edition of the Little House books illustrated by Garth Williams will be out?

I have many inquiries from people who want to give them for Christmas presents. Please let me know when they will be published.

With kindest regards to you and your office force.

Sincerely,

Laura Ingalls Wilder

## *I shall expect . . . to be changed*

*Pa's fiddle brought a steady stream of visitors to the South Dakota Historical Society in Pierre. Many wished to photograph it, and the fiddle was removed from its case for picture-taking. At mid-century the museum staff was somewhat bemused at the attention paid to Pa's fiddle. Laura was incensed that the fiddle was being incorrectly identified.*

OCTOBER 16, 1950

Secretary, State Historical Society

Pierre, South Dakota

Dear Sir,

Recently a friend sent me a copy of the inscription which she says is attached to my father's violin.

As she read it, the inscription is all wrong. The violin was mine. I sent it to the Historical Society. . . .

I have a receipt for the violin from the then secretary, Lawrence K. Fox, dated May 22, 1944. The receipt quotes the inscription as I have given it and promises to make every effort to have the violin played four times a year as I had stipulated.

Rose Wilder Lane is the daughter of Almanzo Wilder and Laura

Ingalls Wilder and the *granddaughter* of Charles P. Ingalls. The violin was purchased by him long before 1879, but was played by him in De Smet at that time. My earliest recollection is of his playing it *years* before. I shall expect [the inscription] attached to the violin to be changed. . . .

The violin was appraised in New York at $50,000. Surely it is worthy of being truthfully explained.

Yours truly,

Laura Ingalls Wilder

## *My trouble was nerves and heart*

JANUARY 3, 1951

Dear Miss Nordstrom,

Thanks for your Christmas remembrance. The book "Horace Greeley" looks very interesting but I have not been able to read it yet.

I have been very ill and am now able to sit up part of the time. My desk is covered with stacks and piles of Christmas mail as yet unanswered.

My trouble was nerves and heart and I am under orders to "take it easy." Which is hard for me to do. . . .

## *I do remember your calling on me*

JANUARY 18, 1951

Dear Mrs. Kelley,

Your Christmas greetings would have been answered sooner, but I have been very ill and could not write. Please give your group of children my love and thanks for their Christmas thought of me.

I am sending autographs that you can paste in my books if you wish. It is more than I can do to attend to autographing and mailing books. I am not very strong. It is too great a task to answer all the mail I get, so please tell your pupils not to write to me for likely they would get no reply.

I am glad you have recovered your health and are teaching again. Yes! I do remember your calling on me.

Love to you and the children,

Yours sincerely,

Laura Ingalls Wilder

## *My mistake in naming the lake*

*Dorothy Smith of Malone, New York, noted that the lake mentioned in* Farmer Boy *was Chateaugay, not Chautauqua. Miss Smith researched the Wilder family, hosted interested visitors to Malone, and founded the organization that restored the house described in* Farmer Boy.

JANUARY 31, 1951

Dear Miss Smith,

Thank you for your letter telling me of my mistake in naming the lake. I have asked Harpers to correct the spelling. It is interesting to know you are a granddaughter of Almanzo's aunt. That would make you his second cousin, would it not?

Perhaps you know Almanzo died in October 1949.

Again, thank you for telling me of my mistake, I am with kindest regards,

Yours sincerely,

Laura Ingalls Wilder

## *I thank them all and send my love*

*Docia Holland was the Wright County, Missouri, librarian. She knew Laura Ingalls Wilder from her weekly Wednesday visits to the Mansfield library. The library staff sent thousands of penny postcards to libraries from coast to coast, asking for greetings to be sent on Laura's February 7 birthday. The response was staggering.*

FEBRUARY 24, 1951

Dear Mrs. Holland,

I thank you for the lovely birthday card. You will do me a great favor if you will explain to library patrons that I cannot answer all cards and letters received. There are between 800 and 900 of them.

Tell them, please, that I thank them all and send my love.

Yours gratefully,

Laura Ingalls Wilder

## *Our old school crowd is vanished*

*Ada Scott Keating attended the De Smet school with the Ingalls girls.*

FEBRUARY 26, 1951

Dear Ada,

It is nice to have your birthday greetings and most especially your letter inside.

You have done a much better job in raising such a nice family than you would have writing no matter how successful you might have been.

My one child, Rose Wilder Lane, is so far away from me, but is planning to come this Spring for a long visit.

It is so lonely without Mr. Wilder that at times I can hardly bear it, but one has to bear what comes.

Our old school crowd is vanished as you say, but we did have good times together, even if we didn't have all these modern things.

With lots of love,

Your old school friend,

Laura Ingalls Wilder

## *I have always been so active*

MARCH 8, 1951

Dear Miss Webber,

I am so pleased with the stationery of the Laura Ingalls Wilder Room and thank you for sending it. . . .

My books have been translated into German, as well as Japanese, but so far as I know that is all.

My health is very good now, but I still have to treat my heart with respect. I have always been so active that it is hard to be careful. . . .

Yours sincerely,

Laura Ingalls Wilder

## *The library here . . . has been named for me*

*Daphne Serton of the children's department at Harper & Brothers was assigned to handle mail sent to Laura Ingalls Wilder.*

MAY 26, 1951

Dear Miss Serton,

I do appreciate your sending replies to letters for me which pass through your office. My eyes are troubling me lately and I cannot answer letters as I have been doing so they go unanswered as there is no one here to write but me.

The library here, a branch of the Wright Co. Libraries, has been named for me—"Laura Ingalls Wilder Library." I would like very much to give a picture of myself to the library, but have none. Please send me one for the purpose.

Except for my eyes I am very well and getting along fine.

We are now having our blackberry winter—the cold spell that comes when the wild blackberries are in full bloom. Almanzo, Rose and I used to gather wild blackberries and I put them up in glass jars for winter. Later I picked them by myself, canned and made jam of all we could not eat fresh. Now I simply eat all I can which I buy from the neighbor boys.

The Hills are beautiful now. Humming birds and bumble bees are feasting on the honeysuckle blooms on the vine over the well at my back door.

With kindest regards to all in your office and thanks for replying to letters that come for me.

Laura Ingalls Wilder


*Please do open and answer all my mail*


JUNE 4, 1951

Dear Daphne Serton,

Thank you for the photos. I will give one to the L.I.W. library here and one to the library at our county seat.

Please do open and answer all my mail and you need not send it on to me unless it is something special. I greatly appreciate your kindness.

My eyes have been overworked and with rest and new glasses I am told they will be all right.

Kindest regards to you and the others in your office,
Sincerely,
Laura Ingalls Wilder

## Please take charge of my house

*Silas and Neta Seal were surrogate children for Laura and Manly. The Mansfield couple provided companionship and security for the aging Wilders. When Manly died, the Seals were the first people Laura summoned. Laura was 84 when she penned this note to Neta. Another note said, "Dear ones, Have dinner with me. It is my turn to treat. Lots of love, Laura Wilder."*

AUGUST 3, 1951
Dear Neta,
    If anything happens to me please take charge of my house and its contents until Rose can do so.
    I am sure Rose will make it right with you for your trouble. Better keep this [note] with the key.
    Laura I. Wilder

## From my heart, I thank you

*On September 28, 1951, the community of Mansfield dedicated their library in honor of Laura Ingalls Wilder. The honoree attended the function and read this message to the crowd.*

Dear Friends:
    I am happy that Mansfield has a public library. Its being named for me is an honor of which I am very proud and that the city I have loved since first I saw it as a little town 57 years ago should celebrate

the dedication and naming of the library as it has done leaves me at a loss for words to express my feelings.

I cannot tell you how much I value your friendship and the honor you have done me. I can only say I thank you all!

From my heart, I thank you.

Laura Ingalls Wilder

## Just as described in Farmer Boy

*Florence Anderson of Grand Gorge, New York, inquired about Almanzo's early home.*

OCTOBER 29, 1951

Dear Miss Anderson,

Your letter forwarded by Harpers has just reached me.

The house where Almanzo was brought up as a small boy still stands on the Vincent Road, east of Malone. It is now just as described in Farmer Boy.

It is described in The Post Standard of Syracuse, N.Y. of Sunday, Dec. 3d 1950.

The barn of Almanzo's boyhood burned down and has been replaced. The house is at the approach to Adirondack Quarries and is as Almanzo left it so many years ago, except for added coats of paint.

Our daughter, Rose Wilder Lane, of Danbury, Conn. saw the place a few years ago.

I hope you will be able to find the old house.

Yours sincerely,

Laura Ingalls Wilder

*I have so many letters and callers*

NOVEMBER 5, 1951

Dear Mrs. Weldon,

I am pleased that you and your pupils like my stories and glad indeed that you love me. The reason the stories seem so real is because they are true.

When I was a small child I lived with my parents and sisters in Burr Oak two years. The reason I did not put it in my stories was that it would bring too many characters. You know in writing a story the reader's interest must be held to the principal people, not scattered among so many. I remember Burr Oak with pleasure. My daughter, Rose Wilder Lane, visited the town some years ago. . . .

Plum Creek is about 2½ miles north of Walnut Grove. I recently had a letter from people who had just visited the place and found the site of our old dugout on the bank.

Silver Lake was ½ mile east of De Smet. It has been drained so there is no lake there now. It was a small lake, fed by springs that were destroyed in the draining.

I have so many letters and callers that I cannot remember any individuals. My memory is not what it used to be.

With love to you and your pupils,

Yours sincerely,

Laura Ingalls Wilder

*Now and then I find a familiar name*

NOVEMBER 19, 1951

Dear Aubrey Sherwood,

Thank you for the copy of The De Smet News. I read every word of it for it carries me back. Now and then I find a familiar name, children and grandchildren of those I used to know, I suppose.

I am sorry but I have not Pa's old ledger nor do I know what became of it. When Spring comes and it is warm enough to rummage in the attic I may find something that would be of interest among the county historical items. If so I will send it to you.

Quite often I have a letter telling of some tourist's visit to De Smet, of how nicely they have been treated by you and shown around to the places of interest.

The postcard you have in mind would certainly be interesting.

With kindest regards to you and yours.

Sincerely,

Laura Ingalls Wilder

## *They are beautiful books*

JANUARY 5, 1952

Dear Miss Nordstrom,

Thank you so much for the books "Dizzy" and "The Home Bible." They are beautiful books, but I have had no time yet to read them, only to look.

Have just finished answering my Christmas mail, 175 cards and letters that I felt I must answer.

Now I shall rest my eyes a bit and then read and read.

Best regards to your office force and a Happy New Year to you all.

Yours sincerely,

Laura Ingalls Wilder

## I am sure you will like it here

*The 1949 translation of* The Long Winter *into Japanese won many readers. The postwar shortages and austerity endured in Japan mirrored hardships in the Little House books. Yoshihiko Sato, a thirteen-year-old boy, corresponded with Laura several times.*

Mansfield, Missouri, U.S.A.
JANUARY 18, 1952
Dear Yoshihiko,

I thank you for your nice letter. You did well with the English.

When you grow up and come to America I am sure you will like it here.

I wish you a year of happy days.

Almanzo would have been pleased with the pretty card you sent him but he died in October 1949. I thank you for sending the card to him. He was 92 years old.

With kindest regards and best wishes,

Your friend,

Laura Ingalls Wilder

## Her choice of names was unfortunate

FEBRUARY 11, 1952
Dear Miss Webber.

I thank you and the children for the beautiful birthday card and I am indeed proud that my name was on so many links of the chain on your Christmas tree.

My daughter's book "Let the Hurricane Roar," is fiction with a background of facts I told her many times when she was a child. The characters in the story have no connection with my family. Her choice of names was unfortunate and it creates confusion. I had no brothers.

There is no one in the family to carry on the name of Almanzo. I am very sorry and wish someone would so name a son. My Almanzo only has distant relatives left and as you know my branch of the Ingalls family ends with me and Rose.

I hope the Laura Ingalls Wilder Room will be carried on to the new building, but am sorry I have no ideas at present that might help. If I should have later, I will let you know.

I would love to visit you in Pomona and will do so if it is ever possible. With love to you all,

Your friend,
Laura Ingalls Wilder

## *More lonely than I can tell without Mr. Wilder*

APRIL 17, 1952
Dear Miss Hillson,

The children's letters were interesting and I thank you for the kind things you say about my books.

All the children who write as well as my publishers want more stories but I am not writing anymore. I have written only the series of eight Little House books.

Our spring weather has been so unsettled, cold one day, warm the next, but no snow or frost.

I am very well, though more lonely than I can tell without Mr. Wilder.

With kindest regards,
Laura Ingalls Wilder

## *I would so love to see Dakota again*

MAY 8, 1952

Dear Aubrey Sherwood,

Thank you so much for your invitation to Rose and me for Old Settlers Day.

If I were only able I would be delighted to visit De Smet at that time but Dr's orders are that I must keep quiet and when I disobey him it puts me in bed. So it is not possible for me to make the trip and stand the excitement however great the pleasure would be.

Things from our old home were scattered as were Carrie's later and I do not know what became of them.

Some were sent me and those are in the museum of State Historical Society at Pierre.

I enclose a clipping from a Springfield [Missouri] daily describing the dedication of the Laura Ingalls Wilder Library here which may interest you. I thought I had sent you a paper of Mansfield Mirror.

The dedication date was September 28 [19]51. The bookmarks were given as favors at the open house.

Pictures of the affair were taken and I am trying to get a set to send you. It has been so long since, I may not succeed in getting them but if I do they will represent me on Old Settlers Day.

I would so love to see Dakota again.

With kindest regards to yourself and family,

Yours sincerely,

Laura Ingalls Wilder

## *Rose is very much pleased*

*Aubrey Sherwood's postage meter in the newspaper office bore the words "Little Town on the Prairie of Laura Ingalls Wilder's books."*

MAY 16, 1952

Dear Aubrey Sherwood,

It has taken me some time to track one down, but I am sending you on this mail a Mansfield Mirror with the write up of the dedication of Laura Ingalls Wilder Library here, which you should have had last October.

Also I am having sent you a marked copy of this week's paper.

Again I thank you for the postmark. It must have taken time and know-how to get permission to use it. Rose is very much pleased.

With kindest regards,

Sincerely,

Laura Ingalls Wilder

## *There must be many changes*

MAY 26, 1952

Rev. R. E. Marks

Sleepy Eye, Minnesota

Dear Sir,

I thank you for the kind things you say of my little books.

The Little House on Plum Creek was just a little way north from the creek which we crossed on our way to the town of Walnut Grove.

I cannot locate it any closer than I have done in the story. You know I was a child and have not seen the place since.

My memory is that the house was in a bend of the creek, which was on the south and east sides, a short distance away.

Across the creek to the east was Mr. Nelson's place to which we went by a footpath and a footbridge across the creek. Our road to town was to the south and a shallow ford across the creek.

I hope this may help in locating the site of the house. It was all so long ago that there must be many changes. . . .

With kindest regards,

Sincerely,

Laura Ingalls Wilder

## It makes me very proud

JUNE 14, 1952

Dear Yoshihiko Sato,

I am glad to have your letter with the good news. It is nice that you introduced my letter in all Japan.

I am sorry I cannot give you a story or a poem.

You see, my dear friend, I am 85 years old and not very well. I cannot write those things any more. I can only send you and your friends my love and good wishes.

Sincerely,

Laura Ingalls Wilder

## Among names of Old Settlers were only 12 familiar to me

JUNE 23, 1952

Dear Aubrey Sherwood,

At last I have been able to get pictures taken at the dedication of the Laura Ingalls Wilder Library here. I am sorry I could not get them in time for Old Settlers Day but think you may like to add them to your collection.

Pictures are numbered. In No. 1 I am standing by myself at right side of window. The others are librarians of the county.

In No. 2 I am standing by a case presented to the library by the state library association. The case is filled with presents sent me by children who have read my books. The dolls on top of the case are supposed to represent Laura and Almanzo.

No. 3 left to right. Paxton P. Price, state librarian, Laura Ingalls Wilder, Docia Holland, county librarian.

No. 4 left to right, Florence Williams, librarian of the Laura Ingalls Wilder Library in Mansfield and Laura Ingalls Wilder at the reception after the dedication of library.

The dedication was on Sept. 28, 1951 and pictures are of course nearly a year old, but people say I have not changed. Even the mumps left no marks.

We are having an awful drought here, the worst on record and the heat has been terrible all through June.

Rose is well and suffering from too much rain.

I hope all is well with you and yours.

With kindest regards,

Laura Ingalls Wilder


P.S. Thanks for the papers that came this morning. Among names of Old Settlers were only 12 familiar to me. Again—Thank you. L.I.W.


*I am well now*

JULY 23, 1952

Dear Mr. Sherwood,

Although rather late I do wish to thank you for the Old Settlers

Day copy of The De Smet News. It was very interesting and pleasant to be remembered.

Notice of the death of Alfred Ely saddened me. I have always thought of him as he was so many years ago, one of the younger boys in school, not realizing that the years had been passing with him, too.

We have had a very unpleasant spring and summer, cold, rainy, with little sunshine until last week, which has been unusually hot and sunny. We at Mansfield are thankful we live on the top of the hills where the floods of 1951 don't reach us.

I hope the storm at Watertown did not reach De Smet and that your weather had not been too bad.

Rose is well, but her part of the country has suffered freak weather as well.

I am well now, my eyes growing stronger as I gained strength after my heart attack.

Please give my best regards to inquiring friends.

Again thanking you and with kindest regards to you and your family,

Yours sincerely,

Laura Ingalls Wilder

*I hope you win the trophy*

SEPTEMBER 29, 1952

Dear Suzanna,

My favorite quotation is from the nineteenth Psalm.

"The heavens declare the glory of God and the firmament sheweth his handiwork."

The whole book of Psalms is a favorite of mine and I can repeat all. Can you?

I hope you win the trophy for the second time.
Sincerely, your friend,
Laura Ingalls Wilder

## Of course Indians are people

A reader wrote Harper & Brothers, protesting that Little House on the Prairie stated that there were no people on the Kansas prairies; only the Indians lived there. "We were disturbed by your letter," Ursula Nordstrom replied. "We knew that Mrs. Wilder had not meant to imply that Indians were not people." When the letters were shared with Laura, she immediately realized that the wording in her book needed revision. Subsequent editions were corrected.

OCTOBER 4, 1952
Dear Ursula Nordstrom,
    Your letter came this morning. . . .
    You are perfectly right about the fault in "Little House on the Prairie" and have my permission to make the correction as you suggest. It was a stupid blunder of mine. Of course Indians are people and I did not intend to imply they were not.
    Thanks for the proofs of the illustrations. They are so fascinating. I'm sure I'll love them in the books.
    With kindest regards,
    Laura Ingalls Wilder

## I autographed 200 books

Samples of Garth Williams's sketches for the new edition of the Little House books were regularly sent to Laura. In this letter

*Laura mentions her book signing in Springfield. Children and parents lined the sidewalk in front of Brown's Bookstore, waiting to meet Laura. When she returned to Rocky Ridge after a full day, she declared she was "tired but happy."*

NOVEMBER 22, 1952

Dear Miss Nordstrom,

I have disarranged the pictures badly. Please excuse it. I like the pictures very much. The little ones are exquisite.

I wish Laura's hair had always been shown in braids. She never wore it with a bow on top of her head or with a bang across her forehead.

The first day of Children's Book Week at Brown's Book Store in Springfield was a great success. It was Saturday the 15th. I autographed 200 books at the store that day and twenty more have since been sent to me to be autographed.

Please give my regards to Virginia Kirkus and say I have not forgotten her kindness to my first little book. . . .

With kindest regards to yourself and your office staff,

Laura Ingalls Wilder

## *So long ago when I taught the Perry school*

*In 1952, one-room schools still operated in the De Smet area. Vera McCaskell taught at the Perry School locale where Laura had been the teacher in 1884. Mrs. McCaskell read the Little House books to her students, and they wrote to Laura. In 1957, Vera McCaskell was a founder of the Laura Ingalls Wilder Memorial Society in De Smet, and spent years as a dedicated volunteer.*

DECEMBER I, 1952
Dear Mrs. McCaskell,

It was indeed a pleasant surprise to have a letter from you and your pupils. It brought back so clearly the time so long ago when I taught the Perry school.

It is kind of you to tell me about father's claim as it is now and that wild geese and ducks still fly over Silver Lake. Your school house is quite different from the one where I taught [the original Perry school had burned] and must be very nice.

With kindest regards and thanks for your letter and picture, I am
Yours sincerely,
Laura Ingalls Wilder


*De Smet has changed a lot*


DECEMBER I, 1952
Dear Children,

I am so pleased with your letters. I don't know how to thank you enough. It is great to know you are going to school where the Perry school used to be and where I taught so long ago.

It surprised me to learn of 42 boats being on Lake Henry. I am glad to learn about the Big Slough and Silver Lake as they are now.

De Smet has changed a lot since it was the Little Town on the Prairie. It is not so little now.

I am glad you like my stories of the way it used to be.

It must be fun to ride a horse to school and I'm sure you have good times there.

Wishing you all a Merry Christmas and a Happy New Year,
With love your friend,
Laura Ingalls Wilder

## With love, your friend

*Edibles, especially boxes of candy, were often sent to Laura from her readers.*

DECEMBER 15, 1952
Dear Steven,
Thank you so much for the box of delicious candy.
Please give my best regards to your mother and father.
With love,
Your friend,
Laura Ingalls Wilder

## Your poem is lovely

*Yoshihiko Sato continued to correspond with Laura Ingalls Wilder. He wrote: "I love American. I am sure to go to American when I am grown up." Many other Japanese children sent Laura letters and gifts.*

DECEMBER 31, 1952
Dear Friend,
Thank you so much for your Christmas gift which arrived on the mail this morning, having just got through customs. The picture is beautiful.

I trust you had a Merry Christmas and I wish you a very Happy New Year.

You have my sympathy in the loss of your grandparent. It is sad to suffer such bereavement.

Your poem is lovely and I am glad you got a prize in the jumping contest.

Your friend,
Laura Ingalls Wilder

## A place where I'd love to go

*Detroit's Wilder Branch Library thrived throughout the 1950s, and moved to a newly constructed building in 1967, Laura's centennial year. Mr. Ulveling and two other librarians, Mrs. Keltz and Ruth Rutzen, updated Laura periodically about the library's activities.*

FEBRUARY 20, 1953

Dear Mrs. Keltz,

It is rather late to acknowledge your kind letter. My mail was so heavy I have been a long time answering it and saved yours for later as a treat not to be taken hastily. Your letter is very interesting and I thank you so much for taking the trouble to write it. I am truly glad to hear such a good report on the Wilder Branch Library. It seems a place where I'd love to go.

Please give my best regards to Mr. Ralph Ulveling and Miss Ruth Rutzen.

Sincerely,

Laura Ingalls Wilder

## Been well, really astonishingly so

*B. Brooks, a California craftsperson, specialized in creating character dolls representing famous literary figures. At the request of Clara Webber, a set was rendered for display in the Pomona Public Library. California librarians wished that Laura Ingalls Wilder could have a set for herself. A set was created and sent for Laura's eighty-sixth birthday on February 7, 1953.*

[MARCH 1953]

Dear Children's Librarians,

The dolls have arrived. They are wonderful! After I have looked at them for some time, I will place them on display in my glass showcase at the Laura Ingalls Wilder Library here.

I don't know how to thank you all enough for such a beautiful birthday gift and kind remembrance of me as I pass the 86th milestone of my journey.

Please convey to all my friends there my grateful thanks.

Spring has come to the Ozarks. The hills are green with new grass, buds are swelling on the trees, spring flowers are blooming. Our winter has been very mild, still I am glad it is over.

I have been well, really astonishingly so. I am still living by myself, doing all my own work. Rose will visit me in April.

With kindest regards and all good wishes, as ever

Yours sincerely,

Laura Ingalls Wilder

## *I am sure his illustrations will be authentic*

*Publishing the new edition of Little House books was one of the most monumental tasks Ursula Nordstrom and her staff had undertaken. Getting Laura Ingalls Wilder's endorsement was essential. Getting Virginia Kirkus's approval was also significant. The powerful children's book guru lunched with Ursula Nordstrom in March 1953; their conversation centered on the Wilder books. Virginia Kirkus suggested that Mrs. Wilder write a letter commenting on the Garth Williams illustrations, to be sent to important librarians across America. Laura promptly wrote the following letter, expressing her pleasure over the major publishing project.*

MARCH 14, 1953

Dear Miss Nordstrom,

I am eager to see the new edition of the Little House Books with illustrations by Garth Williams.

When he visited here he sat surrounded by old family photographs and while Mrs. Williams and I visited he was busy making drawings from the old pictures, so I am sure his illustrations will be authentic.

It is interesting too, that he followed the trail of the Ingalls family from Wisconsin to Minnesota, to Indian Territory, and to Dakota Territory, to what is now South Dakota where it joined with the trail of the Wilders which came from New York.

Eight years is a long time and I am now becoming a little impatient, but I expect to be well repaid for waiting when I see the Garth Williams illustrations in the new edition of my books.

With kindest regards,
Laura Ingalls Wilder


*I had a surprise visit this week*

*Any visitor from the De Smet area who stopped at Rocky Ridge delighted Laura. When Dr. and Mrs. E. J. Failing of Arlington, South Dakota, made an unexpected call, Laura was overcome with emotion. Hazel Gilbert Failing was the daughter of David Gilbert, a young homesteader and mail carrier mentioned in* The Long Winter. *Laura reminisced about each member of the Gilbert family, and confided her secret crush on Fred, one of the brothers. Her pleasure spilled over in a letter to Ursula Nordstrom.*

MARCH 14, 1953

Dear Ursula Nordstrom,

I am pleased that Virginia Kirkus is taking an interest in the new edition of the Little House books. Please give her my regards.

I hope you will approve of the enclosed letter about the books. Use whatever part of it you wish and if you are not pleased with it, I will try again.

Our Spring seems to have arrived early. Weather is delightful. My health continues good and I enjoy being well and active.

I had a surprise visit this week from a daughter of one of the boys in my old crowd in "Little Town on the Prairie." She and her husband came from Arlington, near De Smet, to see me, because of the books. She said her father had told her much the same stories. He was not married when we left De Smet and has been gone for years. Seeing her and talking over the old times made the book come alive again.

Forgive me for rambling on like this.

Best regards to you and your office force.

Sincerely,

Laura Ingalls Wilder

## *It was a lovely place*

*In 1946 Harold and Della Gordon purchased the Plum Creek farm where the Ingalls family had lived in the 1870s. The next year Garth Williams called, camera and sketchbook in hand. He told the Gordons he was illustrating a new edition of* On the Banks of Plum Creek. *From that time on, the Gordons combined farming with hospitality, as thousands of Little House fans sought out the dugout site. Della Gordon wrote to Laura about the farm, and later remarked, "We had no idea the soil here was so rich in history."*

MARCH 20, 1953

Dear Mrs. Gordon,

Indeed I am glad to know of your purchase of our old farm on Plum Creek.

It was a lovely place and I often think of it even yet and of the happy times I had playing along and *in* the creek.

Thank you for writing telling me about it.

With kindest regards and all good wishes.

Sincerely,

Laura Ingalls Wilder

*I hope you will appreciate your gifts*

MAY 1, 1953

Sixth Grade

Peabody School

Dear Children,

Thank you for your nice letters. There are so many of you I can't write to each one separately, so this letter is for all of you. I am glad you like my stories and as you notice how much less I had than you have now, I hope you will appreciate your gifts. But remember it is not the things you have that make you happy. It is love and kindness and helping each other and just plain being good.

I think you have a very nice teacher to read you the books you like. I wish you a happy vacation and with love to you all I am

Your friend,

Laura Ingalls Wilder

## About the minstrel song

*The minstrel show depicted in* Little Town on the Prairie *was a popular entertainment on stages across America at the time. Both Ursula Nordstrom and Laura Ingalls Wilder discussed possible racist overtones of the song lyrics while the definitive edition of* Little Town on the Prairie *was being prepared.*

MAY 21, 1953

Dear Miss Nordstrom,

Your letter with proofs came on yesterday's mail, but as I was away from home all day, I did not get it until this morning. Sorry to have missed a mail with my answer.

I think the words I have added to Galley 20 will prevent any misunderstanding about the upstairs in Pa's building.

The upstairs was an attic. As corrected it reads, "upstairs to the hollow, hot bedrooms under *the eaves of the shingle roof.*"

About the minstrel song. It is an old song and was sung as written. I don't see how it can be changed but the whole song can be omitted or the part mentioning "coons." Do as you think best. It seems no one should be offended at the term "darkies."

Cut out the whole song if you wish.

Sincerely,

Laura Ingalls Wilder

## The books are beautiful

*Ursula Nordstrom was so elated by Laura's complimentary letter that she sent copies to Garth Williams, Virginia Kirkus, and Raymond Harwood, vice president of Harper & Brothers.*

JUNE 6, 1953

Dear Miss Nordstrom,

Thank you so much for the copies of "On the Banks of Plum Creek" and "Little House in the Big Woods."

Though unbound the latter is still my favorite of all!

The books are beautiful and I am so pleased with them.

The illustrations seem to bring the characters to life. Garth has done a grand job in these two books and I am impatient to see the others.

A friend, who has been waiting for the new edition to buy the complete set for her two boys, looked at the books yesterday. She said she is glad she waited and that these books are more than worth the difference in price from the old edition.

Again thanking you and with kindest regards,

Your Laura Ingalls Wilder

## They are beautiful books

JULY 20, 1953

Dear Miss Nordstrom,

In the mail this morning were the four books, Little House in the Big Woods, Little House on the Prairie, Farmer Boy, and On the Banks of Plum Creek.

Thank you! They are beautiful books.

There is a mistake in Little House on the Prairie.

Chapters 15 and 16—Fever 'n Ague and Fire in the Chimney are printed twice. . . .

This might escape your notice [. . .]

## It is fine of you and Mr. Sherwood

*Hazel Gilbert Failing and Aubrey Sherwood envisioned a memorial to the Ingalls family at their old homestead near De Smet. Through Hazel's urging, Edward and Opal May, owners of the land, deeded a corner of the property to the Laura Ingalls Wilder Memorial Society. Aubrey Sherwood located a prairie boulder near Spirit Lake to serve as a monument, and he wrote a text for the marker.*

JULY 27, 1953

Dear Hazel,

I thank you a lot for the pictures, especially the one of your father. . . .

Of course I would be willing and appreciative of a memorial to the Ingalls family, but I fear a duplicate of the claim shanty would not be attractive to sight-seers.

You will find an exact description of it in Chapter 29 of By the Shores of Silver Lake. My memory will yield no more details. I can describe it no better.

It is fine of you and Mr. Sherwood to attempt to commemorate the memory of De Smet pioneers and in your choosing of my family I am greatly honored.

Thanking you again for the pictures and with kindest regards,

Your friend,

Laura Ingalls Wilder

## The new edition has created quite a lot of interest

*The important Kirkus Reviews printed a complimentary review of the new Little House editions. This endorsement assured wide-*

*spread acceptance of the republication of the series. At Ursula Nordstrom's request, Laura composed a simple endorsement. She wrote: "Mary, Laura and their folks live again in these illustrations."*

AUGUST 13, 1953

Dear Miss Nordstrom,

Your wire and the Kirkus report both reached me last yesterday. . . . I hope the wire just sent is what you wanted. It is the best I know how to do.

Miss Kirkus's report is wonderful. Please give her my best regards. The new edition has created quite a lot of interest. Should go over great.

Kindest regards. . . .

Laura Ingalls Wilder

*They do look strange*

AUGUST 19, 1953

Dear Miss Russell,

Thanks a lot for the copies of the Chinese edition of Little House in the Big Woods. They do look strange, but seem to get the spirit of the stories in illustration.

Best regards to yourself and others in your office.

Sincerely,

Laura Ingalls Wilder

*Great interest in the new edition*

*To mark the republication of the Little House books, the* Horn Book Magazine *dedicated its December 1953 issue to Laura In-*

*galls Wilder. Garth Williams wrote of his experiences illustrating the books, Virginia Kirkus described her role in bringing them to publication, and other writers contributed their perspectives on what made it "Christmas all the time" in the Little House books.*

SEPTEMBER 24, 1953

Dear Ursula Nordstrom,

It is indeed grand news about the Christmas Horn Book. Thank you for telling me of it at once.

Mrs. Hatfield of Brown's Book Store in Springfield, has asked me to come to the store and autograph the new books as I did last year. But I am not able to stand a day of excitement and writing so many autographs. I have told her I will write, at home, as many autographs as she wants for her to paste in the books.

There seems to be a great interest in the new edition and the Christmas Horn Book should add to it. I am so pleased about it.

With kindest regards,

Laura Ingalls Wilder

## *I am thrilled*

*Jennie Lindquist, a Harper children's author, was also the editor of the* Horn Book Magazine. *She requested Laura's famous gingerbread recipe to include in the magazine.*

OCTOBER 19, 1953

Dear Miss Lindquist,

Miss Nordstrom has told me of your plan for the Christmas Horn Book. I am thrilled and in a hurry for Christmas time to come that I may see it.

You may use my letter to Clarence E. Kilburn, copy of which you enclosed, if you wish. . . .

I enclose my old gingerbread recipe and wish good luck if you should try it.

Sincerely,

Laura Ingalls Wilder

## They surely deserve some reward

NOVEMBER 12, 1953

Dear Miss Nordstrom,

You may like to send something to the school of the enclosed letter. I have written them that I sent this letter to you.

They surely deserve some reward for living in a place called Bad Axe [Michigan].

Kindest regards to you and your office staff.

Sincerely,

Laura Ingalls Wilder

## New edition is so well launched

DECEMBER 31, 1953

Dear Miss Nordstrom,

Thank you for the books. They look as though they are very interesting.

I thought the enclosed letter might interest you and please tell me if you want me to send you my fan letters.

Geo. Bye has turned over to you somewhere less than a carload, but now that the new edition is so well launched I think perhaps you will not care for more. . . .

## Nice of the kids to buy it for me

*Laura enclosed this undated 1954 note to Rose with a letter from Helen Carpenter, who taught near Malone, New York. Students were so keen to see the Farmer Boy site that Mrs. Carpenter arranged a bus trip to the Wilder farm. The class members collected their spare change to send Laura a gift—some locally produced maple syrup.*

Rose Dear,

I thought you would like to see the enclosed letter and pictures. After you have looked at them I think they should go to George Bye for Harpers. Please do send them.

I hope you are well of your cold.

If you don't feel like writing tell Lydia to let me know how you are.

½ gallon of maple syrup came and I'm eating it clear it is so good. Nice of the kids to buy it for me.

Lots of love,

Mama Bess

## The publicity is great

*Sales of the new edition of the Little House books soared during the 1953 holidays. Garth Williams's illustrations were accepted overwhelmingly. Clara Webber wrote from the Laura Ingalls Wilder Room of the Pomona library, giving her congratulations. She enclosed a swatch of Grandma Moses material, reminiscent of Little House stories, which was used for draperies in the library room. Laura draped it over a chair back in her sitting room.*

JANUARY 2, 1954

Dear Miss Webber,

Please forgive delay in answering your letter. I am glad you like the new edition of the Little House books. The publicity is great.

Sample of cloth you used in your library room came and I thank you for sending it. It is so amusing and fits the stories perfectly. I didn't suppose such picture cloth was made.

I wish you and your little friends a Happy New Year,

Laura Ingalls Wilder


*Glad to have you call me Laura*


JANUARY 25, 1954

Dear Karen,

Thank you for the sampler you worked so nicely. The sentiment is perfectly true. I am sure you are a busy girl with so many hobbies to keep you interested.

I am glad you love my books and me and am glad to have you call me Laura.

"Free Land" is another of my daughter's books I'm sure you would like. "Let the Hurricane Roar" is pure fiction. It has no connection whatever with my family. Her use of Pa's and Ma's names was unfortunate.

I have the verse "If wisdom's ways you wisely seek" in my old autograph album and it has always been a favorite of mine.

[Laura continues her letter with information on the later lives of her family members.]

Thanking you again for the pretty sampler, I am with love

Your friend,

Laura Ingalls Wilder

## *The award will be made in your name*

*On Laura's eighty-seventh birthday, a Western Union telegram arrived at Rocky Ridge announcing the establishment of the Laura Ingalls Wilder Award. Ursula Nordstrom, attending a conference in Chicago, was ecstatic over the news. "I'm so happy about this recognition for her wonderful books," she gloated. "And it is wonderful that such an award will bear her sacred name." Laura shared the news with Rose.*

TUESDAY, FEBRUARY 10, 1954

Rose Dearest,

When I go to town tomorrow I will send you the watch, insured mail. The charm is still attached to it. I was afraid to try to take it off. If the jeweler wants to, he can take it off and throw it away, just so he fixes the watch. The little broken off stem is with the watch. I'm so glad you said to send the watch and hope it can be fixed. I do apologize to the jeweler for such an abuse of his fine work.

Your card came yesterday. I have been thinking and saying that Sunday was my 86th birthday, but it was my 87th, so now I am 87 years old. Seems I've had an extra year I didn't know about. Or have I lost a year? It is too much for me to figure.

This day is hot with just a tiny breeze. Tomorrow is to be a little cooler. No rain in sight. I daren't take off my woolens and they are too hot.

Here is the copy of the wire from California.

Glendale, Calif.

Laura Ingalls Wilder, Phone of dlr today sure, Charges gtd. Rocky Ridge Farm, Mansfield, Mo.

We are honored to confer upon you an award for the lasting contribution which your books have made to literature for children. In future years the award will be made in your name and be called the Laura Ingalls Wilder Award. The award will be made at the American Library Association conference in June 1954.

Birthday greetings to you,

Rosemary Livsey, chairman, Children's Library Association

Should I send the telegram to George Bye?

I'm going now and give myself a manicure, then I will rest a bit I think.

Lots of love,

Mama Bess

## *Everyone is so glad I am 87 years old*

*When Rose visited Rocky Ridge she flew into the airport at Springfield, Missouri, and was met by Laura and her driver, Jim Hartley.*

FEBRUARY 17, 1954

Dear Mr. Bye,

Enclosed, the telegram you wanted.

Thanks for your congrats.

There is some advantage in being my age. Everyone is so glad I am 87 years old. I have had two birthday dinners in celebration while cards and gifts are still overloading my mail.

I am going to Springfield with taxi tomorrow to meet Rose and like "Little Annie Rooney" I am jittery.

Kindest regards to Mrs. Bye and yourself.

Laura Ingalls Wilder

*I am rather overwhelmed by it all*

FEBRUARY 26, 1954

Dear Miss Nordstrom,

Thank you for your kind offer to help me make the trip to Minneapolis, but my health will not permit me to go.

I have to avoid excitement and receiving the Laura Ingalls Wilder award in person would be exciting to say the least, so I must stay quietly at home.

I am rather overwhelmed by it all and greatly pleased.

In my office are between 6 & 7 hundred letters from readers of the books that I am not up to answering, so they will not be answered.

With kindest regards,

Sincerely,

Laura Ingalls Wilder

*Someone who once lived in Walnut Grove*

*Laura was always pleased by letters from her childhood homes. Mrs. Eugene Pollard, a librarian in Marshall, Minnesota, mentioned that she had been a member of the Congregational Church in Walnut Grove, where Laura had been a Sunday school pupil.*

MARCH 1, 1954

Dear Mrs. Pollard,

Your letter is very interesting and it is nice to hear from someone who once lived in Walnut Grove.

I am enclosing an autograph for you to paste in your copy of "On the Banks of Plum Creek." Sorry I have no photo I can send but am referring your letter to Harpers and am sure they will send you one.

　　With kindest regards,
　　Laura Ingalls Wilder

## Keeping as quiet as I can

*When the Twentieth Century Club in Walnut Grove, Minnesota, learned that Laura Ingalls Wilder would be honored in Minneapolis at the American Library Association meeting in June, they hoped to entertain her in her old hometown.*

APRIL 12, 1954

Dear Mrs. Christensen,

　　Thank you for your kind invitation to visit Walnut Grove. I would love to do so but I am not going to Minneapolis and so will not be in Minnesota.

　　At 87 I find my traveling days are over and I must obey my Dr. by keeping as quiet as I can.

　　With kindest regards to you and your club members I remain
　　Yours sincerely,
　　Laura Ingalls Wilder

## I miss him a lot when I go to town

*Ralph Watters edited the Mansfield Mirror from 1936 to 1954. He and Laura Ingalls Wilder were close friends. Her Wednesday trips to town included visits to the newspaper office. Mr. Watters understood her literary career and her passion for current events. Laura was fascinated with the 1950s obsession with flying saucers.*

*A misplaced book on the topic prompted this letter to Jay George,*
*Ralph Watters's brother-in-law.*

MAY 2, 1954
Dear Mr. George,

I am sorry my book and I caused you so much trouble and no apology was needed from you.

It *is* mysterious how the "Flying Saucers" disappeared and reappeared. Just living up to their name I guess.

Please give my kindest regards and good wishes to your brother Ralph. I miss him a lot when I go to town. I always enjoyed meeting you and hope we may not altogether lose touch with each other.

Sincerely,
Laura Ingalls Wilder

## *I send my autograph*

MAY 31, 1954
Dear Dr. Kerlan,

Thanks for your congratulations on the award [The Laura Ingalls Wilder Award] given my books.

However I am sorry to say I will not be able to receive the award in person. Being 87 years old with a tired heart I have to avoid excitement even if pleasant.

The manuscripts of my books have been placed in libraries named for me.

It is difficult for me to rewrap and mail books sent me to be autographed. Instead I send my autograph to be pasted in the books. Eight are enclosed.

Sincerely,
Laura Ingalls Wilder

## *A tribute to the past and a hope for the future*

*Ursula Nordstrom wrote Garth Williams that the Wilder Award "certainly wouldn't have been thought up and inaugurated right now if your pictures . . . hadn't been so perfect that the beauty of the Wilder books was brought anew to influential persons." She also asked Garth to design the award's medal. He agreed, and the finished medal was finally delivered to Laura in 1955.*

JUNE 7, 1954

Dear Miss Nordstrom,

I hope you will approve the note of acceptance. This is all new to me and I am perhaps rather stupid.

As to sending Pa's fiddle to the meeting, I would rather not have it take the chances of shipment. There is always a risk in the shipment and no amount of insurance could recompense for its being damaged or lost. I would rather it remained safely where it is in its glass case.

Would it not answer to have one or more of Pa's old songs played on another violin. There are so many and I loved them all. It is hard to choose my favorite.

"Auld Lang Syne" that Pa sings at the end of "Little House in the Big Woods" would be very appropriate. For a lighter touch, "Pop Goes the Weasel" or "Captain Jinks."

It may be difficult to find someone who can play the old tunes but Pa's favorite hymn is still sung. It is "The Sweet by and By."

I would so like to be there, but as I cannot I would love to have some of Pa's old songs played as a greeting from me.

If two could be played I would like the first to be "Auld Lang Syne" and the second "The Sweet By and By." A tribute to the past and a hope for the future.

Last week I autographed four sets of the books.

With kindest regards and all good wishes.
Sincerely,
Laura Ingalls Wilder

## *Vermont sounds wonderful*

*Alfred and Lydia Morgan were Rose's Danbury friends. They made two car trips with Rose to visit on Rocky Ridge in the 1950s; Laura also grew fond of them. The Freemans mentioned in this letter—Verne and George—were Mansfield friends of Rose's.*

JUNE 13, 1954
Dear Lydia,

This is a warm Sunday morning. It will be 90 again as it has been for several days.

Thank you so much for your letter telling me that Rose is well. It was and is so wonderful that her back is well. I do hope she will be careful to keep it so.

I am sorry Al has not been well and glad he is himself again and that your son is improving in health.

I am quite well usually but must be slow and careful to keep that way. There are days when I lie down most of the time to let my old, tired heart rest.

I autographed 18 books yesterday and 2 the day before.

Wednesday in town I saw Verne and George. They are well as usual.

We have had some rain but not enough and now it looks as though we will have a dry spell. The tourist rush has begun and every day there are accidents and people killed on the highways. There seems to be no way to stop it. Your description of the place in Vermont sounds wonderful. It would be so good to be out of traffic.

My hand is tired and I have more letters I must write, so good bye.
With love to you both,
   Laura I. Wilder


## If I should come to the Newbery-Caldecott dinner

JUNE 24, 1954
Dear Miss Wakefield,
   Your letter should have been answered sooner, but was carelessly
mislaid and only read this morning. Please forgive me.
   Your letter is very interesting. How well I remember that old store
on the shore of Lake Pepin and how beautiful the lake was.
   Thank you so much for your kind offer to meet and entertain me
if I should come to the Newbery-Caldecott dinner. It is sweet of you
and much appreciated.
   I am sorry but I am not able to be there. My doctor says my heart
is tired and orders me to be as quiet as possible.
   With thanks and all good wishes,
   Yours sincerely,
   Laura Ingalls Wilder


## You will be illustrating books someday

*The children's letters never stopped filling the Wilder mailbox.*

JULY 12, 1954
Dear Sharon,
   Thank you so much for the picture you made of Mary and Laura in
the store. It is wonderful that you should have remembered everything

so perfectly. You will be illustrating books someday I'm sure. I am glad
you like my stories and hope you will read all the books.

Love,
Laura Ingalls Wilder

## More mail than I can answer now

AUGUST 12, 1954
Dear Miss Wakefield,

Thank you for your letter and the picture of the Carpenter family.
[The Carpenters were first cousins of Laura Ingalls Wilder.]

It is all very interesting. I am glad to know about them all but will
not write for I have more mail than I can answer now.

My 87 years old hand grows tired soon when writing. Again
thanking you and with kindest regards,

Sincerely,
Laura Ingalls Wilder

## You will especially like "Farmer Boy"

AUGUST 16, 1954
Dear Peter,

I am glad you like my books and hope you read all eight of them.
You will especially like "Farmer Boy."

I am in very good health. Thank you!

Sincerely, your friend,
Laura Ingalls Wilder

## It looks good to me

*A letter postmarked De Smet always pleased Laura. Alice Kirch-meier wrote lyrics for "Sing of South Dakota," which alluded to the Little House books. She sent copies of the song to Laura and Rose. Alice Kirchmeier was a founder of De Smet's Laura Ingalls Wilder Memorial Society.*

SEPTEMBER 18, 1954

Dear Mrs. Kirchmeier,

Thank you for the song about Dakota. I am no musician, so not a judge, but it looks good to me and certainly the words are fine.

I will tell Rose about it and give her one copy.

Again thanking you, I am

Yours sincerely,

Laura Ingalls Wilder

## Doing as little writing as possible

*Harmon Tyler, a bookseller at Jordan Marsh Department Store in Boston, wrote Laura of her Hurricane Carol experience. "I was in the middle of* The Long Winter, *and you and your mother saved me from misery . . . if I can't read I am miserable. With no electric-ity I was reading your description of a button lamp your mother made. I took the top of a spice shaker and soaked a dust rag in cooking fat. I lit it and it worked! It was four days before the lights came on again, and it was you [who] saved me from darkness and misery." Harper created a press release from the incident; Ursula Nordstrom invited Miss Tyler to submit her own story ideas.*

NOVEMBER 16, 1954

Dear Miss Russell,

Today I am mailing you the two sets of books autographed.

The writing of the autographs is not very good for my hands are so lame it is hard for me to write.

Because of that I am not answering fan letters anymore and am doing as little writing as possible.

Miss Tyler's letter was pleasant reading. Thank you for sending it and also for the Chinese editions of books. I am returning the letter [Miss Tyler's] with this.

Sincerely,

Laura Ingalls Wilder


## I will be glad to see you

*Docia Holland, the Wright County librarian, became a close friend of Laura's. One of Mrs. Holland's duties was to drive the library bookmobile to outlying areas. Often Laura joined her on the runs. The route delighted her as the bookmobile swooped up and down the hilly roads. "I enjoy a drive as much as I ever did," she said. Finally, those trips became past pleasures.*


MAY 6, 1955

Dear Mrs. Holland,

I appreciate the interest people take in me and thank them for the friendship they express. But I can no longer receive strangers nor answer their letters. I have done this as long as I can. My 88 years have caught up with me. . . .

So glad to have your letter and the books you sent. I may not be able to get in touch with Virginia [Hartley] before Wednesday but I will not want any more books then. I'm behind in my reading because my eyes got tired and I have plenty of books on hand now.

Ralph Watters gave me a picture of us in the library and I sent it to Rose. I have never had a picture painted by an artist. The one Harpers sends is the largest. I suppose it could be enlarged, but as you say, I don't want any taken now.

Enclosed are autographs for whoever you want them for. My writing isn't what it used to be but I hope you can read it.

I will be glad to see you whenever you can come and I do appreciate your friendship.

With kindest regards and all good wishes,

Laura Ingalls Wilder


## *The poems are lovely*

*Martha Corlett taught in rural schools surrounding De Smet.*

MAY 9, 1955

Dear Miss Corlett,

Thank you for your little book of poems.

I would have written you sooner but have been very ill and only able to be up part of the time now. The poems are lovely and so is the little book.

I am glad you and your pupils love my stories. Please give them my love. I must stop writing now.

With many thanks and kindest regards,

Yours sincerely,

Laura Ingalls Wilder


*In June 1955 Aubrey Sherwood invited Laura to De Smet's seventy-fifth-anniversary celebration and a local stage production of* The Long Winter. *She replied that she would love to be present, but her health would not permit it. Later that year a St. Louis television station honored her during Children's Book Week. Television's popularity prompted Ursula Nordstrom to query, "Why doesn't that foxy George Bye sell the Little House books for a television program?" Laura gave her agent permission to market her books as a possible television show.*

## *I was glad to see you all*

*Dorothy lived on Sunny Slope Farm near Mansfield.*

JULY 21, 1955
Dear Dorothy,

I am pleased that you and your friends enjoyed your visit here. I was glad to see you all and especially you. It makes me happy that I should seem like your own and your love is returned. It is wonderful that you will pray for me. I need it. I will remember you in my prayers every night.

Please come whenever you can. Your letter did me lots of good. Thank you!

With love,
Laura Ingalls Wilder

*Another note to Dorothy was undated.*

Dear Dorothy,

I thank you for your sweet note and shall remember you when I say my prayers. I hope you will do the same for me. One needs the prayers of their friends.

With love,
Laura Ingalls Wilder

*I thank you for your many kindnesses*

JANUARY 23, 1956

Dear Mrs. Holland,

I am sorry that circumstances were such that you thought it best to resign as county librarian. You were doing a good work and I am sure library patrons appreciate it.

I thank you for your many kindnesses and am sorry I have not been able to be at the library to see you now and then.

Most sincerely,

Your friend,

Laura Ingalls Wilder


*I really want to read it*

*Ursula Nordstrom sent* A Hog on Ice and Other Curious Expressions *by Charles Funk as a gift to Laura. After delays, it finally arrived.*

FEBRUARY 4, 1956

Dear Miss Nordstrom,

The "Hog on Ice" you sent must have slipped down somewhere on these ice storms we have been having for it has not come yet. I thank you for your kind intention but am disappointed that the book has not arrived. I really want to read it.

Many thanks for taking care of so much of my mail. I am not writing letters to answer my fan mail.

With best regards,

Sincerely,

Laura Ingalls Wilder

## *Two beautiful, large birthday cakes*

FEBRUARY 6, 1956

Dear Miss Nordstrom,

My fan mail is very heavy and I am not answering it, but thought these few should receive a reply.

Your office is being so kind taking care of my mail that I am encouraged to ask you to answer these. Please!

Among the hundreds of birthday cards came two beautiful, large birthday cakes I would love to share with your office.

Best regards to you all.

Sincerely,

Laura Ingalls Wilder

*Rose arrived to spend the 1956 holidays at Rocky Ridge. On Thanksgiving eve Laura fell ill, so sick that Rose rushed her to the Springfield hospital by ambulance. There she was correctly diagnosed; she suffered from diabetes. With a diabetic diet and medication she improved. Even in the hospital Laura's fame as an author surrounded her. Staff members brought books for her to sign, the newspaper reported on her condition, and thousands of Springfield children signed a huge scroll of good wishes. On the day after Christmas she happily returned to Rocky Ridge, with Rose in faithful attendance. Her ninetieth birthday was approaching. The house overflowed with mail—gifts and greetings poured in from all over. Laura saw the expressions of love and was pleased. On February 7, 1957, ninety years after her birth in the now-fabled little house in the big woods, she slipped into a coma. She died three days later, February 10, 1957.*

*Newspapers and radio stations reported the passing of the author of the Little House books. Sad-faced elementary students brought newspaper obituaries to their equally grieved teachers. The*

*Saginaw, Michigan, public library went ahead with its birthday party honoring Laura's ninetieth. There was fiddle music, ginger-bread, and storytelling, and librarians observed groups of children savoring the Little House books in every corner of the crowded room.*

*Rose remained in the house on Rocky Ridge for two weeks. In her mother's desk, she found a final letter addressed to her.*

JULY 30, 1952

Rose Dearest,

When you read this I will be gone and you will have inherited all I have.

Please give to the Laura Ingalls Wilder Library in Mansfield all that is left in my private library after you have taken from it what you want for yourself. This includes the framed testimonials from Chicago, California and the Pacific Northwest.

My jewelry is unique and should not be carelessly scattered. Do with it as you wish but preserve it in some way if you can.

We were proud of my Havilland china but loved best the English made blue willow ware. Do as you please with all the china, but I wish you might use it.

The persimmon-wood chair and the cypress stand-table that Manly made belong to Silas Seal.

My love will be with you always.

Mama Bess

(Laura Ingalls Wilder)

# AFTERWORD

After Laura's death, Alfred Morgan of Danbury came to Rocky Ridge to escort Rose home. With him was Rose's British friend Elsie Jackson, her extended houseguest. Rose was eager for their company and anxious to leave Rocky Ridge for the last time. She carried out her mother's final wishes, donating Laura's home library to the Laura Ingalls Wilder Library in Mansfield. As she rummaged through drawers and closets, she was amazed at the scope of American history residing with her parents' keepsakes.

When a committee of Mansfield people called on Rose, asking to preserve the Rocky Ridge house as a memorial, the idea was not new. It had been suggested to Laura earlier; she was receptive and pleased. Rose was skeptical. Her parents had sold the farm on a life-estate contract. It was not hers to give. As Rose grasped the local committee's sense of purpose, she eventually decided to buy back the house and several acres from its owner. She turned the place over to the newly chartered Laura Ingalls Wilder Home Association.

With volunteer help, the Association opened the Wilder home for tours. School classes visited and a steady stream of interested readers arrived each summer day. The Laura Ingalls Wilder Historic

Home and Museum became the epicenter of Little House lore, as readers toured the preserved house and the nearby museum filled with artifacts dating from the pre–Civil War era through the latter days of Manly's and Laura's lives in the 1940s and 1950s. Pa's fiddle, the leitmotif of the Little House books, was returned by the state museum in Pierre, South Dakota. It became a centerpiece of pilgrimages to Rocky Ridge Farm.

Also in 1957 Aubrey Sherwood founded the Laura Ingalls Wilder Memorial Society in De Smet. The first of many developments was a monument placed on the old Ingalls homestead, giving visitors something tangible to see. Each of the other Little House sites followed Mansfield's and De Smet's lead. Memorials, restorations, and replications were developed in Pepin, Wisconsin; Independence, Kansas; Walnut Grove, Minnesota; Burr Oak, Iowa; and Malone, New York.

Rose never returned to Mansfield after her mother's death. She remained active in conservative causes as an avid political observer, and was a major influence in the libertarian movement in America. She enlarged her Danbury home again, surrounding it with expansive gardens. She read and wrote omnivorously.

Laura's diary, kept during the 1894 move from De Smet to Mansfield, was found at Rocky Ridge. Harper & Row (as Harper & Brothers had come to be called) was avid for its publication. Rose edited the diary and wrote a setting for the book, which was published in 1962 as *On the Way Home*. She dutifully answered letters from her mother's fans, which still poured in. In 1963 Rose's *Woman's Day Book of American Needlework* was published. Two years later, *Woman's Day* sent Rose to Vietnam for six weeks, to investigate the escalating U.S. involvement there. At seventy-eight, Rose found the State Department reluctant to send "a little old lady" into a war zone, but she was dauntless. Her resulting article appeared in *Woman's Day* in December 1965.

By then Rose was finally retired. She established a second home in Harlingen, Texas. There she observed the ever-increasing reputation of the Little House books, and advised the Rocky Ridge Farm project. At eighty-one, Rose, inspired by her innate curiosity, planned a trip around the world. Like her pioneer ancestors, she felt the lure of unseen lands beckon. But the trip was not to be. Rose Wilder Lane died suddenly in her Danbury home on October 30, 1968, just days before embarking on a last great adventure.

Rose left the responsibility of her mother's literary oeuvre, and her own, to her "honorary grandson," Roger Lea MacBride. As Roger had pondered the collision of increasing government control and individualism, Rose had become his philosophical mentor. Their mutual passion for personal liberty matched that of the pioneering Ingallses and Wilders. Under Roger's direction, the final Wilder manuscript, *The First Four Years*, was published by Harper & Row in 1971. Then came the *Little House on the Prairie* television series, which ran from 1974 to 1983. The weekly network broadcasts resulted in an immense groundswell of new fans. Roger MacBride carried on his duties as the final connecting link to the Wilder family until his death in 1995. Now the Little House Heritage Trust continues to nurture the legacy.

Laura Ingalls Wilder's name and fame continue to resonate around the world. She remains one of America's best-selling, best-known, best-loved authors.

# INDEX

NOTE: Page numbers in *italics* indicate a photograph.

# ABOUT THE AUTHORS

**Laura Ingalls Wilder** (1867–1957) was born in a log cabin in the Wisconsin woods. With her family she pioneered throughout America's heartland during the 1870s and 1880s, finally settling in Dakota Territory. She married Almanzo Wilder in 1885; their only daughter, Rose, was born the following year. The Wilders moved to Rocky Ridge Farm near Mansfield, Missouri, in 1894, where they established a permanent home. After years of farming, Laura wrote the first of her Little House books in 1932. The nine Little House books are international classics. Laura Ingalls Wilder's writings live on into the twenty-first century as America's quintessential pioneer story.

**William Anderson** is a historian, educator, and author of twenty-five books of biography, travel, and history. His groundbreaking research on Laura Ingalls Wilder and her books led to many HarperCollins titles, including *Laura Ingalls Wilder: A Biography*, *Laura Ingalls Wilder Country*, and *A Little House Sampler*. He has also written for *Travel & Leisure*, the *Saturday Evening Post*, the *Christian Science Monitor*, and many other national magazines. Anderson is a frequent speaker at conferences, schools, and libraries. His home is in Michigan. www.williamandersonbooks.com